To

The Whitehorse Community

With best wishes

[illegible] M. Gray

A Fund *of* *Goodwill*

The Story of the International Fund for Ireland

by **Alf McCreary**

First Published in 2008

Cover photographs of Dunfanaghy, County Donegal by Alf McCreary
Designed by Page Setup, Belfast
Printed by Commercial Graphics Limited

The publishers and author have made every reasonable effort to attribute correctly all the visual material, and other references, in this book. If any errors or omissions have been made, we will be happy to correct them in any future edition that is published.

Contents

Chairman's Foreword

For several reasons, it was always inevitable that this book would be written. Among the most important of these is the need to provide a record of the international support in securing peace on the island of Ireland. This is demonstrated clearly by the financial support from the donors: Australia, Canada, New Zealand and the United States of America, all of which have among their citizens a large Irish diaspora, and the European Union. Without their commitment, the positive events described in this book would not have been possible.

There is also, however, a need to record the involvement of a wide range of people in a variety of activities and at all levels in our communities in securing peace over the last quarter of a century.

On occasions, the nature of some of those individual and personal endeavours has bordered on the heroic. As in most of the outstanding stories in human history, the story of the contributions to peace made by those involved in and through the International Fund for Ireland, is one of selfless contributions by men and women of goodwill often in circumstances and times of great difficulty.

Although not all of the individual contributions would necessarily be described as heroic, nevertheless, all were vital in what has been accomplished. This book does not contain all the stories that could be recorded. It includes, however, a representative sample, behind which stands a host of people whose contributions represent the pieces of a mosaic that is now taking shape in the form of a shared peace, acceptable to all. It is the value of all of the individual components and the collective achievement of all of these people that demanded that this book be written.

The chapters that follow, outline the early steps in putting together a Fund that ultimately made a significant contribution to the achievement of peace. When those early steps were taken, the individuals involved had no guiding manual as to the shape of the whole process. Nevertheless, a movement began that enabled the participants to put in place a structure and processes which made a significant impact for the good of all.

Those participants included Presidents, Prime Ministers, Senators, Congressmen and Parliamentarians, across many nations, along with diplomats, civil servants, businessmen and women, who all joined with workers in local communities to encourage and build good relations, peaceful societies and economic progress. Although this book records only some of the more vivid and personal stories of political turmoil in Ireland, the overall effect is greater that the sum of the parts.

There are few places in Northern Ireland and the border counties that have not experienced the benevolent influence of the Fund. As well as being a relentless driver for reconciliation, it has steadfastly built up an enviable capacity in job creation, tourism, community engagement and economic development. This work was undertaken during times when hope and optimism were scarce.

In documenting the stories in this volume, the Board of the International Fund for Ireland wishes to make this book available widely as a testament to what can be achieved when people of goodwill agree to effect change for the better. As the Fund enters its final phase of innovative engagement in these sunset years, I believe it is important to record this remarkable story.
It is hoped that this record can bring hope to other regions of the world that are embroiled in conflict or emerging from it and that it will serve to energise those involved in peace-building to complete the task they perhaps have started. The International Fund for Ireland model is not set in stone. If others wish to adapt it, or draw from it, they can count on us for assistance.

This book would not have been written without the sustained efforts of the award-winning author and journalist, Alf McCreary whose wide experience of writing about bridge-building initiatives gave him a valuable insight for the task.
I want to record my personal thanks to him, to those whose stories and contributions are recorded and to all in the Fund's Secretariat who supported this effort.

I also want to pay tribute to the Members of the Board who took the decision to proceed with this project. I wish to acknowledge their work that has built upon the efforts of those former Chairmen and Board Members who were present in the earlier years of the Fund's work.

This book is intended to complement the Fund's work in support of community peace-building in Northern Ireland and the border counties. It is my earnest desire that the message of hope recorded in the book will itself make a significant contribution to the promotion of mutual respect and reconciliation. The International Fund for Ireland is a remarkable story and one which has now been told clearly and well. I commend it to you.

Denis Rooney CBE

Acknowledgements

As the author, I would like to record my thanks to all those who helped make this book possible. They include the Chairman of the International Fund for Ireland, Denis Rooney, whose idea it was to produce the book, and the Board, as well as former Chairmen and staff, and also the current Joint Directors General Sandy Smith and Eamon Hickey in Belfast and Dublin respectively, and all their Secretariat colleagues past and present.

I would also like to thank the many people on both sides of the Atlantic who gave of their time and experience to relate to me many of the important aspects of the story. They are too numerous to name individually, but they are known to me and I am grateful for their help.

This book has required much research, and I am grateful to the editors of those publications mentioned in the narrative and duly acknowledged, as well as those whose photographs add a visual dimension to the story. I would particularly like to thank John Carson, Rodney Baird, Scott Oliver and Sandra Russell in Belfast and Stephen Ryan in Dublin for their help in providing relevant illustrations as well as Paddy Harte in Donegal and Tom Hobson in Sligo. I would like to thank Carolyn Reynolds for her transcriptions of the early taped interviews. I would also like to thank Beverly McConnell for her considerable help during the final preparation of the manuscript at the production stage of the book.

Special thanks are also due to David Redmond and the design team at Page Setup, Belfast.

Finally, I would also like to record my thanks to my wife Hilary who has given me support and every encouragement throughout yet another long literary journey.

Introduction

When the International Fund for Ireland was established in 1986, following the historic Hillsborough Agreement of the previous year, no-one was quite sure about how long the Fund would last. Few people believed that it would still be in existence more than 21 years later.

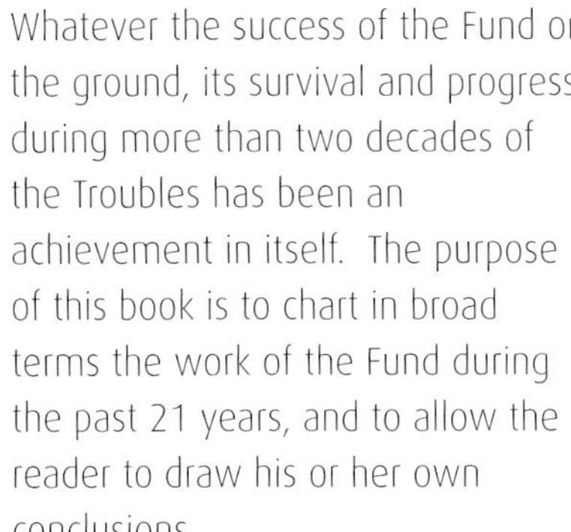

Whatever the success of the Fund on the ground, its survival and progress during more than two decades of the Troubles has been an achievement in itself. The purpose of this book is to chart in broad terms the work of the Fund during the past 21 years, and to allow the reader to draw his or her own conclusions.

This is not intended to be a definitive history, nor could it be. The work of the Fund has been so extensive that a number of volumes would be needed to catalogue all its activities. For those who wish to delve into such detail, the Annual Reports of the Fund provide a wealth of general and statistical information.

My intention in this book is to give a broad-brush account of the story of the International Fund for Ireland which is both authoritative enough for those directly involved, and also accessible enough for the general reader, and all those people interested in this significant period of history on the island of Ireland – and how it has affected the many people elsewhere who were anxious to bring peace to a troubled land.

This is a story of co-operation on many levels, not only politically and economically, but also across the divides within the communities and across the border in Ireland. It is a complex story, but also – to my mind – an inspiring story of how so many people committed themselves to doing their best for each other in the worst of times.

This book is very much a personal observation of a long and important journey, and the conclusions are entirely my own. In that sense it is not an 'official' history of the IFI. There are many major themes, and sub-themes, to the story, but to my mind the main achievement of all concerned has been in widening horizons, and this is reflected in one of the Fund's earliest programmes, which was called 'Wider Horizons'.

It is my hope that this narrative has done justice to the story, and that it leaves an important record of a remarkable institution which emerged from a period of sustained conflict and which played its part in helping to create an atmosphere of co-operation in which peace could blossom.

There is still much to be done to complete what has been poetically-described as the 'healing of history', but the International Fund has played its part in helping to start that process and to help make it a reality. It has been my considerable task, and also my privilege, to help record that achievement for posterity.

Alf McCreary
Belfast

CHAPTER ONE

Setting It Up

THE INTERNATIONAL FUND FOR IRELAND was established on 18 September, 1986 by the British and Irish Governments as an independent international organisation. With subsequent contributions over the next 21 years from the United States of America, the European Union, Canada, Australia and New Zealand, the total resources to the Fund exceeded £600 millions (€849 millions).

The objectives of the Fund were to promote economic and social advance, and to encourage contact, dialogue and reconciliation between nationalists and unionists throughout the border counties in Ireland, North and South. More than 5,500 projects were funded to promote economic development and social advance in disadvantaged areas, and these contributed to making significant progress in cross-community and cross-border areas.

Willie McCarter, a former Chairman of the Fund, noted in his final Report in 2004 "The results of this work can be seen in almost every city, town and village in Northern Ireland, and in the Border counties in the South. Ultimately the credit for all of this.... must go to our international donors whose generous and unflinching support has made it all possible."

Much credit was also due to the IFI staff and the ordinary people who made it work on the ground.

It all seemed so different at the beginning. The concept of such a Fund was mooted at a time when Northern Ireland was burdened with violence, political deadlock and a most unfavourable international image. Sir George Quigley, a distinguished former senior civil servant in Belfast was the then Permanent Secretary in the Department of Finance and Personnel. He was closely involved in the early discussions about the practical aspects of such a Fund.

Willie McCarter, Chairman of the Fund from February 1993 to 2005

Sir George Quigley

He recalled "It stemmed from a desire on the part of people outside Northern Ireland to give support to what one would now describe as the early stages of a peace process. The Americans were clearly anxious to help, and there was also a successful effort to involve Europeans and others as well."

The Fund was being established in a most contentious political atmosphere. Quigley said "Relationships between the British Government and the Unionists in Northern Ireland were probably at an all-time low, so anything which seemed to be bringing the Northern and Southern interests together was regarded as a thoroughly bad thing".

This was hardly surprising, as Unionists of all shades had been alienated by the 1985 Anglo-Irish Agreement, signed at Hillsborough Castle by the then British Prime Minister Margaret Thatcher and the then Taoiseach Dr Garret Fitzgerald. After years of Unionist complaints about 'interference' from Dublin, this Agreement underlined firmly that the Republic – despite them – could and would have a voice in Northern affairs. The Unionists were also enraged because they had not been consulted by the British about this development. On the other hand if Thatcher and her colleagues had told the Unionists in advance, the signing of the Agreement would have been much more difficult.

Nevertheless, one result was that the Unionists, led by the Reverend Dr Ian Paisley, and a somewhat quieter but equally outraged James (now Lord) Molyneaux, literally went on the stomp with their supporters throughout the Province by proclaiming firmly that "Ulster Says No".

Apart from such political trauma, which consolidated the deadlock inside the Province, the almost daily violence went on and on. All of this contributed to a sorry picture of a Northern Ireland at war with itself. The Unionists' rage at the Anglo-Irish Agreement was not conducive to developing a dispassionate view of the International Fund, but there were others in Northern Ireland who saw its potential.

George Quigley, with the cool perspective of hindsight and a clear civil service mind, said later on "At that time, things really were dire. Northern Ireland was cut off from the external world as far as inward investment was concerned. For example, in the terrible year of 1976 only around 400 jobs came from outside Northern Ireland, so we were battling against the odds."

"Our image was appalling, and therefore any country which was prepared to help was very welcome

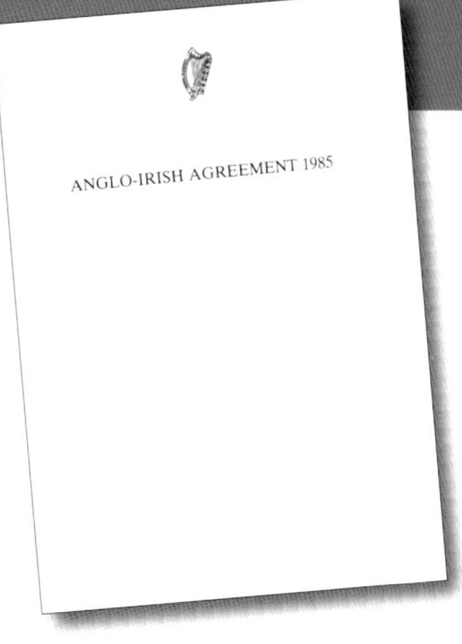
ANGLO-IRISH AGREEMENT 1985

indeed. With the establishment of the Fund we were being connected to the wider world which was actually interested in doing something to improve the situation in Northern Ireland."[1]

The evolution of the Fund, however, was a complex story in itself and it resulted from a long process of lobbying to persuade the American administration that it should take this significant step to provide help for Northern Ireland which had been regarded traditionally by some people as the sole responsibility of the United Kingdom. In the long-term the idea proved to be a winner, but a number of different factors combined to bring it to fruition in the first place.

It is said that success has many fathers but failure is an orphan, and a number of people can be credited with playing a crucial part in establishing the International Fund. One of the names most often mentioned is that of Nobel Laureate John Hume, the Derry MP and MEP who helped to sow the seeds of the peace process long before others saw any hope on the horizon.

Another politician who made an important contribution was Tip O'Neill, a close friend of Hume and the hugely influential Speaker of the

Belfast Telegraph, Saturday, November 16, 1985

The Anglo-Irish summit . . . The Anglo-Irish summit . . . The Anglo-Irish summit . . . The Anglo-Irish summit . . .

Text of agreement between UK and Eire Governments

ANGLO-IRISH AGREEMENT 1985 IN FULL

AGREEMENT BETWEEN THE GOVERNMENT OF THE UNITED KINGDOM OF GREAT BRITAIN AND NORTHERN IRELAND AND THE GOVERNMENT OF THE REPUBLIC OF IRELAND

The historic agreement is signed at Hillsborough Castle.

Picturesque setting for a day of dark bitterness

By Neil Johnston

JOURNALISTS COVERING the signing of the Anglo-Irish agreement were provided with some background information on the venue, Hillsborough Castle.

There were somewhat incongruous references to its having the largest rhododendron bush in the United Kingdom and to the fact that there is also a picturesque lake in the grounds.

As Mrs. Thatcher's helicopter swooped in low over the trees one onlooker suggested a use to which the lake might be put.

"It's a pity they don't open the door and drop her in it," he said to his friend.

Neither of them was involved in the loyalist demonstration up the street at the courthouse.

Bitterness

But the mood yesterday was one of dark bitterness. Words like "betrayal" and "treachery" and "sell-out" were common currency.

Throughout the morning DUP Chief Whip Mr. Jim Allister and other protestors shouted their rage at Mrs. Thatcher through a megaphone from a balcony outside the local council offices. The balcony was draped with a banner emblazoned with the single word "Betrayal".

"No to Dublin, No to Thatcher, No Surrender" proclaimed one of the many placards in the street.

"Ulster will be up for sale in Hillsborough Castle at 11.30 today," they shouted from the balcony.

Inside the courthouse, converted into a Press centre for the day, journalists from all over the world phoned over early stories to the constant chant outside of Mrs. Thatcher's own phrase which the loyalists were now using against her — "Out, Out, Out".

Cloudless

It was a fine sunny morning and helicopters buzzed constantly high overhead in the cloudless sky. It served as a reminder that one of the most popular lines of loyalist graffiti states:

"We will not forsake the blue skies of Ulster for the grey mists of an Irish Republic."

Memories were long. Down the street, beside the statue of the Marquis of Downshire, whose family founded Hillsborough in 1740, an elderly man spoke earnestly to a couple of policemen.

"You boys should be rolling up your uniforms and handing them in," he said.

"That's all very well," said one of them pacifyingly, "but what do you live on? You have to live."

"Your grandfathers did it," the man told them. "And what will you live on? You'll live on less in an Irish Republic. What's their national debt now?"

Refused

There were cheers as the leaders of the two Unionist parties, the Rev. Ian Paisley and Mr. Jim Molyneaux, arrived.

At the gates of Hillsborough Castle they handed in their joint letter of protest.

They refused to give it to any of the N.I. Ministers, with whom they are now refusing to co-operate. It was received by a civil servant.

The letter reminded Mrs. Thatcher of her

The Signing of the Anglo – Irish Agreement

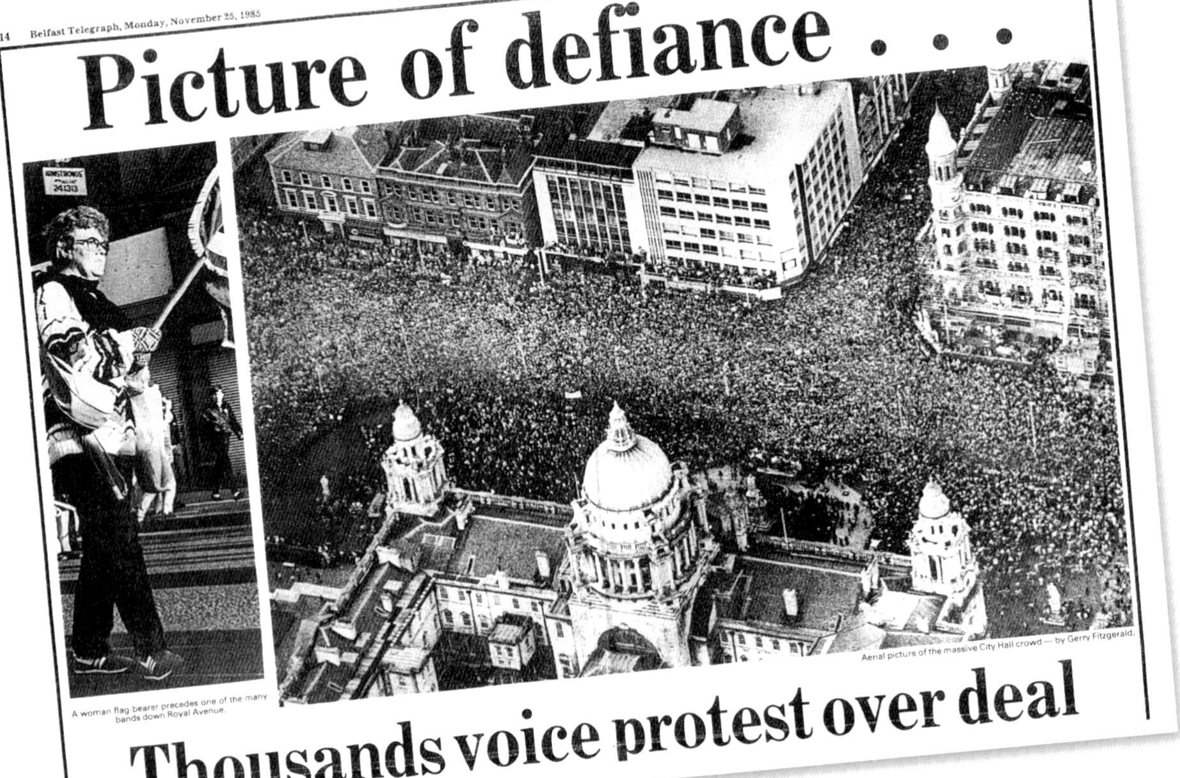

14 Belfast Telegraph, Monday, November 25, 1985

Picture of defiance . . .

A woman flag-bearer precedes one of the many bands down Royal Avenue.

Aerial picture of the massive City Hall crowd — by Gerry Fitzgerald.

Thousands voice protest over deal

Reaction on the streets of Belfast

John Hume pictured with President Ronald Reagan, Tip O'Neill and Senator Edward Kennedy at a Speaker's Lunch in Washington

US Congress. He had strong Irish roots and sympathies towards the land of his forebears. President Jimmy Carter also played an important role, and Ronald Reagan, who eventually discovered his Irish roots, was persuaded by O'Neill and several key Irish-American politicians and others that an innovation like the International Fund for Ireland would be timely and productive. Senator Ted Kennedy was a source of particular support at these early stages and, indeed, throughout the life of the Fund.

On the other hand there were the not inconsequential views of Reagan's close friend and ally Margaret Thatcher, who was reputed to be cool to any intervention by Americans in Northern Ireland which, as a part of the United Kingdom, she regarded as her sole business and that of her Government.

The friendship between John Hume and Tip O'Neill was important. John's wife Pat confirmed this to me during a conversation in their home in Derry. She said "I believe that their friendship was not only close, but pivotal." She said that they were so close that Tip sent John a cheque for 100 US dollars in August 1979 as a contribution to Hume's election expenses. She said "It was rare for one politician to give another one an election subscription like that. John kept it as a souvenir and it has never been cashed."[2]

O'Neill came to Ireland with his wife Millie in 1981 and the Humes brought them to the site of Tip's ancestral family home at Buncrana in Donegal. He was particularly impressed by the visit, according to his daughter Rosemary O'Neill. She told me "He was actually thrilled by the beauty of the place, and the people of the town had organised a fabulous celebration in one of the local hotels. Later there was a picture of the Donegal event in the New York Times and my father said "This looks like some of my cousins back in the States and you can even see the family resemblance!" Ireland was such an integral part of him, and he loved just being able to do something to help."[3] During his visit, Tip was taken on a tour of Derry. Rosemary O'Neill said "My parents noticed all these men standing around the corners and when they asked John Hume why this was so, he replied 'It's because they have no work'. So the idea appealed to my father that you could help to put these people in work, and particularly on cross-border projects which could be beneficial to the economy."

John Hume confirmed this, in a book of tributes by friends and colleagues of Tip O'Neill, which is in the Congressional Library in Washington. He wrote "On the wall of my home in Derry there is a very special picture. It is a picture of Speaker O'Neill, his wife Millie, my wife Pat and myself. Written on it is a very special message from the Speaker 'May you have lasting peace in Ireland...' Throughout his Congressional life, and in particular in the Office of Speaker, peace and justice in Ireland were always at the top of his agenda. In spite of holding one of the most powerful offices in the world, his feet never left the ground. He remained a man of the people. In the city of Derry, or indeed in Ireland, we will never forget him."

President Jimmy Carter. "There are no solutions that outsiders can impose".

The former Irish Ambassador to Washington Sean Donlon who formed a close relationship with Ronald Reagan

Hume underlined that O'Neill's support was unwavering, and that it focused on economics. He also confirmed that on the day after the Anglo-Irish Agreement was signed, Tip O'Neill phoned him from Washington to tell him that the International Fund for Ireland was being set up. O'Neill said "We keep our promises".

However, that sequence of events was the culmination of a process which was not quite as simple as it seems, and the "greening" of the American administrations at the highest level took a long time. A great deal of lobbying had been carried out by O'Neill and by other leading Irish-American politicians, including Senators Kennedy and Moynihan and Governor John Carey, as well as John Hume during his many visits to Washington, and Dublin. Irish politicians and diplomats in Dublin and Washington played an important part in this process.

Paul Quinn, an influential lawyer in Washington with strong Irish-American roots, and a close friend of Hume, filled in some of the background. He said "All of my grandparents were born in Ireland, so my interest in the place was of long-standing. The problems in the North caused me increasing concern and prompted me to do what I could to move things in the right direction."

Many people, including O'Neill, Kennedy and others persuaded President Jimmy Carter to take an interest in Ireland, which he eventually did, with significant effect. On 30 August, 1977 Carter made an important statement on USA policy in Northern Ireland, which in effect internationalised the problem for the first time.

He noted that Americans were deeply concerned about the continuing conflict and violence, and that the United States "wholeheartedly supports peaceful means for finding a just solution that involves both parts of the community of Northern Ireland, and protects human rights and guarantees freedom from discrimination – a solution that the people of Northern Ireland, as well as the Governments of Great Britain and Ireland can support."

Carter stressed that US Government policy on Northern Ireland had long been one of impartiality, and that it supported the establishment of a form of government in the Province which would command widespread acceptance throughout both parts of the community. The President also stressed that "there are no solutions that outsiders can impose."

He added that a peaceful settlement would contribute immeasurably to stability in Northern Ireland "and so enhance the prospects for increased investment." In a key passage he said "In the event of such a settlement, the US Government would be prepared to join with others to see how additional job-creating investment could be encouraged, to the benefit of all the people of Northern Ireland."[4]

It was issued at an odd time, however, when most politicians on both sides of the Atlantic were on holiday. Although one Irish journalist described it as "apparently anodyne" it was, in fact, an historic statement which over-ruled the traditional American line of upholding the "status quo" on Northern Ireland because of the special relationship with Britain.

Ronald Reagan's interest in Irish affairs, initially, was limited. This was partly because of the long-standing tradition of Anglo-American politics that Northern Ireland was the sole business of the British Government.

Some people believed that the establishment of the IFI was the first indication that the Northern Ireland problem was being internationalised, but the breakthrough in Anglo-US policy had already been made by the Carter statement. It seemed obvious that if and when a political settlement emerged, it would be accompanied by some kind of economic package from America, backed by other members of the international community.

Meanwhile there was work to be done, not least in making sure that Carter's successors were clear about the Irish position. In the run-up to the 1978 Presidential election, the newly-appointed Irish Ambassador Sean Donlon made a point of getting to know all the candidates, including Ronald Reagan.

He asked Reagan about his background and suggested "With a name like that you must have some Irish blood in your veins!" Reagan replied that his roots, as far as he knew, could be traced back to London but he asked Donlon to carry out more research on his behalf.

Donlon and his colleagues did this, with the aid of the comprehensive genealogical facilities of the Mormon Church in Salt Lake City, and traced Reagan's roots back to the small village of Ballyporeen in Co. Tipperary -which Reagan later visited as President in June 1984. However Sean Donlon and his colleagues had done their homework well and it was no surprise that Reagan broke new ground for an American President by accepting the Ambassador's invitation to lunch at the Irish Embassy on St. Patrick's Day in 1979. On the way in to the building, Reagan noted the Irish and American flags which were on display and he told Donlon "My great-grandfather would be very proud of this."

Dail to approve aid fund move on Ulster

THE Dail will be asked next month to ratify two international agreements for administering the aid fund set up in support of the Anglo-Irish Agreement.

The United States Government has agreed to contribute 50m dollars this year to the fund to finance economical and social projects in areas of Northern Ireland worst hit by the troubles.

It is expected that additional contributions to the fund will come from Canada, Australia, New Zealand and the EEC.

Names of the trustees who administer the fund are to be announced next week in simultaneous statements from the British and Irish Governments. A number of prominent people in Northern Ireland and the Republic have been approached to serve as trustees.

Review

The Republic's Cabinet, which spent some hours yesterday on a general review of the situation in Northern Ireland, drafted the text of international agreements with Britain and the US which will be brought before the Dail for ratification next month.

The Irish and British Governments will jointly underwrite the cost of administering the fund. Under the Republic's constitution, any international agreement involving State expenditure has to be approved by the Dail.

Although Ministers are concerned at the spread of intimidation throughout the community in Northern Ireland, the Repoublic's Government is satisfied that the Anglo-Irish Agreement has survived its toughest test, the loyalist "marching season" — and that it will bring positive results.

There is satisfaction in Dublin that the British Prime Minister, Mrs. Thatcher, and her Cabinet, are "rock solid", behind the pact, according to a Government spokesman.

Although it is expected that the autumn package of reforms predicted by the Republic's Foreign Affairs Minister, Mr. Peter Barry, and the Minister of State at the Northern Ireland Office, Mr. Nicholas Scott, is not "on," changes in relation to the Flags and Emblems Act, voting rights and the Irish Language, are expected soon. Reforms in the area of the administration of justice and the security system are seen as more long term.

Former Taoiseach Dr Garret Fitzgerald

President Ronald Reagan and Prime Minister Margaret Thatcher – "although he lacked close friends, Reagan had an ideological soul-mate in Margaret Thatcher, whom he first met in London in 1975 before either of them was in supreme office. While he was President and she was Prime Minister, the so-called 'special relationship' between Britain and the US blossomed."[5]

Clearly the American President was "on side" in the approach to the creation of an Anglo-Irish Agreement. Whatever Margaret Thatcher's misgivings about its effects on the Unionists, she was clearly aware of what was taking place. The former Taoiseach Dr Garret Fitzgerald confirmed that senior officials from Britain and Ireland were working on the Agreement, and that the Americans were kept fully briefed. He told me "Margaret Thatcher must also have known about it, and she didn't object, so it was arranged that the Fund would be announced by President Reagan and Tip O'Neill when they came out from the White House to announce their support for the Agreement."[6]

Dr Fitzgerald also emphasised that the Fund was not an attempt to "internationalise" the Northern Ireland problem, but that it was "something that would reinforce the Agreement and eventually make Unionists realise that it was to their benefit." He added that Unionist leaders would not see him, "so I could not explain what we were trying to do. You cannot communicate any other way than personally that you are genuine and sincere about something."

James Molyneaux, at that time the leader of the Official Unionist Party, confirmed to me that he was not in contact with Fitzgerald. He said "Politically I could not have seen him, and I did not do so. The whole thing was on the wrong track politically, and it was totally against my instincts. I poured cold water on all such schemes because there was a price to pay for allowing any foreign power to bring help from outside to only one part of the United Kingdom, and that price was the weakening of the constitutional position of Northern Ireland."[7]

Lord Molyneaux's reaction was typical of mainstream Unionists who were shocked that a British Prime Minister would sign, over their heads, a major Agreement with the Irish Government. None was more troubled than Jim Molyneaux who had a good relationship with Thatcher. He said "Occasionally she and I worked closely and even jointly. Her instinct was also to be careful about any possible foreign intervention in the affairs of Northern Ireland, but she was always under pressure from her civil servants particularly in the Northern Ireland Office who in turn were being influenced from Dublin. I was always opposed to any dangerous flirtations with any foreign country. However I am certain that if the Prime Minister had told us in advance about what was happening, there would have been even greater trouble politically."

Nevertheless, from late 1984 senior officials from the UK and Ireland continued to work hard on the negotiations for what became the Anglo-Irish Agreement. The Irish side asked that President Carter's

1977 offer of economic help to back any Agreement should be included, and this was agreed by the British.

In June 1985, the Irish Government was briefed by the Taoiseach on developments concerning the major thrust of the proposed economic package. Significantly, he indicated that Mrs Thatcher had shown "considerable enthusiasm" about the concept of 'an International Fund'. She felt that apart from the obvious financial advantage of such a measure, it might help to end the international criticism of British policy on Northern Ireland, notably in the US.

Irish Ministers were also told that "a Fund for Reconciliation and Reconstruction in Ireland" was to be established in areas of traditional high unemployment, primarily in the North but also in the South. They were also informed that the details of establishing and administering such a Fund had yet to be worked out.

A few weeks after this briefing Senator Edward Kennedy suggested to Irish officials that one model for US financial aid could be the Cyprus Peace and Reconciliation Fund proposed in 1984 which would provide US funds for Cyprus, in the event of an agreement between Greece and Turkey in their dispute over the island. Kennedy also expressed continuing concern that President Reagan might favour private investment in Northern Ireland, rather than using US tax-payers' money for this purpose.

However, such fears proved unfounded, and tax-payers' money formed the basis of the Fund throughout its lifetime. Reagan and Tip O'Neill gave their public backing to the Anglo-Irish Agreement almost as soon as it was signed. Speaking outside the White House, with O'Neill by his side, President Reagan re-iterated Carter's 1977 promise of financial aid and said "There are many in Congress who have shown their concern and sympathy for the people of Northern Ireland, and I will be working closely with the Congress in a bi-partisan effort to find tangible ways for the United States to lend practical support to this important agreement."

The emergence of a Fund was certain, but its structure was not. However, only days after the Anglo-Irish Agreement was signed, a meeting was held in the Northern Ireland Office in London between senior British and Irish officials to begin detailed discussions on the working of the Fund. The references to the "Cyprus" Fund were dropped, because the title was not favoured by the British, but the penultimate draft of 5 December 1985 referred to "The International Fund for Ireland", and this became its name.

Earlier on, some people had thought of calling it the "American Fund for Ireland" but this was ruled out by the British. Understandably Mrs Thatcher was sensitive about the idea of a purely "American" intervention, and this is why the inclusion of the Commonwealth countries, and later the European Union, was so crucial to the concept of an "International" fund.

The proposals were set out in great detail in a document agreed by the British and Irish Governments and these formed the broad basis of "the International Fund for Ireland." They also became the blueprint for the first Chairman and Board of the Fund.

The major problem had not been money, but rather the political challenges of making such a Fund possible. Peter Barry, the then Irish Minister for Foreign Affairs, told me "We had to grit our teeth and go for it, to bring about structures where Nationalists could feel that their concerns were being addressed and that Unionists did not feel threatened, and these were both equally difficult things to do." [8]

"We knew that the border counties had been badly deprived or damaged for years, and we knew that both Unionists and Nationalists in those areas had to be given some economic lift. The British were not against it, but they were not as enthusiastic about it as we were."

The British Prime Minister was said by some people to be less than pleased with the idea of an International Fund, but this was not

Lord Brooke, a former Secretary of State for Northern Ireland. Margaret Thatcher once said to him "You have the most interesting job in the Cabinet, apart from mine".

strictly the case. Peter Brooke (later Lord Brooke of Sutton Mandeville) who was Northern Ireland Secretary from 1989 to 1992 recalled that Mrs Thatcher was more open-minded about Ireland than she was sometimes given credit for.

He also recalled, for example, that when he went beyond his initial brief from Thatcher, she continued to support him fully. Brooke made a key speech on 9 November 1990 to his constituency party in London in which he stated that Britain had no selfish economic or strategic interest in Northern Ireland. This proved to be deeply controversial, particularly with the Unionists, but it became a fundamental tenet of British policy which underlay all future negotiations.

The Former Irish Minister for Foreign Affairs Peter Barry

Brooke said "Mrs Thatcher asked me to become Secretary of State in July 1989, and she told me 'We have got this institution called the Anglo-Irish Agreement and, frankly, your job between now and the election is going to be an administrative one, to keep things going. Now that we have the Agreement we don't want any new initiatives.' It could be said that I disregarded her advice, but she backed me totally in everything I did."[9]

She also told Brooke "You have the most interesting job in the Cabinet, apart from mine. Mine's even more interesting than yours in terms of scale, but otherwise yours is a more political job than any other in the Cabinet." Brooke added "She was thoroughly supportive, provided the initiative looked as though it was constructive and that it was going somewhere."

Brooke himself was supportive of the first major International Fund initiative in developing the Shannon-Erne Link. He represented the British Government at the official launch of the project, and recalled a lunch afterwards with the then Taoiseach Charles Haughey. He said "Margaret has just resigned and Charlie only wanted to talk to me about her. He was clearly fond of her and admired her. He said that she had created privatisation and now it could be seen all over the world."

Whatever the fascinating nuances and strategies of high Anglo-Irish politics, the bedding down of the International Fund was also the business of senior civil servants on the ground. It was not a particularly easy task, but it provided a unique challenge which was met enthusiastically by State officials on each side of the border. There had been co-operation even in the long gone days of Sean Lemass and Terence O'Neill, but this was something entirely different, namely the establishment of a workable scheme to help people from both communities in the border counties of the island.

The Americans also had an important practical input, and Sir George Quigley recalled the dealings with the State Department in the USA. "I remember going across to some of the meetings in Washington where this was all being thrashed out, and one of the big issues was whether or not there would be strings attached to the money. I don't mean that people were contemplating political strings, but when they give you money, they are keen to restrain the way in which you can use the resources."

"For our part, we at Stormont were keen also to make sure that the money was put to relevant use in Northern Ireland, and not necessarily for purposes that were dictated by the American view of what was applicable worldwide. Overall, I think it was a very well-intentioned initiative on the part of the Americans, and it was fully in line with what they have tried to do in Ireland publicly and privately over the last 25 years or so."

Quigley felt that it was a "tricky time." He says "At the time some people regarded this as quite revolutionary, though in my earlier career I had seen evidence of people capitalising on every conceivable opportunity to do things together on the island. In the Sixties I used to have very productive discussions with my opposite numbers in the Republic, and it taught me that we could learn from each other and that by concerted action we could do more together than we could independently."

The developments since then have demonstrated the validity of this view. "What happened under the Good Friday Agreement to some extent reflected the successful experience of the International Fund for Ireland. It didn't seem to be coming from Mars, but something that was strictly focused on real objectives that were helping real people in real ways."

Nevertheless there were considerable difficulties in presentation, particularly when many Unionists were talking about "blood money" being offered to try to create cross-border structures that might help to bind up the wounds in Northern Ireland.

Clearly a strong figure was needed to chair the Fund, and that figure was Sir Charles Brett, a Northern Ireland lawyer with socialist leanings who had widespread experience of important bodies. 'Charlie' Brett, as he was known, took no prisoners but he faced his arduous task with courage, determination, some necessary muscle, and not a little humour.

Notes

1 During an Interview with the Author in Belfast on 8 February, 2007.

2 During an Interview on 30 January 2008 which, incidentally, was the 36th Anniversary of Bloody Sunday, when 13 people were shot dead by the Army in Londonderry. A 14th person died later.

3 During a Conversation with the Author in the USA in July 2007.

4 John T. Woolley and Gerhard Peters "The American Presidency Project (Online) Santa Barbara, California.

5 "Great Lives – A Century in Obituaries from The Times", published by Times Books 2005, page 647.

6 During an Interview with the Author in Dublin on 22 February 2008.

7 During an Interview in the House of Lords at Westminster on 1 May, 2008.

8 In an Interview with the Author in Dublin on 6 July 2007.

9 In an Interview with the Author in the House of Lords at Westminster on 5 December 2007.

CHAPTER TWO

Making It Work

THE FIRST CHAIRMAN OF THE BOARD of the International Fund for Ireland Charles Brett, had a public-school British accent which made some people assume that he was naturally a "Tory." In fact he had distinct Leftish views and was a former Chairman of the small and 'missionary' Northern Ireland Labour Party.

Sir Charles Brett, the first Chairman of the Fund. "He understood what deprived people and communities had been going through".

Brett was also a former Chairman of the Northern Ireland Housing Executive which did a remarkable job in providing for the basic accommodation needs of people from all backgrounds within the wider community. Charlie Brett may have talked like a "toff" but he understood what deprived people and communities had been going through.

Sir George Quigley recalls "The people who set up the Fund wanted someone who was independently-minded and who wasn't afraid of a challenge. Charlie had been very successful as Chairman of the Housing Executive, and they felt that his heart was in the right place. He was interested in people, and he gave the project the intellectual leadership it needed."

Brett, like many another public figure, was partly a victim of some of his strengths. Quigley says "He brought to the role as Chairman that wonderful quality of acute impatience, which is needed in any pioneering organisation. Charlie did not suffer fools gladly. He wanted things done and he usually wanted them done the day before yesterday. He wanted solutions and not problems, and those are excellent attributes for anyone in a difficult job of getting results and making an organisation credible. He was quite prepared to stir things up and on occasions he could be very demanding of people around him. I see that, particularly in the perspective of history, as a good quality."

The downside of this was the fact that Brett put some people off, but it was a price he was prepared to pay for getting things done. With hindsight, it could be argued that a more sensitive Chairman would not have had the steel to stand up to

One of the early meetings of the Board of the Fund, with Sir George Quigley in the foreground

The first Annual Report of the Fund

the opponents of the Fund, who felt that it was a sop from America, and from those potential friends who had to be told that their pet project did not qualify for assistance.

Sir Charles died several years ago, but he left a small yet significant corpus of material about his work as Chairman. His accounts of the early days of the Fund were written clearly and candidly, and not without flashes of humour. In an article published in 1990 shortly after his retirement as Chairman he admitted to his suspicions that the concept of the Fund "was influenced by a muddled, but benevolent, desire to believe that money could buy peace, even in Ireland. I do not think that the purposes or potentialities of the Fund had been at all clearly worked out before it came into existence. "Its objects and functions were diffused; even the primary objectives 'to promote economic and social advance and to encourage contact, dialogue and reconciliation' constituted a tall order, on a not unlimited budget." He added "The fruitful distribution of large sums of money, especially other people's money, is neither as easy nor as popular as might be supposed."[1]

The first seven-man Board appointed jointly by the British and Irish Governments had a wide business, professional and administrative experience. Brett recalls that there were "no politicians, ecclesiastics, or representatives of special interest groups. All, myself included, were part-time appointments; we were busy people; we came under heavy strain. Four were Catholic, two Protestant, and there was one interdenominational anticlerical-me! But the Board never, in my time, divided along sectarian, or North-South, lines; it developed into one of the strongest and most united bodies I have known."[2]

In his first Chairman's Annual Report published in 1987, Brett underlined that while the Board had "complete independence", there were "a number of express or implied constraints, resulting from its constitution, and the wishes expressed by the donor countries." The Board was required to have regard to the principles of equality of opportunity and "non-discrimination in employment, without regard to religious affiliation."

Brett stated "Clearly, it ought not to support any project which may be to the advantage of one community, but only at the expense of the other. It will not support, directly or indirectly, those who exploit instability by recourse to violence. Nor will any part of its funds be

The twelve Counties within the IFI's remit

applied to policing, military or judicial purposes. Indeed, more generally, the Board considers it to be axiomatic that it should not substitute the money derived from the taxpayers of the donor countries for the money of British or Irish tax-payers."[3]

Some of the Programmes selected were a direct consequence of the provisions under which the Fund had been established. These included investment companies, and the encouragement of business development and local self-help schemes, as well as agriculture and fisheries, inner-city urban development, and relevant scientific and technological development which, it was hoped, could provide commercial benefits reasonably quickly. Another important development was the establishment of a Wider Horizons Programme and the provision of training and work-experience overseas - which was a preference expressed by the Government of Canada.

The Board was also keenly aware that the USA had indicated that it wanted its contribution to be used principally for the stimulation of economic growth and prosperity in the private sector, with an emphasis on practical projects which would produce measurable results. Notwithstanding such stipulations, or certainly strong indications, from the respective Governments, the Board was determined to remain strongly independent.

This major imperative, common to all the Boards, was neatly summarised by Sir Charles. He stated "While it is certainly true that the establishment of the Fund derives from the Anglo-Irish Agreement of 1985, the Fund itself is in no way political. The seven members of its Board are all non-political figures. The Agreements expressly provide that the Board Members are not to receive instructions from the two Governments as to the exercise of their powers, and their independence is guaranteed." He also stressed that the Board was determined to carry out its functions "with absolute impartiality and integrity" and "without regard to political, sectarian or religious considerations."[4]

The American President's authorisation of the first US contribution was signed on 17 March, 1987, and the first payment was received six days later. In the first Annual Report, it was disclosed that the Fund had received during its first year two payments from the USA, totalling $85 millions. New Zealand made a single payment of NZ$300,000. These sums amounted in total to £53,035,000 sterling or IR£59,184,000.

Canada paid Can$4.1 million. The somewhat temporary nature of the funding was underlined by the promise of further $35 millions from the US, for payment in 1988. Although Australia and the European Union would come on board later, the situation at the end of the year 1987 was that no further contributions from anywhere else were promised.

Sir Charles Brett, however, was clear that the Board was charged with the "equitable distribution" of the resources available, and not with fund-raising. He stated that "The sum of £53 millions is a substantial one, but it has to be spread fairly over a large area, and a sizeable population. What can be achieved needs to be kept in proportion; this amount.... is equal to only about one-fifth of the combined budgets of the Industrial Development Agencies North and South in one year alone."[5]

Brett also outlined clearly the Fund's geographical remit. It covered "the six counties of Northern Ireland, and the six Southern 'border counties' of Donegal, Cavan, Monaghan, Sligo, Leitrim and Louth", which had a total population of some two million people. Brett further stated that "The Fund is enjoined to spend approximately three-quarters of its resources in Northern Ireland, and approximately one quarter in the south. It is not specifically required to give any special preference to the border areas; but it is to have regard to the needs of those areas which have suffered most severely from the consequences of the instability of recent years."[6]

Shortly after the Fund's first meeting on 14 December 1986, advertisements were placed to invite applications from those seeking assistance. This was to test the market and to find out the potential demand on the Fund. Within the first three months, more than 2,000 application forms had been issued, and around 1,200 had been completed and returned. The response, according to Brett, was "extraordinarily varied, and in some ways disconcerting."

A large proportion were judged to be ineligible for support, within the Fund's remit. "Some.... were for grandiose multi-million pound schemes; others were modest, and occasionally touching. Amongst them, however, was an appreciable number of sensible and businesslike projects, even if not all of them had been properly worked-out or presented."[7]

Sir Charles later gave some clues to the kind of applications which he may well have found "touching "or, in his own description "pathetic." Writing in the Political Quarterly several years later, he noted that a great number of the early applications "were from people seeking money for such things as a travelling fish-van; a lorry;.... the making up of a farm lane described as 'a contribution to the local infrastructure'; or 'for keeping Jimmy as a helper which I cannot otherwise afford'; in one case, even, 'a new suit a clothes.' "[8]

The former senior civil servant John Hunter recalls the story of an undertaker who wanted to replace the family's ageing hearse. "When he was asked how this project would contribute to cross-community reconciliation, he indicated that he would bury people from both sides of the community!" This story has a distinct ring of truth in a society where even death was a kind of segregation. In the main, there were "Protestant" and "Catholic" graveyards, and undertakers from either side of the community tended to be given the business by members of one or other main denomination. This was not an absolute rule, nor was it deliberately sectarian. It was part of the traditional customs, where Catholics and Protestants tended to choose undertakers on denominational or tribal lines.

Some of the applications to the Fund may have looked like frivolous attempts by some people to try to cash in on, literally, "money from America." Others may have been genuine requests to help small businesses in a big way. Sir George Quigley notes "Small things can make a difference between somebody being in or out of a job, or being able to provide a second job. We often quoted the example of a barber who wanted to have a second chair, or somebody who was delivering sandwiches around the neighbourhood and wanted a better van, or whatever it may have been."

The Fund spread its largesse over a significant range of activities in the first year. It committed £5.5 millions to Urban Development Programmes in 24 towns in the North and 12 in the border areas of the South; it provided £3.5 millions to Agriculture and Fisheries, and £6.5 millions to Science and Technology. Another £6.5 millions were allocated to the Wider Horizons Programme. The Board earmarked £7.55 millions for a Business Enterprise Programme over a 2-year period, and £8.9 millions to a Tourism Programme.

The first Annual Report carried several (now-dated) photographs of projects which had been helped – including Newry and Mourne Co-Operative Ltd, Dundalk Enterprise Co. Ltd., proposed Business Incubator Units at the Regional Technical Colleges in Sligo and Dundalk, potential development sites in Omagh and Dungannon, the emerging Navan Fort at Armagh, and the Irish Institute for European Affairs at Louvain. There were also important contributions to Business Enterprise ventures, including a Translation Agency in Belfast, a Hairdressing Salon in Ballyclare and a Designer-clock workshop in Edenderry.

The Fund also wisely set aside a reserve "partly to allow for the redeployment of funds if a pattern of take-up departs from that expected, and partly to fund a restricted number of exceptionally worthwhile projects which do not fit neatly into any of the Programmes." Sir Charles ended his first Chairman's Report with the reassurance that the Board "has been anxious not to be rushed into handing out money in a way which, with hindsight, might come to be seen as having been ill-judged. The amounts at its disposal, though sizeable, are not unlimited."[9]

Though Brett did not say so, it had been a good year's work. However, in the necessarily businesslike tone of his first Chairman's Report, he did not indicate his personal strategy of developing the best possible personal relationships between the Members. John Hunter recalls "The Chairman was conscious that these were all successful people who were undertaking a considerable time-commitment with relatively modest payment, and he felt it was appropriate to treat them well. Sir Charles was keen that they should get to know each other over the dinner or lunch table, and it worked. The chemistry was good."

Sir George Quigley concurs "These were tremendous ice-breaking sessions where people were bantering, and talking about

John Hunter- A former Senior Civil Servant who recalled one of the first Board Meetings in Malahide Castle

everything under the sun, and good relationships developed accordingly. People were genuinely engaging with one another."

These meetings were not without their darker side. The first gathering of the Board-designate took place on 23 November 1986 in Fivemiletown, but the first meeting proper of the Board was in the Tyrone Guthrie Centre at Annaghmakerrig in Co. Monaghan on 14 December 1986. Quigley recalls "Charlie was determined that this was a Board that would have quality and ambition, and he was insistent that the first meeting should be at Annaghmakerrig, with its aura of the arts."

"I remember travelling across the border on a Sunday morning, and suddenly, near Annaghmakerrig, four or five rough-looking guys carrying machine-guns popped out of the hedgerows. My colleague and I in the car thought that our last hour had come. Actually, these were members of the Southern security forces who were making sure that the meeting went off well. They were positioned around the house during the entire weekend, and that tells you something about the atmosphere in which the International Fund for Ireland was launched."

The first Board meeting at the Tyrone Guthrie Centre, Co. Monaghan, with Chairman C E B Brett, Board Members Sir Ewart Bell, Sir Gordon Booth, N V McCann, G P Dempsey, J Doherty and A McGuckian. Also pictured are Mr Bob Bell Deputy Assistant Administrator, US Agency for International Development (USAID) and Mr Michael Phillips, QC, the Canadian Observer

There was also an element of symbolism in the venues where the Board met. Hunter recalls that one meeting took place in Malahide Castle. He says "It had imposing portraits of some of the ruling family who had lived in the Castle. Some of their members had sat down for breakfast in that building before setting off to support the army of King James at the Battle of the Boyne in 1690, and very few of them returned. Another Board Meeting was held at the Bank of Ireland in College Green, Dublin, formerly the Irish Parliament, before the Act of Union, which had marvellous tapestries of the Battle of the Boyne. There were also important venues in the North, and the symbolism of holding our meetings in places which had a significant historical dimension was significant for Charlie, as Chairman."

Brett was markedly optimistic in his Chairman's report for 1987/88. He noted that the Fund's portfolio had developed steadily. He stated "There is now a considerable amount of progress to be seen on the ground; expenditure is building up steadily, and the commitment of funds runs well ahead of expenditure."

He also noted that "projects tend, like buses, to travel by stops and starts, and each stage has its own tariff in time, if not in cash. Not every case is long-drawn-out; some are quite simple and straightforward. But every application needs to be handled with equal care and, if waste and abuse are to be avoided, short cuts may prove foolhardy."[10]

By 30 September 1988 some 858 offers had been made, representing a total sum of £26,579,000 (IR£31,174,000). Brett noted "This represents a formidable total of obligations, the more so when it is recalled that the Board is prohibited from entering into financial liabilities which exceed its resources."

The Chairman also underlined that it was "notoriously difficult" to estimate the number of jobs created. His best-estimate was of around "4,500 permanent, new full-time jobs as well as additional part-time or seasonal jobs; 4,000 construction jobs of varying duration', and jobs "for at least 1,500 people in rural areas who might otherwise be forced to emigrate."[11]

Navan Fort, one of the Fund's first Flagship Projects

In translating theory into practice, Brett said, the Board had encountered "many vexing problems. For example, the comparative size, number and value of the projects to be supported; their spread in terms of geography, of demand, of population, of category; the balance between comparatively poor and comparatively well-off areas or applicants; the extent to which leverage has been insisted on; or to which it should be dispensed with."[12]

In September 1988, the Board reviewed its work. The timing of this was important, following a third US payment of $35 millions, and the announcement of proposals for a European contribution of 15 millions ECU in 1989, and in each of the two ensuing years. The US also proposed a fourth, unspecified, contribution in 1989. The Board itself decided to seek a more focused contribution to a regeneration of the most disadvantaged areas through its existing programmes, as well as a new Community Economic Regeneration Scheme, and special projects.

It also resolved to embark upon "a modest and experimental venture" into community relations, and in response to the wishes of the British and Irish Governments to carry out detailed appraisals and feasibility studies of such "Flagship" schemes as Navan Fort, and the refurbished Ballyconnell Canal which later developed into one the jewels of the Fund's crown, namely the linking of the Shannon-Erne waterway.

With hindsight, it is possible to trace the steady progress in the early years, but also to detect – mostly from the reminiscences of Brett – the uncertainties under which the Fund continued to exist. The Chairman acknowledged this bluntly in his 1988 Annual Report. He wrote "The Board's task is not made easier by uncertainty as to its future lifespan and funding prospects. It is constrained, therefore, to live within its means from year to year."[13]

Sir Charles, when he left office, was altogether more revealing. "My greatest fear, throughout my term of office, was of a total breakdown in Anglo-Irish relations. If Mrs Thatcher had reacted to some new event with another outburst of 'out, out, out', as she had done to the Report of the New Ireland Forum; if Mr Haughey had reverted to the extrovert Republicanism of his earlier days, the Board could easily have been deprived, at one stroke, of the administrative assistance of the Government agencies on one or both sides of the border, and of the services of the seconded civil servants who provided its sole executive arm, and of the flow of resources from the donor countries. I made my contingency plans for such an event; to my vast relief, it never happened."[14]

Brett also revealed that the administration of the Fund "took a lot longer than some impatient American legislators had hoped." The advertisements for applications raised hopes to "even more unrealistic heights than before", and the announcement of the Board's Programmes and policies caused much consternation, especially from those "who found their projects declared ineligible."

The publication of the second Annual Report in December 1988 caused, in Brett's own words, "the poached egg to hit the fan. There was an onslaught of criticism from all sides.

Prime Minister Margaret Thatcher. "It is not the lack of money that is the matter with Northern Ireland."

Certainly, when I took on what I had thought as a fairly non-political post, I little expected to find myself under attack, almost simultaneously, from Unionists and Paisleyites; Seamus Mallon MP of the SDLP; Gerry Adams MP of Sinn Fein; the Orangemen, the Hibernians, the Irish Congress of Trade Unions, and churchmen of various brands; normally sympathetic sections of the media; and a number of US senators, congressmen, and pressure groups, some (not all) of them ill-informed on the issues.

"One of Senator Moynihan's staffers in Washington once told me that he was a para-politician, on the model of para-medics and para-legals. I reckon that that description fitted me pretty well too."[15] Brett also describes colourfully some of the personal pressures of his early days as Chairman. "The extreme Protestant view was that the Fund was 'blood-money', a mere slush fund for Republicans and their collaborators. Dr Paisley denounced me as a traitor for accepting the Chairmanship; my professional office was picketed, and my home the scene of a demonstration by extreme Unionists, within a month of my appointment.

"The extreme Republican reaction was slower, but did not fail to come.... The Alliance Party was non-committal. Almost the only local supporters of the Fund were John Hume's Social and Democratic Labour Party; and even some of them (certainly not John Hume himself, who behaved most honourably in all his dealings with the Fund) gleefully shared the Unionist delusion that it was meant to be a slush fund for their especial benefit. On the British side, behind the scenes, it seemed that Mrs Thatcher was no great supporter of the Fund. Her only comment when I met her was the laconic, but incontrovertible one – 'It is not the lack of money that is the matter with Northern Ireland.' "[16]

Despite all the challenges, and setbacks, Brett and his Board carried on with courage and foresight, at a time when the Fund was still in an experimental stage, and when Northern Ireland remained in the midst of turmoil and political deadlock. It provided a firm foundation on which the successors to the pioneers could build, and over the years the Fund established its credibility and reputation with people on all sides.

In one of his last formal Reports, the Chairman was almost prophetic in his analysis. He stated "When the last dollar, pound, cent and penny have been spent, and whenever that may be, I believe that the International Fund will be seen to have made a significant contribution to the economic and social regeneration of the twelve Northern counties of Ireland."[17]

It did much more than that, in helping to provide a way forward for the whole island.

Notes

1 In an article published by The Political Quarterly Volume 61, No.4, dated October-December 1990 Pages 431-2.
2 Op.Cit. Page 433.
3 IFI Annual Report 1986/87 Page 4.
4 Ibid Page 3.
5 Ibid Page 2.
6 Ibid Page 2.
7 Ibid Page 5.
8 Op. Cit. Page 434.
9 Op. Cit. Page 8.
10 IFI Annual Report 1987/88 Page 4.
11 Op. Cit. Page 4.
12 Ibid Page 5.
13 Ibid Page 6.
14 The Political Quarterly, Op. Cit. Pages 432-3.
15 Ibid Page 435.
16 Ibid Page 432.
17 IFI Annual Report 1987/88 Page 6.

CHAPTER THREE

Good Pogress

SIR CHARLES BRETT WAS SUCCEEDED as Chairman in 1989 by John B. McGuckian, a prominent North Antrim businessman who had an impressive record at senior level with a number of major Northern Ireland institutions. These included Queen's University where he was senior Pro-Chancellor, and also Ulster Television where he was Chairman.

John McGuckian the second Chairman of the Fund. "It created an awful lot of good in all sorts of deprived areas".

In his first Annual Report he paid tribute to his predecessor, and noted that his work "was instrumental in the significant successes of the last three years." John McGuckian was clear about his reasons for accepting the Chairmanship of the Fund. He said "I became involved because of the political aspect. In my view its work was fundamental to the whole peace process because it involved the two Governments and it also had an international dimension. "It was a political phenomenon as far as I was concerned, and vital in the context of bringing the whole process forward. I thought it was worth doing, and in its political essence it created an awful lot of good in all sorts of deprived areas, and all sorts of cynics became enthusiastic in all sorts of places."[1]

McGuckian had a different personal style to Brett. He recalled that "Charlie was a man for whom I had the highest regard, and he worked his heart out. He took an awful lot of the heat at that time because he understood profoundly what was happening. He was a very able man and he achieved phenomenal things."

One of the early challenges facing the Fund was to encourage the Unionist community to apply for grants. McGuckian recalls a meeting with the then Joint Directors General who were told that there was a growing resentment among some Unionists who felt that they were not getting their share of the IFI money.

He said "I shocked them somewhat by telling them that I was pleased by this news, even though it appeared to be negative. The fact that Unionists were complaining in this way meant, in fact, that we were beginning to develop our own profile across the entire community. That was a great achievement, as far as I was concerned."

McGuckian remembers one cross-community meeting in a predominantly nationalist area of Tyrone where a local Orange Grand Master and his wife were helping to provide the refreshments for people from both main communities. "It was nice to see this happening in a place like that. I was always delighted by the enthusiasm in so many areas where people were keen to get together and to do things for the community. I just knew that eventually we would get it sorted out, and that given the right circumstances, people would forget their divisions."

Even today, only a few years after the worst of the Troubles ended, it is easy to forget the scale of violence and political deadlock that existed during the early years of the Fund's existence. In the broad period of McGuckian's Chairmanship, from

Secretary of State for Northern Ireland, Peter Brooke, MP, (left) Fund Chairman, John B McGuckian and Minister for Foreign Affairs Gerard Collins, TD

1989-1992, there were 317 deaths due to the violence, 3,893 injuries, 2,128 shootings, 843 explosions, 602 unexploded devices, 12,971 house searches by the security forces and 476 recorded paramilitary "punishment" shootings.[2]

Politically there was little or no progress in breaking the deadlock. In July 1989 Charles Haughey was re-elected as Taoiseach, with support from the Progressive Democrats. Nearly two weeks later in a Tory Cabinet reshuffle Tom King, the Secretary of State for Northern Ireland, became Defence Secretary, and he was succeeded by Peter Brooke, the Conservative Party Chairman. Despite the Anglo-Irish Agreement, the continuing difference in attitudes between London and Dublin on major issues was symbolised starkly by comments from two senior politicians.

Prime Minister Thatcher visited Northern Ireland and praised the "bravery" of the Ulster Defence Regiment, while in Dublin Ray Burke, a senior politician, underlined that the Republic's Government wanted Britain to justify 'the very existence' of the UDR. On December 31 that year, an Observer newspaper poll showed that 51% of people in Britain wanted the withdrawal of troops from Northern Ireland, while 36% wanted them to stay.[3]

The IFI carried on its work undaunted. In his first Annual Report published in 1989, John McGuckian underlined the "significant progress" that had been made and said that the Fund had "begun to make a serious impact on the economic and social landscape of that part of Ireland which has been so seriously affected by the Troubles of recent years."

He added "The achievements of the past year, in particular, demonstrate that an impressive momentum of activity has now been established in addressing the aims of the Fund in the fields of economic and social advance, and reconciliation." The Report noted that the Fund, to date, had approved assistance for a total of 1,261 projects. McGuckian expressed his pride that it had "contributed to the generation of more than 8,000 permanent full-time jobs – 4,000 of them in the past year – plus a considerable number of part-time and construction jobs."[4]

The Chairman drew attention to the Disadvantaged Areas Initiative, which arose from a strategic review undertaken in 1988, and one of the most important developments was the Community Economic Regeneration Scheme. The aim was to assist local community groups, with limited resources, to undertake imaginative projects which would help to regenerate the economy.

The Board also considered the formal establishment of a Community Relations Programme which would give "a more focused expression to this very important aspiration, and to concentrate specifically on improving relations between the divided communities of Northern Ireland, and between the communities North and South."

The Chairman added "The experimental nature of the initial Programme enabled it to become involved in, and to assist, community groups in projects which might otherwise not have happened. I am convinced that we can now build with confidence on what has been achieved in this important endeavour."[5]

The Annual Report featured a large number of projects which were being helped by the Fund. They ranged from micro-electronics to horse-breeding, and from tourism and fisheries, to international trade and local business development. One picture in the Report neatly highlighted a core objective of the Fund – with the Mayors of Derry and Galway and their senior colleagues discussing joint export promotion.

John McGuckian was no less enthusiastic in his second Annual Report, published in 1990.
He noted that it had been a year "of innovation, progress and considerable practical achievement, in which we have continued to give top priority to bringing new economic life into those localities and neighbourhoods which have suffered most from the communal strife, deprivation and destruction of the past two decades."[6]

In line with its mandate, the Board focused on promoting economic re-generation "to the direct benefit of the entire community, particularly in the most disadvantaged areas, where over two-thirds of the Fund's resources are concentrated. We have especially welcomed proposals with a cross-community dimension or involving practical cross-border co-operation, and have developed a number of important All-Ireland initiatives. We have also vigorously advanced the International Fund's quintessential message of hope, and illustrated the real scope for peaceful, constructive change through working together."[7]

One of the most striking examples of this was the development of the Erne-Shannon Link, with Taoiseach Charles Haughey and Northern Ireland Secretary Peter Brooke pictured together with John McGuckian, and also the Chairman of the Electricity Supply Board Professor C.T.G. Dillon at the launch of the project.[8] The Report also demonstrated the continually wide variety of projects supported by the Fund, ranging from Business Development Units in Derry to the harvesting of clams in Sligo, as well as Donaghmore Heritage centre in Tyrone, improved streeting in Buncrana, and training for mushroom growers in Keady, Co. Armagh.

One particularly important development during 1990 was the introduction of the Community Regeneration and Improvement Special Programme, known as CRISP. This was aimed at smaller towns and villages in the disadvantaged areas. Where the elements of CRISP dealt with physical regeneration projects, including community-led economic projects, urban development and environmental improvement, the Fund's investment was matched pound-for-pound by the Department of the Environment for Northern Ireland.

John McGuckian launches the Community Regeneration and Improvement Special Programme - known as CRISP - in Belleek Co Fermanagh

The town of Coalisland in Co. Tyrone, which had suffered severe economic depression since the early 70's and at one time had an unemployment rate of 50%, was the first place to be awarded CRISP status. The local District Development Association received a £2 million grant - half of which was supplied by the Fund, and matched by the DoE.

The main elements in the Coalisland package were to include the renovation of a derelict corn mill into a community resource complex, a fully-serviced industrial investment zone, new workspace facilities on the site of a former weaving factory, the encouragement of private sector investment in the town's regeneration, and the transformation of Coalisland's visual image by improvements in landscaping. Preparatory work on a series of CRISP proposals for other towns and villages in disadvantaged areas was also taking place.

During 1990, the Fund approved assistance for a further 386 projects, which brought to 1,647 the total number since its establishment. The Chairman reported that "The projects selected for support during the year are expected to result in about 3,400 additional full-time permanent jobs, plus a significant number of construction and part -time jobs."

McGuckian emphasised that the Board had achieved "considerable momentum as the many projects it has supported over the four years of its existence become increasingly

Coalisland CRISP before work started (left) and the finished project (right)

Canadian Prime Minister, Mr Brian Mulroney (right) visiting Fund projects with the Taoiseach, Mr Charles J Haughey, TD (centre) and the Fund Chairman (left), while on an official visit to Ireland

visible on the ground." He also stressed that the Board was determined to maintain that momentum "and to channel the resources available to the Fund into the right projects, as quickly and as effectively as possible."

McGuckian remained upbeat in his third Annual Report, published in 1991. He wrote "As Chairman, I am profoundly of the view that by concentrating on the most disadvantaged areas, by bringing communities together in a productive partnership, by reaching out to individuals and groups who have long felt marginalised and neglected, by helping local enterprise and small business to make a fresh start in deprived urban and rural areas, by promoting innovative cross-border and all-Ireland initiatives and – in all of this – by adhering closely to the principles of non-discrimination and fair employment, the International Fund is clearly making a significant impact of the political and economic landscape."[9]

John McGuckian with Senator Ted Kennedy

There were many examples of high-profile picture opportunities, with the Chairman being photographed at various Fund projects with – among others – the Taoiseach Charles Haughey, the Prime Minister of Canada Brian Mulroney, the Northern Ireland Secretary Peter Brooke, the Irish Minister for Foreign Affairs Gerry Collins, John Hume MP MEP, and the Hon. Tom Foley, Speaker of the US House of Representatives who was visiting Northern Ireland with a US Congressional delegation.

Equally important, however, there was much work continuing on the ground, with support being given to many projects including those at Poleglass-Twinbrook in West Belfast, a Business Enterprise Park on the Shankill Road, an angling project in Co. Cavan, help for the Inner City Trust in Derry, and improvements in landscaping at Downpatrick, Warrenpoint and Dungannon.

Overall, John McGuckian reported that a further 600 projects had been supported in 1991. He wrote "The story of the Fund's success in tackling the deep-rooted problems of the disadvantaged areas is really the story of many courageous and dedicated individuals and groups who are prepared to devote their

John McGuckian with the Hon Tom Foley, Speaker of the US House of Representatives

time, energy and talents to the economic and social regeneration of their own areas. Throughout these areas on both sides of the border, the Fund's team of locally-based Development Consultants has worked with such groups and individuals, helping them to prepare regeneration projects related to local needs and potential which the Fund can support."

In his final Chairman's Report in 1992, John McGuckian maintained his note of strong appreciation of the success achieved by the Fund, and his hopes for the future. The record of the Fund was, by that stage, a good illustration of success breeding success. During 1992, for example, approval was given by the Board for assistance to another 500 projects, bringing the grand total to 2,800 since 1986.

It is worth noting that in the earlier Annual Reports prepared by the first Chairman and Board, there was also a note of achievement and of optimism, but as well there was an uncertainty about the level and scope of future funding.

By the end of McGuckian's tenure of office, that sense of uncertainty had disappeared, and it was replaced by an enthusiasm about the scope for further achievement. This change in mood was not just due to one single factor or to the distinctive contributions from each of the first two Chairmen and their Boards.

The success of the Fund was essentially a collective effort, not only from those who provided funding but also from others who distributed the resources, and the recipients who made the projects work.

McGuckian in the 1992 Chairman's Report underlined that "The unique role which we have been able to develop, both North and South of the border, stems from the fact that the Board.... is directly appointed by the British and Irish Governments and from our uniquely independent mandate to administer funding in both jurisdictions.

"The Fund enjoys special status, too, as a result of the on-going international support which it receives, as well as the recognition given to our efforts and achievements on the ground in both parts of Ireland, where it is addressing the needs of both communities with complete equality of opportunity and without regard to political or religious affiliation."[10]

He noted that since its inception, the Fund had provided assistance to almost 60 projects in or near Belfast, ranging from a grant to a Dairy Farm regeneration scheme on West Belfast's Stewartstown Road, to an Argyle Street Enterprise agency on the Shankill Road, the Ashton Street centre in the New Lodge area of North Belfast, a Bryson Street employment project in East Belfast and the East Belfast Development Agency.

The Fund provided a total of £15 million for the 60 projects in Belfast, which in turn had a leverage of some £50 millions from other sources. The Chairman stated "These and other projects demonstrate the value of co-operation between the Fund, local communities, private businesses, regional authorities and Government over a wide range of activities."[11]

Other initiatives included further support for ACUMEN, a project to foster stronger ties between commercial and economic interests, North and South. A three-year programme was also planned to develop the first all-Ireland economic planning model, and a further series of joint marketing promotions were held to help tourism and trade on an all-island basis.

Carlingford – where the Border Towns and Villages Scheme was launched in 1992

The CRISP Programme developed rapidly, with funding for another 11 major projects in 1992. These included grants for improvements to Derrygonnelly and Garrison in Fermanagh, the development of the Plantation Centre in Draperstown as a major tourist attraction, the establishment of a heritage centre in Cullyhanna in South Armagh, and a regeneration package for Portaferry at Strangford Lough "to make the most of its location in an area of great natural beauty." There were also grants for Stewartstown which was considered to be "one of Co. Tyrone's most run-down and depressed communities", and Plumbridge in the Sperrin Mountains, which "suffered a gradual decline in recent years."

The rationale for the Plumbridge grant illustrated the essence of the CRISP Programme. The £0.34m to help halt the decline included the acquisition and development of a derelict property in the centre of the town as workshop-retail units and office suites, and a programme of environmental improvement and urban development to improve its appearance. The Annual Report emphasised that "It was anticipated that these new measures would 'stimulate commercial activity and breathe new life' into the village.[12]

In 1992 the Board also introduced a Border Towns and Villages Scheme. They included £IR328,250 to Carlingford, attractively situated on the Cooley peninsula across the Lough from Warrenpoint and Rostrevor. This money was to help exploit the town's tourist potential, to stimulate commercial activity and "to contribute to the regeneration of a town which, due to the community's commitment, has begun to reverse its decline in recent years."[13] These, and other investments and hard work, paid off handsomely, and Carlingford today is an upmarket centre, much different from its image of the not too far distant past,

Another noteworthy grant under the scheme was £IR 0.12m to Inniskeen in Co. Monaghan, the birthplace of the poet Patrick Kavanagh. This grant was to help restore a disused church as a heritage centre in order to feature the work of Kavanagh and other Ulster writers, and to help with environmental improvements to the village which suffered from high unemployment.

A third investment of £IR0.1m for Kiltyclogher in Co. Leitrim was for measures to help the town become more attractive to visitors. In the Board's opinion, Kiltyclogher had "suffered from its proximity to the border and from being cut off from its natural hinterland in Co. Fermanagh." These small pen-portraits provide an insight into the thinking of the Board, and the way in which relatively small sums were used to start projects in border areas where the Troubles and other factors had led to a decline or lack of confidence, and sometimes both.

In return, many of the beneficiaries of such grants paid tribute to the Fund. The Chairman and others received letters from individuals and institutions where Fund money had made a big difference. There was appreciation from the people of Coalisland, and Jim Canning, Chairman of the local Development Association, wrote to John McGuckian to assure him that the work being funded in the £2.7 million project was well underway.

It had resulted in major changes in the town, including "the removal of dereliction, the provision of much-needed employment and a complete change in attitude of the people. They have been given a new enthusiasm, and they look forward to the future with great hope. None of this would have happened without the help of the International Fund, both financial and the assistance of the development officers and secretaries. I would like to record the thanks of the people of Coalisland for the kind generosity of the American people, and to inform them of the enormous help their money has been in the regeneration of a very disadvantaged community in Co. Tyrone."[14]

Another letter from ROSA, a group working for the Regeneration of South Armagh, illustrates how outside help gave hope and stimulus to an area which was often featured in the media as for all the wrong reasons. Tom McKay, the Chairman of ROSA, summarised the dire situation within the area in 1989. He wrote "No economically-oriented groups active; climate of economic nervousness generated by the Troubles; private sector unwilling to move; no opportunity for positive action; label of 'Bandit Country'."

By 1992, however the situation had changed for the better. "Fourteen groups actively implementing economic projects; four 'bricks and mortar' projects have received IFI grants; three community businesses 'up and running'; five community-driven projects close to application stage; a very positive climate of growing confidence and co-operation; private sector beginning to move."

McKay paid tribute to the Fund's appointment of Joe McNulty as a local Development Consultant, who helped in the formation of the ROSA group itself and in formulating local strategy. Mr McKay also recorded the growing response of the Government to match the CRISP funding, and by the firm commitments of senior civil servants and others to the area.

He added "As a result a whole new positive arrangement has been established in an area where apathy and misunderstanding was the general status quo. More important is the fact that the Fund has been the catalyst in empowering local communities to have a role in the regeneration process, activating committed skilled individuals in a

Members of the Fund's new Board appointed by the British and Irish Governments. L-R (back row) Mr Irvine Devitt, Joint Director General, Mr Denis Calvert, Mr John Craig and Mr Donal Hamill, Joint Director General. Front row: Mr Willie McCarter, Mr Neil McCann, Mr John B McGuckian, (Chairman), Mr Paddy Duffy and Mr Pat Kenny positive co-operative way to drive job-creating viable projects, and through this to change the image of the area. Quite simply, none of this would have happened without the Fund."[15]

Another positive letter, this time to Senator Edward Kennedy, was written by Kevin Gilmartin, Chairman of the Development Trust for Belleek in Co. Fermanagh, which received a CRISP grant of £1.88m to help regenerate the village and the local district. Partly as a result of this, the Trust attracted inward investment of £2.4m, and according to Mr. Gilmartin "this has directly leveraged an additional £2.5m from the private sector for a series of projects which are being carried out in the next 2-3 years."

Kevin Gilmartin ended his letter to Senator Kennedy thus; "We would like to thank both yourself and the members of Congress for your commitment to helping to solve the conflict in Ireland, North and South, and for the financial support to the International Fund for Ireland. We can assure you that your efforts are very much appreciated here."[16]

This was not just a polite thank you from a group that had received largesse from the Fund and its sponsors. It was a sincere response from those people who felt that the help from the Fund had made all the difference. Not all the grants, of course, worked quite so well, and mistakes were made, but the general air of goodwill on both sides of the Atlantic, in the European Union and elsewhere, helped to create and to cement relationships and networks which made an important grass-roots contribution to the eventual peace.

In his final report John McGuckian summarised his "genuine sense of achievement from having been associated with this unique body, which is proving to be such a powerful force for change through its very practical contribution to peace and prosperity."

McGuckian had decided firmly from the outset that he would serve as Chairman for only one term, but he resolved also that he would give much of his time to the Chairmanship when in office. He did so, at a period in his career when he had many other pressing responsibilities and interests, but he found that his work with the Fund was eminently worthwhile.

He recalls "It was a truly great experience, and I loved every minute of it. We were seeing people working together and achieving so much on the ground. I probably could have stayed longer and still have enjoyed it, but I believed that I had achieved all I had set out to do.

"I knew that I would miss it, but there has to come a time in everything when you move on. I have done and enjoyed all sorts of things during my career, but there's nothing I have done before or since my time as Chairman of the Fund that I enjoyed quite so much".

In stating this, he was also underlining a central factor about the Fund and its operations. Essentially it was all about helping people and communities to help themselves.

Notes

1 In an Interview with the Author on 11 June, 2007.
2 Northern Ireland – A Political Directory by Sydney Elliott and W. D. Flackes, published by the Blackstaff Press Pages 680-689.
3 Op. Cit. Pages 44-47.
4 Annual Report 1989 Page 5.
5 Op. Cit. Page 5.
6 Annual Report 1990 Page 5.
7 Op.Cit. Page 5.
8 This Flagship Project will be Discussed in more detail in a later chapter.
9 Annual Report 1991 Page 5.
10 Annual Report 1992 Page 5.
11 Op.Cit. Page 6.
12 Op.Cit.
13 See Separate Panel on Carlingford.
14 Op.Cit. Page 28.
15 Op.Cit. Page 36.
16 Op.Cit.Page 32.

Carlingford

Carlingford in Co. Louth was the first place in the South to benefit from the new Border Towns and Villages Programme which was set up in 1992.

The Fund announced that it had allocated a multi-million pound budget over two years to benefit 16 border towns and villages which had been adversely affected by the Troubles. They were located in Donegal, Leitrim, Cavan, Monaghan and Louth, and were chosen not only because of their geographical location but also in association with the Fund's Development Consultants and the Local Authorities.

The Scheme was launched at Carlingford on 2 September 1992 by the Taoiseach Albert Reynolds who paid tribute to the "vision and efforts" of the people of Carlingford, and to the Fund's commitment to working with communities.

Cross border tourism and development programme for community groups in the Holy Trinity Heritage Centre, Carlingford, Co Louth.

The Chairman John McGuckian underlined that the Fund could help people to overcome the negative effects of the Troubles but "only if the communities themselves are involved, as they are in Carlingford." The Fund approved assistance to Carlingford Lough Heritage Trust for an integrated development in the town, and for environmental improvements, in association with Louth County Council.

The Trust had considerable success in developing Carlingford as a centre of tourism, given the town's rich and archaeological heritage, and its location in the beautiful Cooley peninsula. The Trust's Chairperson Ciaran McGoey, speaking at the Carlingford launch, thanked the Fund for its support which, he said, would enable the group to continue its regeneration work.

Carlingford's extensive historical heritage includes remnants of the 12th century King John's Castle, the 15th century Taaff's Castle, and The Mint, dating from 1467. The well-preserved Tholsel or gate-tower was a medieval customs-barrier. There is also a fine Heritage Centre and the remains of Carlingford Friary, which was established by a Norman Lord early in the 14th century.

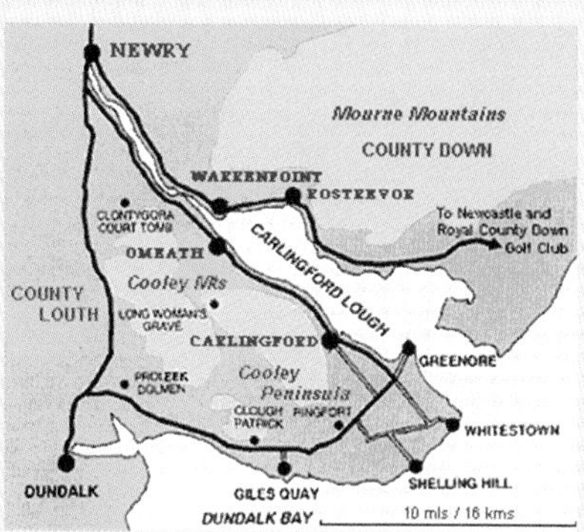

The Carlingford Waterbus.

The area's heritage also includes a legend myth about the giant Finn McCool who reputedly lived in the region around Carlingford and decided on his last day to lift a huge clump of earth and to throw it into the sea. This allegedly became the Isle of Man, and having thus changed the geography of the wider area Finn McCool lay down and died. It is said that that Slieve Foy mountain resembles the outline of his body, but the point to remember about Irish myths is that the facts may be quite different.

Happily, however, there is no "myth" about the progress of Carlingford, through the initiative of its people and with help from the International Fund and others at the right time, and that success story continues to the present day.

CHAPTER FOUR

Vital Link

DURING JOHN MCGUCKIAN'S PERIOD as Chairman, the Shannon-Erne Waterway was one of the first Flagship projects of the International Fund and it proved to be of considerable practical, economic and symbolic importance. This re-development of the disused 19th century Ballyconnell and Ballinamore Canal opened up once again a link between the Lough Erne and Shannon Waterways and brought regeneration to an area that had suffered from long-term economic neglect.

This initiative by the Fund, which was taken well before the paramilitary ceasefires or political breakthrough seemed possible, provided a tangible link across the border and demonstrated that economic progress and greater understanding between all the communities could go hand in hand.

More than a century and a half earlier, the original link between Upper Lough Erne and the River Shannon had seemed a good idea. Both waterways had proved to be an effective transport system for commercial goods and people in an area which had a poor road system. It seemed obvious that a new waterway link would be a resounding success.

This optimism was expressed by the engineer William T. Mulvany in his 1839 Report to the Shannon Commissioners, a year after the original survey had taken place. Mulvany wrote thus of the proposed link; "No doubt can be entertained of its remunerative nature, and especially when it is considered as the means of connecting neatly all the Inland Navigations of Ireland."

The Canal took four years to plan and 14 difficult years to build. It was back-breaking work, and the costs constantly exceeded the budget. The construction was complicated by the twin objectives of dredging a navigation canal and also improving land-drainage, but it was a considerable feat of engineering.

However, there was one major drawback - by the time that the Canal was opened on 4 July 1860, the newly-developed railways which were faster and more efficient were making the waterways commercially obsolete. Only eight vessels passed through the Canal in more than eight years - roughly one a year - and in 1869 it was abandoned, as a commercial disaster. The last-known passage was made in 1873,

Over the next 122 years or so, the locks rotted and the silt and vegetation gradually reclaimed its former territory. Ironically, the Canal which had been constructed to bring people together, eventually created a new physical barrier, which divided local communities and even farms. Instead of being a flourishing waterways hinterland, the area became literally a backwater, with the local population being forced to move elsewhere for employment.

The Troubles deepened the sense of isolation within the region. The border area was dangerous, and impossible to secure effectively from either side. Short of constructing a kind of "Berlin Wall", which would have been impractical and politically impossible, the people on both sides of the border had to live with the uncertainties and inconvenience of a long paramilitary campaign directed at the North and sustained by activists on both sides of the border.

Although much of the Canal's basic infrastructure seemed sound and there had been talk about a possible re-opening, this remained only talk. Given the intensity of the Troubles, it did not seem an opportune time to consider re-opening a waterways link in the midst of such unpromising times and terrain.

Ballinamore & B'Connell DISTRICT.

RETURN of all Persons, except Gangers and Labourers, employed in the above District, during the Month of January 1854 whether paid on Salary Forms or Labour Sheets.

(Directed by Circular No. 87.)

NAMES, (With Christian Name in full.)	Rate of Pay.	Date of Appointment.	In what capacity employed.	Whether paid on Salary Form or Labour Sheets.
Thos. J. Mulvany	£500 per an.	21 June '49	District Engineer	Salary Form
James Joyes	10/- per day	1 July '46	Pay Clerk	"
Francis Green	7/- "	1 Mar '48	Asst. Engr. & draftsman	"
Wm. H. Kelly	7/- "	5 Oct '46	Office Clerk	"
Richd. Ironson	4/6 "	31 Jan '53	Asst. Ditto	"
Edward Morris	3/4 "	5 May '47	Ditto	"
Marshal S. Thornton	3/- "	19 Sept '50	Yard & Store Clerk	"
Michl. McGuinness	3/4 "	29 Jan '53	Store Keeper	"
Robert Armstrong	10/- "	3 Mar '47	Assistant Engr.	Salary Form
John Quigly	5/- "	13 Sept '47	Overseer	Pay List under Circular 90
John Macdonald	3/6 "	May '47	Check Clerk	"
Patk. Caffrey	3/4 "	7 Sept '46	Ditto	

District Office Staff employed on the B & B and L. C. District

COURTESY: NATIONAL ARCHIVES

Labour Sheet dated January 1854 for the Ballinamore and Ballyconnell Canal.

However, the idea of re-opening the Canal had some powerful supporters, including the Taoiseach Charles Haughey and senior officials in the European Commission. The International Fund had been approached as a suitable body to "kick-start" such a project, but there was by no means an instant decision to press ahead.

Willie McCarter, at that time a Board Member and later Chairman, recalls the thinking behind the project. He said "Most people thought that the idea was completely mad, and there seemed to be no appetite for it at all. However, a consensus began to form."[1] People who had been sceptical began to come on board. In 1989 the Fund put forward £1 million for a feasibility study of the costs and possible benefits of the proposed restoration of the Canal.

This was a complex operation which examined the engineering, environmental and economic aspects of the proposal, but eventually the study presented a strong case for re-opening. This was based on the likely tourism opportunities at a time when waterway recreation was developing generally. There was also the powerful symbolism around the

An aerial view of the Shannon Erne Waterway

Dermot Gallagher, Secretary General at the Department of Foreign Affairs in Dublin

potential for an all-island economic venture. The Fund then provided another £5 millions toward the capital investment in the project which cost a total of some £32 millions, after claims by contractors were finally agreed.

The other funding came from the EC, the Electricity Supply Board, the Northern Ireland authorities, and the Irish Soldiers' and Sailors' Fund. The new Shannon-Erne Waterway also provided an early model for the Fund, and demonstrated its potency as a lever of economic development projects for the border counties.

Dermot Gallagher, at that time Assistant Secretary in the Irish Department of Foreign Affairs – and later Ambassador to the United States, and eventually Secretary General at the DFA – was Chairman of the Southern Project on the Canal Flagship project. As such he had the task of raising the large amount of funding which was needed.

He told me, during a conversation in his office in Dublin on 3 March 2008, "I went to the then Taoiseach Charles Haughey and told him we needed this money. He had the vision for it, and he was very supportive. He said to me 'I want this to happen.' " Gallagher, a Leitrim man, understood the mood of people in the border areas, and their need for help.

He said "While Governments and politicians were trying to move things forward at their level, it was very important that, at the grass-roots, there were building blocks as well to show people that they were not going to be left behind as part of this new arrangement, and that there was going to be meaningful change."

Although the feasibility study had been positive, one of the turning points from the International Fund's point of view was a meeting in a Dublin hotel with a Tourism sub-committee which was discussing the Canal project. The discussion reached stalemate, and at that point the two IFI Board Members withdrew for a private discussion. They came back later to announce that they would recommend that the Board should support the project and provide another £5 millions in due course – bringing the Board's total commitment to around £6 million, which was a considerable sum at that time.

Dermot Gallagher, who played a major role in delivering the project and keeping it within budget and within target-time, said later "It needed the feasibility study initially, and all the other money as well, but it was a good example of how the Fund could put 'first money on the table' and help to leverage finance from elsewhere. It was able to make something happen, that most likely would not have happened otherwise."

The restoration of the Canal was itself a considerable technical achievement which involved the renewal and repair of some 40 miles of waterway, including 16 locks. This required a mixture of new technology and traditional skills. The original cut stone was magnificently restored, and new locks were operated by the latest

Lord Mayhew, former Secretary of State for Northern Ireland

Former Taoiseach Albert Reynolds TD

"smart cards" – all of which presented an intriguing blend of 19th century engineering and architectural charm, and 20th century technology.

The reconstruction began in 1991 with a pilot contract, and from the outset the aim was to adhere to the highest standards of engineering, conservation and safety. As well, much attention was paid to minimising the environmental impact of the work.

The Official Opening on 23 May 1994 was a grand affair. Willie McCarter, who by then was the Board's Chairman, recalled "It was hugely symbolic. It took place before the paramilitary ceasefires, so that various people had to be taken to Ballyconnell by helicopter, including the then Northern Ireland Secretary Sir Patrick Mayhew. There was a huge gathering at Ballyconnell and then afterwards at the Slieve Russell Hotel. It was really a very dramatic day altogether."[2]

The Shannon-Erne Waterway project had the enthusiastic support of both Governments, and senior figures expressed their admiration in letters to the Chairman. Sir Patrick Mayhew stated, on 27 April 1993 ".... the British Government is proud to be associated with this project, and all those involved for the progress they have made in bringing this project to its present stage of completion deserve congratulations. The contribution which the International Fund has made is something which the British Government greatly appreciates."

Several weeks later, on 17 May 1993, the Taoiseach Albert Reynolds wrote to McCarter in a similar vein "I wish to express the Government's appreciation for the major contribution which the Fund has made to this outstanding project. The reconstructed canal will constitute an important new tourism asset on the island of Ireland, and should also be a catalyst for significant economic growth in the region which it serves.

"I am deeply committed to the success of this project. I wish to see effective management and marketing structures put in place which will ensure maximum benefit both for the present, and for future generations of Irish people."

Although the project was completed in 1993, the Fund was already aware of the serious challenge of exploiting the economic potential of the unique infrastructure. A North/South Task Force was established between the relevant statutory and agency bodies, and in 1992 the Fund agreed to part-finance a major marketing operation.

The main aims, according to IFI Development Officer Tom Hobson, were "to build awareness, to explore new marketing potential, to encourage product development and to provide a lead in quality assurance. The Fund also supported a Canal Villages Programme to provide a stimulus to the private and public sectors, in order to upgrade the infrastructure and to establish commercial projects."

One woman for whom the re-opened waterway made a huge difference is Joan Bullock, who lived with her family in a 17th century thatched house beside the Woodford River, on the Northern side just across from the small town of Belturbet. In 1972 the Troubles raged fiercely, and violent attacks were inflicted by extremists from both sides on innocent and vulnerable people. Joan told me about the night that year when she and her family had to flee from assailants who blew up the bridge which carried the main road from the North into Belturbet.

The violence deeply affected her wider family, and on 21 September 1972 armed men attacked the home of Joan's second cousin, by marriage. Thomas Bullock, who served in the UDR, and his wife Emily, were shot at point-blank range by people who broke into their home, and they died almost instantly. They had been watching television, and a neighbour later told an inquest that he had heard a shot, and had seen a car full of men going towards the border. He then went to the Bullock home and found the bodies. He described the scene as "a shambles."[3]

Joan Bullock remembers the day after the funerals, when armed men returned to the area and blew up their family's petrol station and tyre depot – allegedly in retaliation because a television report claimed that a close relative had seen the terrorists who had blown up the bridge at Belturbet. Later on a Bailey-bridge was built to connect the town with the North, but it, too, was blown up by unknown assailants.

Joan Bullock recalls "About a dozen men came to our house around 1.40 am and told us to get out. We left in our night-clothes, with our two children who were then only two years and six months old respectively. It was terrifying."

Joan Bullock and the remains of the blown up bridge at Belturbet. "We had a pulley system to bring things across".

The Bullock family later returned to their thatched house and despite the dangers, they refused to be driven from the area by violence. The destruction of the 19th century stone bridge nearby, and its modern successor, had a two-fold effect. It made the family feel safer in their isolation, but it also cut them off from Belturbet where they had many friends, and where had bought their groceries and supplies, and had attended the local Methodist Church.

Joan recalls "If our neighbours wanted to get in touch from the other side, they would drive down to where the bridge had been, and toot their car horn loudly. We would go out and talk to them, and if either of us wanted something we had a pulley system to bring things across. We also had a small boat on the river."

This almost surreal way of life was enlivened by a small number of foreign tourists who travelled to the area, even in those days of depression and danger. Their road maps did not indicate that the bridge had been blown up, so they naturally called in at the Bullocks' farmstead to find out what had happened.

Joan says "We usually made them a cup of tea, and we met some lovely people." She showed me postcards,

Graham Thomas – "There was a lot of character in the barges and each one had a log burning stove. So there was a bit of romance in it as well".

including one from a couple of young girls who addressed it to "Joan, Amer Lane (Between the Post Office and the 'Bust' Bridge to Cavan - NI").

The Bullocks continued to live their lives in such unusual circumstances, but one of the first signs of a possible return to normality was the beginning of the reconstruction of the old Canal which flowed past their house as the Woodford River. Joan says "There was still no bridge over the road until several years later, so the opening of the Shannon-Erne link was for us one of the first signs of new life.

"In the past the only sounds we heard was when road traffic came up near our door, but now you could hear the sound of river traffic, and that was lovely. I thought that it was a wonderful project, and it was great because it also brought new tourists. You never knew who you were going to meet, and that was really nice."[4]

Joan Bullock's story underlined the dangers in the border areas during the worst of the Troubles, and also the immense courage of 'ordinary' people who lived as best they could in the circumstances. As Joan Bullock talked to me in almost matter-of-fact tones about what her family and others had experienced, it was hard to realize just how difficult it had been. Joan said "It was scary", and simply left it at that.

The development of the Shannon-Erne Waterway helped many other people in less dramatic ways, but it changed their lives economically. In 1971 Ray Thomas, who describes himself as 'half-English, half-Welsh, moved from Berkshire to Leitrim with his wife Violet, a Cavan woman. They bought a large house with 85 acres and set up a dairy herd.

Ray says "In March of that year, I was working in a bank in England, and in April we were hand-milking three cows in Leitrim and beginning to re-paper the house."[5] Farming was difficult enough, even in those days. "It was a culture shock, and hard work, but also enjoyable. Some of the prices collapsed, and in the winter of 1974 cattle were selling for 50 pence each. However we were prepared to listen to an agricultural adviser, and when Ireland joined the EU we achieved 'development farmer' status, and worked up our herd to 23 milking Friesians."

The family also developed a guest-house business, which depended greatly on visiting fishermen and Americans searching for their Irish roots. However, the reconstruction of the Waterway opened up possibilities in the boat-hire business. Graham Thomas, Ray and Violet's son, recalls the early days of the reconstruction.

He says "The old Canal had been falling apart and was reduced to a trickle, except in storms when it became a raging torrent. When the building work began, it was a huge job and much bigger than we had expected. The whole front lawn was stripped of topsoil, and there were diggers as big as we'd ever seen, working down there. They would pour 40 loads of concrete into the bottom of a bog before they'd start putting up a side wall. It seemed unreal!"

There was a general welcome throughout the area for the idea of a Canal re-construction, and the possible new benefits it would bring. The Thomas family decided to expand into the boat-hire business. They had been leasing out smaller boats, but there had been drawbacks. Graham says "We had to learn to smile at some of the call-outs. We had to deal with people, with the cord pulled out of the engine or a fuel filter that had dropped into the water, and there was no screw to put it back again because they had tried to fix it while hanging over the back of the boat!"

The Thomas' new business was to be entirely different. With the help of funding from the IFI they became barge holiday operators at Riversdale where they had set up their farm and guest-house. Ray says "We'd seen traditional narrow-boats in England with a seven foot wide restriction, but we wanted something different. There were no such restrictions in Ireland, and we proposed to operate our own barges which were 10 feet wide."

Graham says "There was a lot of character in the barges, and each one had a log-burning stove. So there was a bit of romance in it as well." The IFI grant was for no fewer than 10 barges. "They told us that this would be a viable number, and we accepted that, because there was no point in taking on something that would not be viable. We started with four barges, and the rest were phased in. These were vessels which you could not buy 'off the shelf'. They had to be built to order, with staged payments, so the IFI's approach was very suitable for our needs."

The Thomas family has expanded further into building their own barges, and they have developed a marina at Riversdale to cater for their own customers and others who need mooring facilities. The 2007 season was one of their best, and despite the downturn in farming and the challenges of the guest-house business at a time of increased hotel accommodation at competitive prices, the future looks even brighter.

Ray Thomas notes that "Without the IFI initiative, there probably would be no barges here today. It was recognised early on as an ideal Flagship for a cross-border venture. There was existing boating on either side of the border but this came just at the right time. When the Waterway was completed, people started to trickle down from the North and discovered that down here we did not have horns, and the same applied in the other direction. People would say 'You know, it's

Seddie McGovern, Chairman of the Ballinamore Development Association. "This required a great deal of time and input, and it was an act of faith by the local people".

A Natural Boating Paradise

very nice over there.' A lot of it was perception, and we were perceived pretty badly. The new Waterway did a huge amount to improve the reputation of this area."

The Flagship Project helped not only individual families but also entire communities. Seddie McGovern, Chairman of the Ballinamore Development Association, talked to me about the days when the old Canal was only a small stream running through a large green field, which was known as "the priest's field." This later became the site for a splendid marina and boat-yard.

He explained that when the Canal was being developed, the local community sat down to plan how best it could exploit the new infrastructural development for the benefit of the town and hinterland. This gave rise to the formation of the Development Company.

Given the location (the mid-point on the Waterway) and the fact that the site was available for purchase with Canal frontage, it was decided that a cruise-hire facility was an option. The Development Company employed consultants who carried out a feasibility study and business plan, which concluded that the Marina was a viable project. The Development Company received some IR£423,000 from the EU Inter-Regional Fund and IR£123,000 from the IFI for the project.

The community also raised a significant amount of its own funding. Seddie McGovern says "This required a great deal of time and input, and it was an act of faith by the local people." The Development Association had also decided to lease out the marina to a commercial operator, and it became an Irish base for the French company Locaboat Plaisance which hires out vessels to a large international range of customers. The Company's promotional material draws attention to the many rural attractions of the area, including fishing and bird-spotting, and also underlines – rightly – that "here you are at the heart of one of Europe's last unpolluted natural paradises."

The success of the marina and the boating business has had an important spin-off for the local area. Seddie says "It has helped to bring a new dimension to our thinking. It is commonplace, for example, to walk along the street in Ballinamore and to hear people speaking French or German, and this makes us feel part of a wider European community. It has made us all more open-minded, and more aware of what a united community can achieve."

The IFI has provided further funding for the completion of a large boat-servicing area beside the Canal. Mr McGovern, like many others, pays tribute to the IFI's role in the general development of the Waterway and the surrounding area. He says "They were the catalyst, and they had the ability to make swift decisions, with the minimum of procedure. This was refreshing, in comparison with some other agencies."

The benefits were not confined to the Southern side of the border alone. Eddie McGovern, the Tourist Development Officer with Fermanagh District Council, remembers as a boy from Derrylin bringing the family donkey to be shod in a forge at Ballyconnell. He says "It was right beside what used to be the Canal, and the guy who shod the donkey told me that there used to be barges on that stretch of water. I looked over this overgrown

The benefits of the re-opened waterway were seen almost immediately

weedy stretch, but the next I remember about it was in the early 1990's. I was then working for the Council and I went on a bus trip with a group of local people and IFI representatives who were proposing that the Canal should be re-opened."

Around that time, canals were being restored in England, and Eddie McGovern had hopes that that the old Canal stretches would also be re-opened, one day. He says "There were some people who thought it was a madcap idea, and suggested that any money available would be better used to improve the border roads.

"To me, however, it seemed a matter of time that the canal would be restored, but it happened sooner because of the IFI. If they had not stepped in, the project might have been delayed for a considerable period, maybe for more than a decade. There comes a right time to do a thing, otherwise the opportunity might be lost, and I believe that the IFI got it right."

The benefits of the re-opened Waterway were seen almost immediately. "There was an instant increase in the number of boats appearing on Lough Erne, and the Upper Lough, which had lagged

Joe Gillespie, Northern Ireland Regional Manager of Waterways Ireland.

behind, also showed signs of improvement. Of course, the political significance was huge, but as a tourist project and as a catalyst for the development of a border area, it would be difficult to overstate its importance."

Economically it was an undoubted success. The Waterway was expected to attract 400 craft in its first season, but no-one foresaw that the figure would reach over 3,000. The commercial impact was immediate in other ways, with local pubs, restaurants and shops around the Canal basin reporting significantly increased business. An initial Indecon Study projected an economic return to the area of some £1.5 millions, in 1991 values. However, another study taken in 1995 estimated a return in excess of £1 million during that season alone, with some 2,000 trips recorded.

In its 1994 Annual Report, the IFI summed up the benefits of the development as follows; "an area that perceived itself as forgotten, has suddenly found itself a future. People are planning for next year. The forward-looking view is at its most tangible in the Waterway corridor, but even the towns 20 to 25 miles away are feeling the benefits."

The belief in the quality and impact of the project was tangible. "Until the Waterway opened, Ballinamore was a ghost town. Last summer, it was full of life. The supermarket took on extra staff, the hardware store boomed and grass-seed, to name but one commodity, was sold by the truck-load."[6]

Another significant outcome of the Waterway opening was the development of cross-border co-operation in tourism. Eddie McGovern says "During the Troubles a lot of the border roads were closed. It wasn't the case that people living within a few miles radius were unaware of one another, but there was very little connection between North and South in terms of tourist development. However, the success of the new Waterway and the all-island marketing it involved, became a model for co-operation."

Joe Gillespie, is the Northern Regional Manager of Waterways Ireland, a North-South Implementation body established in 1999 under the Good Friday Agreement. He was previously a monitoring engineer on the project, and he later became the Waterways engineer. He recalled the enthusiasm of the boating fraternity at the Leitrim end who could hardly wait to be among the first to use the new Canal.

Some 14 boating seasons after the opening of the Waterway, he listed its considerable economic benefits, including the developments in boat and barge hire, holiday homes, waterfront apartments and extended public moorings and new marinas.

Significantly, he also recalled the human dimension, and said "I talked to a woman in her Seventies who was moved almost to tears at what had happened. She told me that she never thought that she would see boats moving up and down the Canal again in her life time. There was a sense of wonder among the locals that something that had fallen so much into disuse could be developed again in this way. People in the border areas were very impressed and were indeed amazed at seeing such large sums of public money being used in this way and on their own doorstep."

No doubt, William Mulvany the engineer who forecast the benefits of a working Canal in the mid-19th century, would have also been impressed by the restoration of the Waterway. With the help of the International Fund and many others the "remunerative nature " of the former Canal, to which he had referred, and the new joined-up Waterway became a self-fulfilling prophecy. Mulvany's initial vision was overtaken by the then new technology of the railways, but the even newer technology of the 20th century proved more effective. Even if Mr Mulvany was more than 150 years ahead of his time, he was proved right in the long-run.

Notes

1 In an Interview with the Author in Dublin, in July 2007.
2 Ibid.
3 From "Lost Lives" by David McKittrick, Seamus Kelters, Brian Feeney and Chris Thornton, Published by Mainstream Publishing in 1999, with Reprints, Page 267.
4 In an interview with the Author in her new home near the Old Bridge, in September 2007.
5 In a conversation with the Author at Ballinamore in September 2007.
6 IFI Annual Report 1994 Pages 11-14.

CHAPTER FIVE

Consolidation

THE OFFICIAL OPENING OF THE Shannon-Erne Waterway link in 1994 was one of the highlights of the early years of the Chairmanship of William McCarter. He had taken over from John B. McGuckian, and in his first Annual Report, he drew attention to the historic re-opening of the Waterway and noted that the Fund had played a "pivotal role" from the outset.

In 1994 the Board announced a Fishing Villages Initiative

There was much else of note in the Fund's programme, including the development in 1994 of a Fishing Villages Initiative, in association with the Department of Agriculture for Northern Ireland. This was to provide assistance for community-led regeneration projects in Ardglass, Annalong, Kilkeel and Portavogie. Other noteworthy achievements in 1994 were the opening of a 15-bedroom hotel on Tory Island, off the Donegal Coast, assistance for accommodation on the nearby Arranmore Island as noted elsewhere, and a provision for self-catering facilities and a Dive Centre on Rathlin Island, off the Antrim coast.

The Chairman also highlighted a new initiative called the Community Leadership Programme, which is intended to help mobilise the energies of local communities in the most deprived areas, and to allow them to address their own needs in a new context. Flexibility and "community ownership", which were among the keystones of the Fund's approach, were fundamental to this initiative.

While the Board continued to oversee a wide variety of developments, the Chairman – like his predecessors – continued to carry out a leadership role. Willie McCarter was an ebullient figure, and a successful businessman whose family textile firm of W. P. McCarter and Company had developed from a Donegal-based concern into a partnership with the large American company Fruit of the Loom.

Rathlin Island

Inner City Trust Area in Derry/ Londonderry

Willie McCarter recalls "I became involved with the Fund in 1989, when I was asked to become a Director. At that point I was busy with Fruit of the Loom, in which we were ultimately to invest $200 millions in Donegal and Derry, and I was up to the tonsils in building a business that eventually employed around 3,000 people. So I didn't think I would have much time for anything else, but my boss at Fruit of the Loom, John Holland said 'Oh, you'll be able to manage working with the Fund as well! So I took it on'."

McCarter had a good cross-border pedigree. He was born into a Church of Ireland family in Derry and he understood the Northern "Unionist psyche." He had been educated at Coleraine Academical Institution, Trinity College Dublin and the MIT in Boston, and his business roots were deeply in Donegal. He was well-qualified, through his upbringing and experience, to become Chairman of the Fund.
He paid tribute to his predecessors who helped to shape the Fund which he inherited. He said "Charles Brett had done a remarkable job in starting out with a plain sheet of paper and a pencil, and a very willing group who decided what the Fund should be doing. Then John B. McGuckian, his successor, made a major contribution, and not least by focusing the Fund on the disadvantaged areas."[1]

One of McGuckian's key strategies was to involve the Unionist community with the work of the Fund, and this was continued by Willie McCarter. He says "A lot of Protestants were excluding themselves from the kind of help which we could provide, and one of the first things I did was to enlist the help of the church leaders."

"One evening I went to a function in Dublin Castle, and I spoke to the then Church of Ireland Primate Archbishop Robin Eames, who was flanked by the Presbyterian Moderator and the Methodist President. I said to them basically 'This is a time for all good men to come to the aid of the Party,' and asked if they could help to do something about the Protestant communities' self-exclusion policy."

Chairman Willie McCarter with former Prime Minister Sir John Major

McCarter also met Protestant Community leaders on the Shankill Road in Belfast, and he found that there were "at least" 25 different Protestant denominations in that area alone, which made it even more difficult for local communities to focus on the need for help. Nevertheless, the Fund made steady progress in engaging with the Protestant communities to accept that it "was a fair and equitable dealer, that it had no political values, and that it was there to help people in the best way it could."

Derry/ Londonderry where people have a deep pride in their culture

McCarter believed that the Fund was successful because "It met the real needs of people. It started to deliver jobs, and to give people a structure whereby they could do things. The Fund started out by focusing on economic ventures, and when people have a vested economic interest, they tend to develop relationships as people."

He told the story about Sir Charles Brett who, as a young journalist, attended one of the early sessions in Paris when the precursor of today's European Union was being set up. "Charlie said that many people thought that they were mad to try to do this on a continent that had been wracked by war, but, of course, they were not 'mad.' If you try to get economic things together, then people want to buy into this, even if they have been knocking hell out of one another only a few years previously. In turn, that process of working together leads to the development of ordinary human relationships which in turn leads to the development of stable civil society."[2]

Another important factor was the continued support from the British and Irish Governments, and the other main sponsors. "You had civil servants from Northern Ireland and the Republic working together on Fund Programmes for a long time, and because of that, a great many people got to know one another and developed good working relationships.

"The contribution of the British and Irish Governments in providing administrative staff was also important because it meant that we could go to our donors and say that every Dollar or Euro which they provided was going straight into the projects, because the two Governments were picking up the administration bill."

These "hidden" elements are not always as easy to recognise or to appreciate as the tangible success of bricks and mortar, but there was no better example of the latter than in Londonderry, which had borne the brunt of so much of the violence virtually from the onset of the Troubles.

In one sense the city had long been a litmus-paper test of much of Irish history, ranging from the 17th century Siege of Derry and the Williamite Wars, down to the civil rights protest marches of the late 1960's. The people on both sides of the community had a deep pride in their culture, but the name of the city itself underlined the divisions. The Catholics called it "Derry", after the ancient Gaelic name "Doire", but the Protestants referred to as Londonderry, following the 17th century Plantation of Ulster. More recently it was often referred to as "Derry/Londonderry" which led to the local broadcaster Gerry Anderson cleverly dubbing it "Stroke City." This important differentiation in title and culture was recognised by the International Fund which set out to help people on all sides of the community. The scope of projects was wide, and one of the key factors was to encourage local pride and achievement. Part of the regeneration was to develop community-owned shopping centres and the encouragement of tourism in a region of great natural beauty, and with one of the best walled-cities in Europe.

One particularly important development was the work of the Inner City Trust led by Paddy Doherty in the restoration of the Bishop Street area, which was badly damaged during the Troubles. This included the opening of a Craft Village, the establishment of an important Genealogical Centre and the opening of a large self-catering hostel.

An historic tower which had been destroyed long ago was rebuilt on its original site and developed into a theme museum. As the Fund noted "This project was much more than a piece of tourist infrastructure. It is part of a healing process in Londonderry and here, for the first time, the people of the City and elsewhere could see the display of both traditions and come to understand how things were and how they came to be the way they are. The leadership of both traditions endorsed the museum. Each saw in its displays a source of comfort and of communal healing."[3]

Another significant initiative was the development of shopping, commercial and leisure centres in local communities which were given a sense of ownership. A good example of this was in Shantallow, where the occupiers of every third house on the estate were visited door-to-door and consulted about the things which most affected them.

The survey revealed that a large number of families in Shantallow were spending significant sums each week on taxis to take them to shopping centres outside their own area. As part of the regeneration, major stores in the city saw the advantage of locating their branch outlets on the estate.

In turn, the communities like Shantallow had a vested interest in making their centres successful by ensuring that profits were ploughed back into other shared projects. Another major community business scheme was undertaken in the Waterside area of the city where a former shirt factory was redeveloped to provide office and workspace and creating new jobs in the process. The Fund made the point that virtually every project it undertook in Londonderry included people who had been affected by the Troubles.

It concluded "This involvement in a creative venture not only restores their sense of worth, but it also stimulates their productive skills, and ensures that they can identify with the newly-emerging Derry, a much more hopeful place than the city they once knew."[4]

As the Fund moved into its tenth year of operation, its Chairman reported that it had spent on average some £30 millions annually since 1986, and had assisted more than 3,200 projects. Mr McCarter commented "Whether it be the revitalisation of urban or rural areas, fostering cross-community reconciliation, creating a network of business enterprise centres, or training young people, the Fund has played a significant role in helping disadvantaged communities which have suffered badly over the past decades. This long and rewarding experience has left the Fund in no doubt as to the real value of what it is doing."[5]

Outside agencies also affirmed that solid progress was being made. The Board commissioned the independent KPMG Management Consultants to assess its contribution to cross-community reconciliation and employment. It reported that by September 1994 nearly 17,000 jobs had been created in IFI-supported projects, with over 7,000 further "indirect and construction" jobs. The report also indicated that 441 organisations had been helped in promoting social and economic developments and that there had been a total investment of more than £700 millions, including more than £450 millions from other sources.

The KPMG report concluded that "To a large extent, the IFI has approached its reconciliation objectives through the process of economic regeneration. This is one of the most distinctive aspects of the work.... The Fund has also focused specially on working at local level, and in the most disadvantaged communities." [6]

One of the undoubted advantages of the 1990's was the steady improvement in the political situation, which itself helped to dampen down the worst of the violence. The Downing Street Declaration of 1993 was a significant breakthrough, and much credit for this was due to the British Prime Minister John Major and the Taoiseach Albert Reynolds. This laid the foundation for progress towards the successful negotiation of the Good Friday Agreement of April 1998. It took nearly another decade of an uneasy, and often ill-tempered, "peace process", which was punctuated by violence, until the historic Stormont Agreement was endorsed publicly in May 2007.

Even at this short remove, it is easy to forget how little was happening politically prior to the Downing Street Declaration of 1993. Lord Eames, the former Church of Ireland Primate who made a major contribution behind the scenes, with others, in helping to make the Agreement a reality recalls "It was my duty under God to do everything I could to try to bring an end to the death and destruction among my people and their neighbours.

"We were living in highly unusual and dangerous times, when lives were being lost, and if I was asked to be part of the process of trying to bring this to an end, I felt that there was no way in which I could stand aside."

Lord Eames, the Former Church of Ireland Primate. "We were living in highly unusual and dangerous times and I felt as if there was no way I could stand aside".

He further recalls "The Downing Street Declaration was an historic document whose time had come, and it was seen as part of a greater and a developing understanding between the two sovereign governments. I had lived through the years of megaphone diplomacy across the Irish Sea and I had witnessed at a high level the events which were bringing the two governments together. Without the Downing Street Declaration there could have been no Good Friday Agreement."[7]

The paramilitary cease-fires were far from complete, but they engendered a level of violence that was less intolerable than in the past. This diminution of the conflict helped people to begin to think once again about the possibilities of developing tourism in Northern Ireland and the

President Bill Clinton at an International Fund project with the Chairman on his right and Jim Lyons, the US Observer, on his left

border counties in the South, which is one of the most beautiful places in the world, with a wide range of landscapes, coastlines, lakes, mountains, rivers and places of historic interest.

The International Fund had made tourism a priority from the start, and it sought to maximise the opportunity to attract new visitors and to stimulate private sector investment in tourism, particularly in disadvantaged areas. The Fund continued to support joint marketing initiatives by the Northern Ireland Tourist Board and Bord Failte, now known as Fáilte Ireland, and also the development of closer contacts and co-operation within the tourism industry. Other priorities included the training of skilled staff, and the provision of quality tourist accommodation.

It is important to note that part of this Programme was underway even in the dark days of the Troubles, and this foresight by the IFI paid dividends. As the Board noted, after a good tourist year in 1995, "The happy combination of a peaceful environment and perfect holiday weather created an unprecedented demand for accommodation. At peak periods, establishments from Derry City to Leitrim were only able to cope because of the previous prudent investment."[8]

In 1995 the IFI Board met the then US President Bill Clinton during his historic visit to Northern Ireland. It seemed symbolic of the resurgent hope in the North, and the situation was much more encouraging, compared to the difficult days when the IFI was established.

The outside assessments of the Fund's work continued to be encouraging. In 1996 the British Irish Inter-Parliamentary Body carried out its own review and expressed its support. The Committee was impressed by the work of the IFI and by the "unique and distinctive role it has developed for itself in promoting reconciliation and economic regeneration in the region." Significantly, the Committee also recommended continued support for the Fund by the British and Irish Governments and the donor countries.
Irrespective of such independent appraisals, it was important that the Fund itself should assess its achievements over the first ten years of its existence, and this was a done at length in the 1996 Annual Report, which began by setting out the bleak picture when the Fund was set up in 1986.

The Report pointed out that paramilitary violence and civil unrest had raged for more than 17 years, with no apparent end in sight. Some 2,500 people had been killed and injured during those years, and there had been more than 27,000 injuries - with some 6,000 casualties in the 1980's alone. Community relations remained at a low ebb, and there was little sign of reconciliation between the Nationalist and Unionist communities.

President Bill Clinton with Prime Minister Tony Blair during their visit to Northern Ireland

In 1986 unemployment reached a peak of 17% of the labour force, and although the border counties in the Republic were less damaged, their economy remained depressed, and particularly so in tourism. In many small towns and villages, trade was badly affected because of the permanent border road closures.

The Fund concluded, however, that ten years on "the outlook is incomparably better, even if many of the underlying issues remain to be resolved. While political and social relations between the two communities might seem uneven in some respects, a large number of cross-community and cross-border contacts have been built over these years, and there are now many examples of Nationalists and Unionists working constructively together."[9]

The Board reported also that exports had risen by 33% in the four years prior to 1996, tourism in the border counties of the South had grown rapidly, and the economic environment had improved for cross-border trade. Naturally, the Board did not claim all the credit for this, but suggested that "the work of the

Help for Rathlin Island, fom left, Colm Kavanagh, Catherine McFaul, Rathlin Island Trust, Jane Morrice, Head of Office, European Commission Belfast and Board Member John Craig

Troubled Belfast

Fund has undoubtedly been a major influence in these developments."

However, there was no sense of euphoria, and the Board concluded realistically that "much remains to be done. Many people remain out of work, and many of these are concentrated in chronically-deprived areas. In many cases the two communities in Northern Ireland continue to live in distinct and often segregated areas. The task of promoting contact and reconciliation remains as important as ever."[10]

While acknowledging that the Fund intended to continue its flexible approach and the development of new and effective programmes, it underlined one of the most important lessons of all-namely that innovative programmes and successful ideas would be taken up by Governments and by European and other agencies with often greater resources than those available to the Fund itself. Nowhere was there a greater success story than in Donegal County where the people had their own particular problems, challenges and skills. These are examined in more detail in the next chapter.

President Bill Clinton, during his historic visit to Northern Ireland in 1995, gave a ringing endorsement to the work of the IFI. He said "One of the most successful things that has been done, even in our own country, was starting the International Fund for Ireland. It works better here, what you are doing through these community groups, than almost in any other place that I am aware of, in the world."

Notes

1 In an Interview with the Author in Dublin, in July 2007.
2 Ibid
3 IFI Annual Report 1994 Pages 15-18.
4 Ibid
5 IFI Annual Report 1995 Pages 6-7.
6 Ibid
7 "Nobody's Fool, the Life of Archbishop Robin Eames", by Alf McCreary, and published by Hodder and Stoughton in 2004, Page 176.
8 Ibid Page 16.
9 IFI Annual Report 1996 Pages 10-18.
10 Ibid Page 18.

CHAPTER SIX

Donegal *Delights*

DONEGAL IS ONE OF THE MOST BEAUTIFUL COUNTIES in Ireland, and one of the most delightful places in the world. Its range of rugged scenery, from the coastlines to the highlands and islands, is ever-changing in the lights and shades of the variable weather, so that no two visits to Donegal are ever quite the same.

The people are courteous and friendly, and the visitor is welcome to share in the traditional entertainments of music and song, as well as dancing and story-telling. For those who wish to be alone there is the spacious wildness of clean, sandy beaches or the higher reaches of mountain, moorland and bog. Donegal still retains the rural romance of Ireland, allied to the benefits of modern technology.

However, for those rooted in Donegal, the reality has often been less than romantic. For generations, people have had to wrest a meagre living from the harsh landscape, or snatch a dangerous harvest from the turbulent seas along the rocky coastline. Many from previous generations had to leave Ireland for ever, and to send back money from America or Australia, or places in between, to help a struggling family at home.

The restoration of The Old Courthouse (above) was a key element in the regeneration of Lifford

In the post-war years of the 20th century, the situation gradually improved, as the Irish economy started its slow and at times uncertain journey towards the economic phenomenon of the "Celtic Tiger." However, before that journey gathered apace, the outbreak of the Northern Ireland Troubles also affected Donegal, which had been cut-off so brusquely by the partition of Ireland.

Prior to 1969, when the Troubles started in earnest, Donegal had enjoyed a strong tourist trade, supplied largely by visitors from Northern Ireland and Scotland.

However, once the violence spilled across the eastern counties of Ulster, and into the headlines of the world's media, they spread across the entire region, and cast a dark shadow over the 12 border counties.

Donegal suffered particularly badly. Its people had already felt themselves neglected by the politicians in Dublin, and given the fact that only some nine kilometres of its border – at Leitrim – is shared by the rest of the Republic, there was an added sense of isolation from Dublin and most of the island. It is therefore not difficult to imagine how the Troubles added to Donegal's already strong sense of being neglected.

The battle-smoke from Northern Ireland hung over the border counties, and nowhere more so than in Donegal. There were a number of incidents at times of heightened tension, when the holiday caravans of Northerners in Donegal were attacked, and people were ordered by violent elements to "go back home".

There was particular tension in the eastern part of Donegal where the fault-lines in the local social and political geography were more

The restoration of the Old Courthouse and its development of a heritage centre was important symbolically

Gillian Graham, Manager of the Old Courthouse

apparent. It is to the credit of many people that those fault-lines did not widen into serious cracks, and then dangerous chasms, as they had done in Northern Ireland with disastrous consequences.

In this context, credit is also due to the International Fund for Ireland and its partners who helped to steer Donegal through the effects of the Troubles, and to nurture in its people a self-confidence that was vital to its future. This also helped it build upon its innate sense of entrepreneurship and hard work.

From the earliest days, the Fund decided that one of the most obvious places needing help was the Lifford-Strabane area which became one of the Fund's first projects. Strabane, in Northern Ireland, was the natural County town for the rural hinterland, including Lifford which was just across the River Foyle, in the Republic. However, with the onslaught of violence, both areas experienced the worst of both worlds.

Strabane was literally bombarded by violence, while Lifford was cut off by one of the biggest Army checkpoints on the border. In the days of peace it had been commonplace for people from Lifford to go across to Strabane on a shopping errand, or to have a hair-cut, or even to go to church there. To do so they had to travel through Customs check-points, and although money was made by some people on each side through smuggling and allied activities, the economic "border" was never a major hindrance to easy movement between the two places.

However, the Troubles changed all that, and the "iron curtain" of the military presence, and the permanent check-points, created all sorts of difficulties. A cross-border errand which might have taken only a few minutes in the days prior to the Troubles, soon turned into a frustrating marathon which, on bad days, could last up to 90 minutes. There was also the irritation for local people in continually having to provide evidence of their identity to ever-changing groups of British solders at the check-points.

It was against this complex background that the International Fund had to work out the best way to start helping the region to help itself. After preliminary soundings with people on the Republic's side of the border, it was decided to restore the historic Old Courthouse in the centre of Lifford to its former glory. This seemed a curious decision by the locals, in that the Old Courthouse was the symbol of the British legal

The Canal Basin Strabane

system in the days before partition, but the building's 250 year history was integral to that of Lifford and its environs.

The decision to refurbish the historic building was also seen as a lever to encourage private development, and one of the notable successes in the context was the establishment of modern offices by private developers, which in turn encouraged Donegal County Council to retain its main offices – and the resultant jobs – in Lifford, rather than transferring its headquarters to Letterkenny. The restoration of the Old Courthouse and its development as a Heritage Centre was also important symbolically.

The regeneration of the Lifford area was funded in 1992 by an IFI grant of IR£1,520,000 under the scheme for Special Projects in Disadvantaged Areas. The Fund also decided, however, that it was important to establish new developments that would help to build bridges not only across the river but between the communities on either side.

Accordingly, in 1993 the Fund decided to make the Strabane-Lifford initiative a Flagship Project, and donated a further £1 million to the regeneration of the Canal Basin at Strabane. This was matched by equal funding from the Department of the Environment in Northern Ireland.

Donal MacLochlainn, left, and Winston Patterson, members of the Strabane-Lifford Development Commission.

The Board of the Fund underlined that "Taken singly, each of the projects in Lifford and Strabane would have contributed significantly to the regeneration of their respective areas. Together, however, they offer substantially greater potential for the complementary development of the area on a cross-border basis."[1] It was an imaginative scheme, and it worked. It was also a courageous move by the Board of the International Fund to undertake what was regarded as a high-risk development at a time of sustained violence and political deadlock.

The Fund had also taken an important decision earlier to assist a new Strabane-Lifford Development Commission, and in 1992 it granted assistance of IR£100,000 for the employment of a project manager and administrative facilities. The manager appointed was Alan Moneypenny, and with two senior colleagues he outlined the rationale that had helped to drive the Commission. He said "We set up various initiatives and community-building projects, and we just got on with our programme. We reckoned that by keeping a relatively low PR profile, we would minimise the potential for political upsets."[2]

The Commission was carefully chosen to reflect not only local ability and entrepreneurship but also the main community backgrounds. Donal MacLochlainn, a Lifford-born accountant who later became Chairman, said "There was always a need for a body like the Commission. We were facilitators with a broad overview. When the local communities saw that the initiative was working, they backed it more and more, and Councillors and others gradually began to see us as partners rather than as people who were somehow trying to upstage them."

Winston Patterson, a Commission member from Lifford who also became one of its Chairmen, said "The locals took comfort from the fact that an international body like the Fund was directly involved. In a sense the IFI was the chicken and the Commission was able to germinate the egg to produce more chickens, and that is how we made progress. This is an area where people were not born with silver-spoons in their mouths.

Cathel MacSuibhne, Regional Manager of Udaras na Gaeltachta, the State Development Authority in Donegal.

Denis Rooney, Chairman of the IFI, left, Father Brian O'Ferraigh and Pat "The Cope" Gallagher having fun at the opening of the Dobhar Community Enterprise and Resource Centre

"We were brought up by families who had learned to survive through their own efforts, but the IFI helped us all to move forward together." Local initiative was important, as was the increasing European dimension which was symbolised by the local MEPs who became Patrons - Pat "The Cope" Gallagher from Dungloe in Donegal, and John Hume from Derry who had helped to initiate the project based on models he had witnessed within the European Community.

What is striking about the work of the Strabane-Lifford Commission is not only its practical achievements, but also the enthusiasm which continues to drive its members some 15 years after its formation. As we talked in a small cafe near the restored Old Courthouse it was all too easy to imagine the dereliction and rubble of the past, and to marvel at the prevailing sense of hope for the future. For very different, yet allied, reasons both Strabane and Lifford had suffered from neglect and structural decay, but today they are much more vibrant and forward-looking.

Part of the success story is that the IFI underlined the international interest in providing help, and the Fund's ability to provide grants with a minimum of bureaucracy proved crucial. Much still needs to be done, particularly in dealing with social issues among young people involved in alcohol and solvent abuse, but there is little doubt that the Fund's Flagship Project at Strabane-Lifford and its encouragement and support for the local Commission have been successful.

Another important part of the Fund's work in Donegal was to help to rebuild the local tourist infrastructure in the wake of the major setback caused by the Troubles. Significant amounts were provided for hotel and guest-house developments and accommodation, as well as the establishment of Visitor and Heritage Centres and other amenities, not only in Donegal but also in all the 12-border counties, and further inland.

Bands are a feature of the cultural life of Donegal

There was also much emphasis in Donegal on the development of local communities within the Irish-speaking Gaeltacht area of the more western and southern parts of the county. Cathal MacSuibhne, Regional Manager of Udaras na Gaeltachta, the State Development Authority, worked closely with the IFI and other agencies on a number of tourism, community and economic projects.

He said "One of the advantages of working with the International Fund is that once they came on board, it was easier for other agencies to follow. To that extent the Fund was often an important catalyst. There were a lot of development ideas which were hanging round this area, but which were going nowhere until the IFI came along."[3]

A good example of self-help is the Dobhair Community Enterprise and Resource Centre in Dore in the west of Donegal, following the initiative of a number of women who needed a building to help provide a focus for the local area. An existing building was in disrepair, so the women's group applied for IFI funding for a new centre, costing Euros 835,000 - which was a small fortune in local terms. However, the Fund donated

A welcome from "Bart Simpson" at the St. Patrick's Centre.

Rannafast in West Donegal is an area where the purest "Ulster-Irish" is spoken

some 50% of the cost and the rest came from development agencies, and the community itself.

The St. Patrick's Centre currently caters for a wide range of activities, from computer classes to provision for toddlers' groups, as well as Irish dancing and yoga. Most important, it provides a new "heart" for a widely-based rural community which in the past depended heavily on fishing and agriculture and which has had to concentrate on other activities and means of securing incomes.

What is striking about these projects, like similar ventures in the area, is the determination of the local people to make them work. Mary Coyle, the manager of the St. Patrick's Centre, was one of the original five women who applied for an IFI grant. She told me "It is very important that everyone feels included in this project. We were determined from the start that if the Fund would support us in providing a centre of such excellence, it would not become a white elephant. We wanted it to be open and accessible to people at all times, and this has been happening."

There are plans to extend the Centre further and the local curate Fr Brian O' Ferraigh talked enthusiastically about a proposed new project. He said "We hope to retain and sustain the rich heritage of the region, and to maintain a musical archive as well as encouraging people to provide music themselves." He did not exaggerate when he talked about the rich local tradition which world-renowned Irish artists such as Enya and Moya Brennan, and also the groups Altan and Clannad (an abbreviation for 'Clann as Dobhair'- family from Dobhair).

The St. Patrick's Centre at Dore is clearly fulfilling a need, and its extension will pose further challenges to those who realise that they cannot rest on their laurels, even if they wish to do so. Significantly, however, their enthusiasm shows no signs of waning, and that is perhaps the best indication of a further positive outcome.

The International Fund has helped to set up several other community projects and centres in the Gaeltacht area, including those at Kilcar and the Crannog, as part of the Disadvantaged Areas Initiative. All of those have helped the local communities to find a renewed focus and identity at a time when the traditional forms of livelihood have been in relative decline. In the field of tourism the Fund also played a major role in helping to fund a regular ferry from the mainland to Tory Island, which became literally a lifeline for that community. The Fund helped with the development of a hotel in Tory and also in providing assistance to Arranmore Island, near Tory.[4]

The funding of buildings and boats is important and tangible, but one of the most significant developments in recent years has been the Fund's new emphasis on tackling conceptual issues. A good example of this is the development of the Rannafast Resource, Education and Heritage Centre (Aislann Rann na Feirste Teo) on a site in west Donegal which is owned by the local community.

Monreagh Church was established in 1644 and is part of the rich Presbyterian heritage in Donegal

This is in an area where the purest "Ulster-Irish" is spoken, and where the language is also protected and preserved. The project has the support of the Donegal County Development Board, the Ulster Scots Agency, the local groups Oideas Gael, and Forbairt Feirste in Belfast, and also a range of schools and colleges on a cross-border and a cross-community basis.

One of the main aims is to encourage reconciliation and good relationships through the use of Irish and to promote pro-actively the language and culture of other traditions. This may be a surprise to outsiders, particularly to many Protestants and Unionists in Northern Ireland who have looked on the Irish language as a divisive

The "Jeanie Johnston" sets off from Rathmullan to commemorate the 400th Anniversary of the "Flight of the Earls".

influence because, in their opinion, it has been hi-jacked by elements of the Republican tradition who have used it for political objectives.

Historically, however, Irishmen of a Protestant background have played a distinguished role in the language movement. Douglas Hyde, later the first President of Ireland, had been a founder of the Gaelic League. Even at the height of the Troubles, a number of Northern Protestants maintained this interest and some of them would visit the Gaeltacht, particularly in the Rannafast area, to help develop their fluency in the language.

For example the Irish Language Summer College in Rannafast has attracted thousands of Northern Ireland students from all backgrounds since its foundation in 1926, and they have stayed with local families, not only to learn Irish but also to build up lasting friendships.

This convention of treating all traditions and backgrounds with equal respect is one of the cornerstones of the new Rannafast project, and it will build on reconciliation activities which will be carried out in Irish and English. Until now such reconciliation occurred more by accident than by design, but the latest initiative is an attempt to further reconciliation along clearer guidelines. The marketing strategy will be aimed at Protestant as well as Catholic students and their

Paddy Harte (right) with Alf McCreary on location in Donegal.

parents from Northern Ireland, and in association with the Tyrone Donegal Partnership, the topics will include "Examining the Legacy of the Conflict", "Eliminating Discrimination" and "Removing Barriers to Reconciliation."

All of these are weighty topics and should indeed be tackled, but the significant point about the new development is the way in which Protestants are being encouraged to take part, as opposed to the bad old days of the Troubles when Protestants from Northern Ireland went across the Border to learn Irish but did not necessarily want to tell too many people back home about it.

For example, the story is told of an Orangeman from Northern Ireland who regularly travelled to the Rannafast area during the Troubles to give tuition to a local "marching" band, but due to the sensitivity of the situation, that particular exercise was a well-kept secret on all sides.

Allied to the imaginative Rannafast project, and almost as a cultural counter-balance, another venture is being developed to encourage people to explore the Ulster-Scots dimension in Donegal. This concept may well be as much a surprise to outsiders as the previously-mentioned project. For many years it was believed by most people in Northern Ireland that the Ulster-Scots legacy belonged to the eastern (and heavily Unionist) part of the North, but in fact this tradition obviously extended to Donegal which, with the six counties of the North, were all part of a united Ireland under British rule. The ties with Scotland had been developed for many years by Donegal people who had travelled over there to find work, and also strengthened later on by the large numbers of Scottish holidaymakers who came to Donegal.

The Ulster-Scots heritage long predated the border, though with the "border mentality" resulting from Partition, many people did not realise that the Ulster-Scots heritage was also established in the west, with the "marching bands" in the Gaeltacht, which were not unlike those in some areas of Northern Ireland.

The proposed Ulster-Scots Education and Heritage Centre is being developed in a former Presbyterian manse at Monreagh, near the border and close to Derry. It has the backing of the local Education and Heritage Association, as well as the Institute of Ulster-Scots Studies at the University of Ulster, and other local associations. Part of its brief is to promote the language, culture, heritage and understanding of the Ulster-Scots in the border counties.

The influence of Ulster-Scots Presbyterians was strikingly apparent in the American Declaration of Independence of 4 July 1776, and the hardy pioneering spirit of the settlers from that same tradition helped to mould the events that eventually led to the establishment of the United States as a nation. It is still not known widely enough in America, and elsewhere, that a significant number of US Presidents came from Ulster-Scots stock.

The fact that the new cross-community project is being established in a former Presbyterian manse is further evidence of a growing understanding of the need to explore different cultures and

The elegant sculptures by Maurice Harron and titled "Let the Dance Begin" are a sign of hope for the future

traditions. A similar cross-community project was mooted for Raphoe in the mid-1990s, but this foundered because of a number of factors - and not least the Drumcree stand-offs which polarised the entire community in Northern Ireland and had ripples further afield. The development of the Monreagh project underlines that the overall climate of public and political opinion is always important, and that for many of these sensitive and innovative projects, timing is all.

The Monreagh development, situated on land within one of the oldest Presbyterian communities in Ireland, will also underline the contribution which Donegal people have made to Christianity worldwide and also to the concept of "religious freedom." These range from the impact of St. Columba from Derry and the other Irish missionaries in Europe to the Reverend Francis Mackemie from Donegal who emigrated to the USA and has been rightly described as "the father of American Presbyterianism."

Donegal is so rich in heritage and history that the continuing dimensions are being acknowledged in new ventures and developments almost all the time. In the autumn of 2007, the Donegal County Council in association with local agencies and the IFI promoted an essay competition among schools to acknowledge the 400th Anniversary of the "Flight of The Earls" in 1607. These were the last of the ancient Irish Chieftains - the O'Neills and the O'Donnells - who were defeated by the English at the Battle of Kinsale in 1601, and which marked the beginning of the end of the old Celtic order. The Earls sailed from Rathmullan in Donegal for continental Europe in September 1607, and were never to return. That voyage was commemorated 400 years later in September 2007 by the vessel the Jeanie Johnston, a replica of a former Irish Famine ship which itself played an important role in the Wider Horizons Programme sponsored by the International Fund. The historic occasion was marked by a ceremony in Rathmullan, which was attended by the President of Ireland Mary McAleese.

The developments in Donegal, perhaps more than in any other border county, have exemplified the range, depth and imagination of the many funding Programmes which have been initiated, nurtured and developed by the International Fund. Over 21 years some Euros 65 millions were given to 450 projects, with a leverage of a further Euros 100 millions. This assisted in the creation of some 3,000 jobs and directly involved another 2,500 people in its work. All of this adds up to a significant record of achievement.

Paddy Harte, the Fund's Regional Development Officer in the area was featured as one of the 2006 "Donegal People of The Year Award." This was a deserved personal honour, but also a recognition by the people in Donegal of the help given by the Fund and its 21 years of achievement.

Paddy Harte said "It's been massively rewarding to meet with people, to hear their aspirations, and to help them to deliver on those aspirations. Some people were in at the start, others at the middle and some at the end. But with the IFI you got all of the experience. This wasn't just the money, which was very measurable, but it was also a vote of confidence in local people by major international donors."

He added "I also believe that the many generations of Irish emigrants who contributed socially, politically and economically to their host countries created the depth of goodwill which enabled the Governments of these countries to make contributions to the International Fund".

So this diaspora has been a significant player in the Peace Process, through the work of the Fund. The challenge is to put in place measures to ensure that this valuable network, fostered by the Fund, can become sustainable. I really do believe that "Rotha mór an tSaoil" (the Donegal Irish saying for the Great Wheel of Life) is there for the Fund to complete."

One of the most tangible and symbolic memorials to the work of reconciliation and peace in Donegal and across the border in the Strabane area is a group of tall, elegant sculptures which dominate a busy roadside site at the Northern Ireland border with Lifford.

These are known by the locals, typically, as "The Tinnies", and the significance of their presence is that they stand in an area formerly called "The Camel's Hump". This was the site of the large British Army checkpoint which caused so much frustration, irritation and delay to the local people on both sides of the border for so many years during the Troubles.

The proper name of the elegant sculptures by Maurice Harron is "Let The Dance Begin." One of the figures is playing a flute, another is beating a drum, while the two remaining figures are preparing to dance. The symbolism is powerful - the "Orange" tradition of the flute and drum, with the musical tradition of the Irish culture, and the two figures ready to dance to the rhythms and instruments they have in common. Winston Patterson said simply "This shows that the war is truly over, and none of us wants it to occur ever again."

Hopefully the war dance is indeed over. Let the dance of peace and prosperity really begin.

Notes

1 IFI Annual Report 1993 Pages 39-40.
2 In an Interview with the Author in Strabane in August 2007.
3 In an Interview with the Author in August 2007.
4 The Tory Ferry is mentioned in more detail elsewhere in this Chapter.

Tory Life-line

ONE OF THE MAIN PRIORITIES OF THE INTERNATIONAL Fund has been to help communities in disadvantaged areas. A good example of this was the assistance given in 1992 to the establishment of a regular ferry between the island of Tory and the Donegal mainland.

Lying 12 kilometres off Bloody Foreland, this is one of the most remote inhabited islands off the Irish coast, North or South. It is some four kilometres long and one kilometre wide, and it has a range of attractive features - including its long history from the Stone Age and the Bronze Age, as well as remarkable examples of flora and fauna, and also of bird life.

Time, however, has not been not kind to Tory. Its former peat bogs were used up, and its inhabitants had to earn a difficult living from its poor land and also the dangerous seas around the island. Many people were forced to emigrate to find jobs, and at one point it seemed as if this continual outflow would eventually render the island totally uninhabited.

One of the key factors in helping to prevent this was the self-help attitude of local people, both on and off the island. This led to the establishment of a regular ferry service, and also the construction of appropriate harbour facilities on Tory and at the picturesque Magheroarty Bay on the north-west coast of Donegal. There always had been contact between the island and the mainland, and throughout each generation, hardy sea-farers combined fishing with taking basic supplies to the island.

However in 1992 the International Fund helped to establish a regular ferry, with a grant of IR£128,000, which was some 25% of the cost of a new vessel. Around IR£215,000 was supplied by "Udaras na Gaeltachta" - the Development Agency for the Donegal Gaeltacht, and the remainder came from Donegal Coastal Cruises, the pioneer operators. The 58-feet vessel the Tormor was built in Killybegs and was capable of carrying some 72 passengers. It was also well-equipped to bring essential oil supplies and foodstuffs to the island.

The Tormor went into service in July 1992, and it has been operating successfully ever since. One of the partners in the operating company is Padraig O'Dochartaigh, a Donegal-based former school-teacher, businessman and local councillor who comes from a sea-faring family.

He recalls "One day I received a phone call from the then curate from Tory Island, Fr. Eddie Gallagher, who was stranded on the mainland

Padriag O'Dochartaigh: "The ferry has been an absolute lifeline".

by bad weather. Eventually we got him across and on the way, the conversation turned to the need for a regular ferry. He told me that the mail contract for the island was coming up, and we applied for it successfully. So we combined this, with a bit of fishing, but the need for a regular service remained."

Padraig O'Dochartaigh and his business colleagues began to look for financial backing but this was proving difficult, and a number of agencies were reluctant to commit themselves at that stage. However, the proposal had considerable merit, and the International Fund recognised this by its grant in 1992. Once this primary funding was underway, others literally came on board, and the project proved highly successful.

The service developed steadily year by year, and in the 2006-07 season alone, the vessel carried some 7,000 passengers. These included tourists from many countries, including China, Argentina, India, Iran, Russia and Finland, and also from the Republic and Northern Ireland.

Padraig O'Dochartaigh says "The tourists come for a large number of reasons, including solitude and also to discover the traditions of Tory, such as song, dance, story-telling, the beautiful scenery and the wild birds. In the summer of 2007, one of the Finnish visitors was a university professor, and I was amazed at the quality and range of his fluency in Irish. He was an accomplished linguist, but he had to learn Irish without the help of a language laboratory and he told me it had taken him 10 years."

The crossing to Tory, amid gorgeous scenery, usually takes 45 minutes. On the day that this writer travelled to the island and back, the sea was gracious, with only a gentle swell, but at certain times the crossing can be difficult. Mr O'Dochartaigh says "There are lots of storms and gales, and there are big sea-surges in Tory sound. You need to know what you are doing."

The regular skipper, Jimmy Sweeney, is a sailor with vast experience, and the Tormor is in good hands. The journey is worthwhile, and as well as the attractions mentioned earlier there is a lively cultural scene on the island, including a thriving Tory community of artists, with the colourful Patsy Dan Rodgers who holds the honorary title of King of Tory. Accommodation is available in the island's hotel and in local guest houses, and a visit to Tory is an experience in itself.

Undoubtedly a key to the resurgence of interest and participation in the life of Tory has been the regular ferry, which in turn was a major factor in the establishment of the island's hotel - which was also supported by the International Fund. In recent times the Fund has also helped with a local community and medical centre.

Currently there are about 200 people living on Tory, and although there are always challenges in an island way of life, the community's future seems secure.

Padraig O'Dochartaigh sums up "These can be difficult waters to cross, and at one time there was a real sense of isolation concerning Tory. We were looking for money for a ferry boat and we tried many agencies, but the impact of the IFI funding cannot be overstated. It provided the seed capital to allow us to process a business idea to its successful conclusion.

"We might have gone ahead anyway, but it would have taken a couple of years longer. The success of the ferry has encouraged people to go back to Tory, and it has also introduced thousands of visitors to the island, as well as encouraging islanders to go back and live there. For Tory it has been an absolute lifeline."

CHAPTER SEVEN

Good *News*

THE WORK OF THE INTERNATIONAL Fund was allied closely to the political and security situation in Northern Ireland, as has been noted already. It was established in 1986 during one of the worst periods of the Troubles, but by 1998 the tide began to turn towards peace.

The Good Friday Agreement which was achieved in April of that year was a significant milestone, though it would take another nine years of wrangling before a more permanent peace began to settle over Northern Ireland. Quite rightly, however, the IFI Chairman William McCarter underlined this significant development.

He stated "1998 has been a momentous year for the island of Ireland. We have seen the Good Friday Agreement negotiated, and passed by referendums North and South, which has brought hope and optimism to all who want lasting peace. The Fund is looking forward to playing its part in helping the Agreement to take root, and achieve its promised beneficial effects for all."[1] McCarter pointed out that the new institutions set up by the Agreement would require nourishing and support in the early years, and that the Fund "with its many unique strengths" had a role to play in this process. He added that the basic economic and social conditions, out of which the Fund's Programmes had grown, were continuing to generate strong demands for "the kinds of assistance, economic and reconciliatory, which we have innovated."[2]

An independent KPMG Report, which reviewed the Fund's activities up to September 1997, revealed encouraging developments. Up to that point, the Fund had committed £314 millions to 3,627 projects; some 89% of the Fund's expenditure had been in Disadvantaged Areas; over 7,600 people had taken part in cross-community projects, and 4,700 in cross-border ventures. The Fund had also helped to generate 31,629 full-time equivalent jobs, and some

The Chairman William McCarter is pictured with Her Majesty Queen Elizabeth, the First Minister Peter Robinson, the former First Minister, the Rev Dr Ian Paisley, and the President of Sinn Fein Gerry Adams

1,400 businesses had taken part in cross-border business development programmes.

The KPMG Report concluded "Simple summaries such as those set out.... cannot fully capture the integration of the various strands of the work of the Fund across its priorities, the demonstration effect which the Fund has had in establishing new working models, and have been adopted by Government and EU Programmes as a distinctive 'way of working', or the inter-relationship between the Fund's economic regeneration and its work on contact dialogue and reconciliation."

The Report also concluded "In this way, the Fund has made a major contribution to the development of an economic and cross-community dynamic which has had an important role in underpinning the Peace Process in Northern Ireland."[3] One significant statistic in the Report revealed that "for every £1 spent by the Fund, a further £2 had been levered, producing a total investment of £948 millions".

L-R: Cllr Bernard McGuinness, Chairman North West Region Cross Border Group, José Palma Andres, Director DG for Regional Policy European Commission and Chairman Willie McCarter

William McCarter underlined the importance of such "leverage." He said "When I left as Chairman in 2005, there were more than 5,000 projects which the Fund had been involved in from the start. Given that the leverage was roughly 2:1 and that the Fund had handed over more than £500 millions, you are talking about a total investment of about £1.5 billions, or nearly Euro 2.25 billions. As my father used to say 'These are not inconsequential sums!' ".

McCarter stressed that the Board "except in very special circumstances was not dependent on Government where basically everything is subject to someone's decision at ministerial or Cabinet level. One important factor was that the Fund could put money on the table first, as with the Shannon-Erne development, and this could be used as leverage. The principle of first money on the table was key to the Fund's operations, and once people realised this, they were able to make progress."

The Fund, he said, had clear parameters, but they were flexible. "If someone made a good case for doing something, and this fell broadly within the objectives of the Fund, we tried to be flexible. There were controls, and the Board had the reputation of being a relatively lean machine, as well as being flexible and straight up. The Fund's Development Consultants really came into their own because they were the people on the ground, and they were in touch with real needs in areas with serious violence and high unemployment."

Sometimes things didn't work out "just like in any organisation, but once people feel that they can buy in to the output of the thing, then there's a real chance that in the ordinary process of developing relationships the process starts, and that it will continue. I used to see this time and again when I visited projects and listened to people talking. It was not always a perfect solution but it was a solution to a lot of the process of trying to develop reasonable working relationships between people, and in my view that is what the Fund was all about."[4]

Left to right: Former Secretary of State for Northern Ireland Dr John Reid MP, Des Brown MP, Defence Minister, Taoiseach Brian Cowen TD and the Chairman, Willie McCarter, at the launch of the Fund's 2001 Annual Report at Hillsborough Castle

During his period of office William McCarter and the Fund welcomed a large number of visitors, and the Chairman was pictured on separate occasions with Queen Elizabeth, the Prince of Wales, President Mary McAleese, Taoisigh Charles Haughey, Albert Reynolds, John Bruton & Bertie Ahern, Prime Ministers John Major & Tony Blair, President Bill Clinton and Hillary Rodham Clinton, President George W Bush, Presidents of the European Union Jacques Delors & Jacques Santer, EU Commissioners, Prime Ministers and Ambassadors from the Commonwealth, and also Irish and British political leaders.

Willie McCarter was a popular figure on Capitol Hill, and he in turn paid tribute to the work of his US colleagues in helping to maintain the financial and moral support for the Fund at certain times when some people felt that there were other more important priorities on the agenda.

He says "This support was bi-partisan, and very senior people stuck with us through thick and thin. People like Senator Mitch McConnell and Senator Pat Leahy helped keep the Fund alive, with support from Congressmen Jim Walsh, Richie Neal, and others."

McCarter recalls meeting Senator McConnell in Washington just after the start of the paramilitary ceasefires in Northern Ireland. "I said to him, in retrospect naively, that if we had two or three more years' support we would have the job done. The Senator said 'I'm going to continue to support you, because – apart from anything else – you are the only man who has come in to my office and has said that there's an end to anything!".

However, this story has a sequel. Some years later Senator McConnell, who has family roots in Co. Down, visited Fund projects in the North. McCarter recalls "He stood up at a

The Chairman in Washington with the former US Vice-President Al Gore and Senator Patrick Leahy, a strong supporter of the Fund

dinner in Dublin and, waving his finger at me, he said 'It's quite a long while since you told me that two years more funding would be enough, but I have seen the kind of projects you support, and I'm satisfied that the money is being well spent. I will continue to support you.' " McCarter added "People in USAID used to tell us that we delivered the biggest 'bang per buck' in terms of what they did all over the world, and that they were pleased with the way in which the Fund handled their money."

William McCarter also paid tribute to the help from the EU, and also the support from Canada, Australia and New Zealand. He added "The Fund received great support from politicians across the board in Northern Ireland and in the Republic, as well as the British-Irish Parliamentary Body and from members of the European Parliament."

The continued support from such a varied range of sources was confirmation that the Fund was making a worthwhile contribution to the slow peace-building process in Northern Ireland, but the Board was always keen to canvas independent professional assessments of its work. In 2001 yet another KPMG Report carried out a number of different case studies of projects supported by the Fund. They included those in the broad areas of economic development, contact, dialogue and reconciliation, and focusing on disadvantaged areas.

From the study, the Report indicated that there were a number of distinctive characteristics of the Fund's operation. These included the importance of long-term relationships and flexibility, the encouragement of innovation, the emphasis on helping the most disadvantaged communities and areas, and the work of the Fund's Development Consultants who had a special role in providing local knowledge, and in drawing attention to and helping specific organisations.

The Report also highlighted the Fund's sponsorship of enterprise, its development of international networks, its cross-community and cross-border work, its emphasis on sustainability, and its partnership with other funding organisations, often providing the "first money on the table" - as mentioned previously.

All of this, according to the KPMG Report, was illustrated by three separate themes which made the work of the Fund "distinctive and particularly valuable." These were the integration of the impacts across the Fund's three priorities, its capacity-building which assisted deprived communities to help themselves, and using market-based techniques the ability "to contribute to the development, growth and sustainability of both private enterprises and social economy organisations."[5]

The Chairman with President Mary Robinson visiting Pettigo in 1995.

This assessment by KPMG was necessarily in the language of management and consultancy, but the work of the International Fund is most vividly understood in the human and social dimension, and particularly in those projects which brought widespread benefits to a large number of people, as well as to individuals.

One such project was the assistance given to the Lough Foyle Car Ferry which came into operation on 14 June 2002. This roll on/roll off service provided an important link between Magilligan in Co. Londonderry and Greencastle in Donegal. The journey normally takes about 20 minutes each way, and saves the traveller from making the much longer land-journey through Londonderry. The benefits of the Ferry are not only economy of time and effort but also in the remarkable effect this link has had in introducing the people from across Lough Foyle to one another.

The Fund contributed around £0.9 million to the project, and the balance of the cost was provided by the European Union Special Support Programme for Peace and Reconciliation, the Irish Government, and the relevant councils on each side of the border - namely, Limavady and Donegal. The rationale for the Ferry was to provide direct access to two areas where few previous links had existed - apart from recreational sailors who would travel from the Causeway Coast area over to Greencastle for a short stay.

It was hoped that the new Ferry would encourage tourism, and that its existence would stimulate local business on either side of Lough Foyle. Some six years on, at this time of writing, the benefits are obvious to Greencastle which is now a thriving community with a good range of tourist facilities.

The benefits on the Northern side are less immediately obvious, in that the Magilligan area is sparsely populated - apart from the inhabitants of the local HM Prison, situated on the main road from the Ferry. However, tourism has greatly increased in Northern Ireland in recent years, and towns like Coleraine and Limavady have indubitably benefited from the greater North/South access.

The uptake of the service exceeded all expectations. In the first few months alone, some 43,000 cars and 150,000 passengers had used the new service. Shortly after its inauguration, Willie McCarter said "This project is here to stay. It has become almost overnight an integral part of the infrastructure which is not only creating jobs, but also creating hope for the future. Like many other ferry projects, people wondered what the take-up would be, but in this case it has been fantastic and full marks to the

Anyone who has used the Ferry regularly, as this writer has done during visits to Donegal with a Coleraine-based walking group, will appreciate its immediate benefits, not only in the range of facilities now in Greencastle and the surrounding area, but also in discovering the cultural background to the region.

The uptake of the new ferry exceeded all expectations

operators and everyone who has been involved."

Significantly, the Ferry was the first Flagship Project which was jointly supported by the Fund and the European Union, and was quickly recognised as a "resounding success." The Director of the DG Regional Policy European Commission José Palma Andres joined Willie McCarter and others at the launch in 2002.

He said "One of the key aims of the Peace and Reconciliation Programme is to allow the local economy to take advantage of the new opportunities offered by a resolution of conflict. The Lough Foyle Ferry is a prime example of a cross-border initiative working effectively to enhance economic progress, tourism and the transportation infrastructure of a small, yet highly important, region in the North of Ireland."

The economic importance was underlined by Michael Heaney, the Director of Community, Culture and Enterprise with Donegal County Council. He said "It is easy to forget how isolated we felt. Some 20 years ago you might not even have been able to buy a bag of chips in Greencastle. In the 1980's we had plenty of good ideas, but we had no money to develop them.

"The community demonstrated a lot of voluntary effort, and there was never a lack of a willingness to try things. Development means having to effect change, but this also requires initiative and the right mindset. Without help from the IFI all of this would not have happened. That's the long and the short of it."

Gemma Havlin is the Manager of the impressive Maritime Museum and Planetarium at Greencastle which has also been supported by the IFI and which houses many important artefacts. She underlines the social importance of the Ferry. "Magilligan and Greencastle are only about a mile apart, but in reality they were much further apart. The Ferry has literally been a bridge-builder. People now cross over either way, and they get to know more about one another.

"The Ferry is the best practical example of peace-making that I have come across. It is not as if someone had written a report, which is gathering dust on a shelf. This is a living, working project and I see it in operation every day, so I know how it has changed people's perspectives."

Gemma showed me one of the Museum's most prized possessions. It is a copy of a letter written on 9 August 1950, by a D. Blakely,

Gemma Havlin: "The ferry is the best practical example of peace-making that I have come across".

Principal Keeper of St. John's Point Lighthouse, in Co. Down. He is complaining bitterly about the workmanship of a painter in the service of the Lighthouse Authority.

Blakely writes "No work was carried out by him yesterday. I also have to report that his attitude here is one of careless indifference, and no respect for Commission property or stores. He is wilfully wasting materials, opening drums and paint tins by blows from a heavy hammer, spilling the contents, which is now running out of the paint store door....

"His language is filthy and he is not amenable to any law and order. He has ruined the wall surface of one wall in No1 dwelling by burning. He mixes putty, paint etc with his bare hands and wipes off nothing.... Empty, stinking milk bottles, articles of food, coal, ashes and other debris litter the floor of the place which is now in a scandalous condition of dirt.... He is the worst specimen I have met in 30 years service. I urge his dismissal from the job now, before good material is rendered useless, and the place ruined."

That painter was none other than the legendary Brendan Behan, who later made his name as a dramatist. The discovery of such a letter was in itself worth a visit across on the Ferry.

The Lough Foyle service, which began with the aptly-named Foyle Venture in June 2002, was an act of faith, and not least for the operators. Jim McClenaghan, the Managing Director of the Lough Foyle Ferry Company Ltd which operates the service, said "We took a risk, but I always thought it would work out. However, the results exceeded even my expectations, and it has opened up the entire peninsula."

In this writer's experience, the effect on the people on both sides of the border has been psychological as well as economically beneficial. My wife's parents used to live in Portstewart, and I recall staying in their house on Strand Road, which had a commanding view of the ocean across to Donegal. It seemed to me a little odd that this particular county belonged to the Republic, and yet it was "North" of "Northern" Ireland.

Many an evening I would watch the lighthouse beyond Greencastle, and wonder what kind of a place it was, what the people were like, and how much – or how little – we had in common.

Having been brought up in South Armagh, I had experienced the "border" attitude and, for me, the delight of being able to travel South with different currency, and meeting people with different accents. After such close proximity to the South in my boyhood years, the "border" seemed just another road-crossing. Yet up in the north-west the "border" between the Republic and Northern Ireland was a large stretch of Lough Foyle, opening up in to the Atlantic Ocean. In that setting, the border seemed impassable, and the Inishowen peninsula and its people appeared accordingly remote.

In that sense the "border" seemed very real, but in the more peaceful times the Lough Foyle Ferry changed all that. Suddenly the Inishowen peninsula, and that hinterland of Donegal, became not only more accessible, but also more attractive. As has been noted earlier, the Lough

Jim McClenaghan. "The ferry has opened up the entire peninsula".

An Irish Times cartoon drawing of the Chairman shortly before he stepped down

Foyle Ferry not only crossed the physical Border frequently every day, it also helped to soften the "border mentality" in people's minds.

Willie McCarter recalls talking to people from North Antrim about the "Magilligan" Ferry. He says "They had no idea that I was connected to this in any way, but they told me that once the Ferry started they would go to Donegal, whereas they would not have driven through Derry and areas in the city where they felt unsafe. I found that very interesting."

The Lough Foyle Ferry, through the funding of the IFI the EU and the local councils, and also the entrepreneurship of the vessel's operators, has become one of the best examples of cross-border co-operation on the island. This is not only in providing an economic link but also in introducing different communities and people to one another. This lies at the very heart of the work of the IFI.

William McCarter stepped down as Chairman in February 2005, and was succeeded by Denis Rooney, a chartered surveyor and a successful Belfast-based businessman. McCarter had a distinguished record of more than 15 years of service with the International Fund since 1989, as a Board Member and then, from 1993, as Chairman. During this

Brendan Behan

time he had witnessed significant changes in the political and social landscape of Ireland, North and South.

In his final Chairman's Report he noted that "In the politically-charged atmosphere of the early days of the Fund, we worked long and hard to demonstrate our impartiality, and to build strong and durable relationships with all communities. Those days are long gone, and the Fund now enjoys sound working partnerships with representatives from all political shades and persuasions."

The Chairman also recorded that by the end of 2004, just before he retired, the Fund had channelled some £527 millions (Euros 768 millions) to more than 5,500 projects. This was no mean achievement, and the Chairman claimed, with justification, that the Fund was one of those factors which had led to wide-scale improvements in the peace process and that "it could share in the credit for what had been achieved."[6]

He also stressed that "The work of the Fund touches the lives of a large number of people in all parts of Northern Ireland and in the Southern border counties. Without the participation of people working in all of those communities, our work would not be possible, nor would we achieve such high levels of success."

In a newspaper interview, shortly before his departure as Chairman, William McCarter summed up the ethos and the achievements of the body with which he had been so closely associated and to which he had given such faithful service.

He said "The Fund was a subtle way to bring people from both communities together. Instead of giving them cups of tea and saying 'Let's get reconciled', it used job creation to give people an economic focus.

In a low-key way, the Fund brought people from both communities into projects to provide a human dynamic and to develop relationships that would not have existed in a divided society."[7]

How right he was, and the following chapters in this book help to show how the support from the Fund helped to change lives and to build networks within communities and across the divides. It provided some of the very best of help in some of the very worst of times.

Notes

1 1998 Annual Report Page 6.
2 Ibid Page 7.
3 Ibid Page 9.
4 In an Interview with the Author in July 2007.
5 IFI Annual Report 2001 Pages 8-16.
6 IFI Annual Report 2004 Pages 6-9.
7 Irish Times, 4 February 2005, in an Interview with Siobhan Creaton, Page 28.

CHAPTER EIGHT

Wider *Horizons*

THE WIDER HORIZONS PROGRAMME WAS ONE of the first to be established by the IFI, and it remained an integral part of the Fund's impetus and outreach. The Board allocated, in the early stages, an initial £6.5 millions to help young people in Ireland North and South to learn new skills by obtaining work experience, training and education, and in providing personal development opportunities at home and abroad.

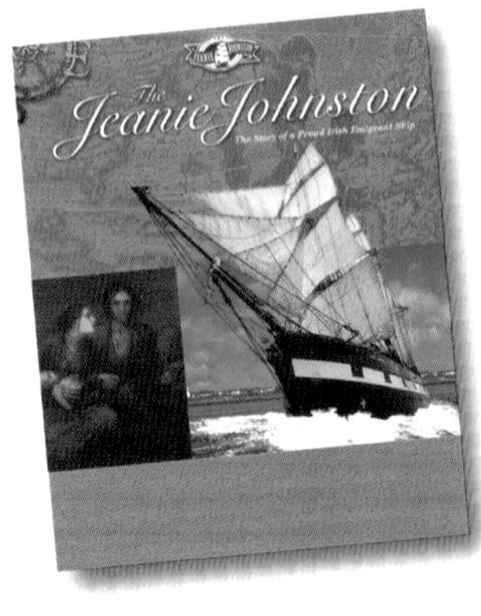

The central philosophy of the Programme was, literally, to provide wider horizons. The opportunity to travel overseas, mostly to Canada and the United States, and also to Europe, was to help young people to look with more perspective at their own communities, with their long-established prejudices and cultural attitudes, and to try to understand how this might be contributing to the problems of society in general.

It was felt that by working together on common projects, trainees from different religious and political backgrounds could discover that they had much more in common than they had assumed previously. One of the most important and symbolic examples of this was the Jeanie Johnston project, which featured the construction and utilisation of a replica of a graceful, triple-masted sailing ship built in Quebec in 1847,

The Jeanie Johnston on a recent visit to the Port of Belfast, with the iconic Harland & Wolff Cranes in the background

and which carried Irish emigrants from Tralee in Co. Kerry to the United States and Canada.

The original vessel had created its own, almost legendary, reputation. Its maiden voyage began in April 1848 and it carried nearly 200 emigrants who were seeking a new life in North America. During the next seven years, this distinctive and sturdy wooden vessel made a total 16 trans-Atlantic voyages to Quebec, Baltimore and New York and carried across some 2,500 people from an Ireland that had been ravaged by the Famine.

During this entire period, the Jeanie Johnston achieved the remarkable feat of not experiencing a single loss of life on board. Even after a collision in 1858 when she began to sink in the North Atlantic with a load of timber, all those on board were rescued by a passing Dutch ship – thus retaining her remarkable record of preserving life.

The construction of the "new" Jeanie Johnston is a story in itself, and one which lies outside the direct interest of this volume, but it is sufficient to note that the process required to carry out the work needed considerable funding and support, as well as exceptional technical skills. The vessel was rebuilt in Co. Kerry, and in 2003 she embarked on a number of voyages around Ireland, prior to her departure for the United States.

The International Fund was supportive of the Jeanie Johnston venture in a number of ways, though it did not make a contribution to the capital costs of the project. However, it supported young trainees from North and South who worked on the construction of the vessel, under the direction of an international team of skilled shipbuilders. The Fund also provided support for Wider Horizon trainees to take part in trans-Atlantic voyages.

A key objective of the Wider Horizons Programme was to foster mutual understanding and reconciliation among young people between the ages 18-28, and it particularly targeted people from areas of economic and social disadvantage. In nearly all cases, the volunteers found this to be a worthwhile and inspiring exercise. One of these was Stuart Moffett, from North Belfast, who took part in a voyage on the Jeanie Johnston from Quebec to St. John's, Newfoundland in the autumn of 2003.

Stuart was one of a group of 14 young people who were chosen from different backgrounds in association with a Springboard Opportunities project which was established in 1992. Its purpose, like that of the Wider Horizons Programme, was to help young people from the different communities North and South to develop their skills and employability and also to foster an exchange of cultural beliefs, and an understanding of communities as well as an understanding and an appreciation of diversity.

The voyage was preceded by a residential programme in Rostrevor to give the participants an opportunity to get to know each other and to help them bond as a group before they went overseas. Stuart Moffett, an articulate young man from a Unionist background, recalls some of the highlights of that particular adventure.

"We were a group of Protestants and Catholics from North and South and there was a good mixture of boys and girls. The southerners were a bit hard to understand, though I had met some of them on a previous course. They used different slang words, but there was never a feeling of 'them and us.' The voyage was lovely, and also exciting. Sometimes it was bitter cold, with the sky calm and beautiful, and porpoises gliding alongside the boat. That was amazing."[1]

Stuart said that the trainees were "basically deck-hands. We worked as look-outs and we helped to steer the ship, with commands from the Captain which was fun – because you asked yourself 'When would I ever get a chance to steer a boat, apart from this time?' It was definitely for real. The Captain would tell you how far he wanted to go, and you just had to keep measuring the distance."

"Although other people were watching out for us, just in case, it was all quite exhilarating, just knowing that you had a good-sized boat under your control, with all the people in it. Sometimes the seas were rough but we were lucky, although one night we had to weigh anchor close to the coast and just sit it out."

Stuart, however, had added challenges to contend with, including his fear of heights and of deep water. He says "I went up as far as the second tier of sails, which scared the living daylights out of me, but I'm really glad I did it. I was also scared of deep water, but there was a small net at the front of the ship, and when it was nice and calm you could hook yourself on to the net and just relax, with the water splashing up beside you. I still have phobias about heights and depths, but I'm not afraid of them any more. I'm willing to experiment now."

Stuart says that the voyage helped to teach him that "There should be no 'what ifs?' in your life - if you want something, you just do it." On the Jeanie Johnston he travelled with friends he had known previously, but he also met new people. He says "One fella I did not know was from the South, and he had brought the Irish national flag with him. I was always curious about the Tricolour, and what it meant. He explained to me that the green was for Irish, the orange was for the Protestants and the white in-between was for peace." Incidentally, the colour is from the Coat of Arms of the House of Orange-Nassau.

This impressed him, because in the Loyalist area of the North where he was brought up, the Irish Tricolour was viewed very differently. Stuart says "It was looked on as a bad thing, but that was not its real meaning at all. So when they were burning the flag on the July bonfires they did not really know what it meant. Now I try to let people know about these things, because I don't like discrimination."

"That's another thing I learned about being on the Jeanie Johnston - you can't discriminate against people

Stuart Moffett, left, and Tony Clarke, who learned a great deal from their voyages on the Jeanie Johnston, are pictured at the Lagan Weir in Belfast

because they could be a friend of your friend or your brother. You could end up by discriminating against someone in your own family, if you carry it on. I have learned, above all, that if you discriminate against someone, you are actually discriminating against yourself, and against your own future."[2]

Clearly Stuart Moffett learned a great deal from his various courses and his experience on the Jeanie Johnston, and with a mischievous smile he also confided in me what he had also picked up from the journey – "I also learned to say 'Kiss my backside' in Gaelic!." That might not be the way that the International Fund would measure progress, but for this young trainee on the Wider Horizons Programme it was a clearly a learning experience in more ways than one!

It was not just the trainees who faced challenges, but also some of the trainers like Tony Clarke from the Poleglass estate, a Nationalist area on the outskirts of Belfast. He himself had been a Springboard trainee and later became involved with the organisation as a trainer on some of the Jeanie Johnston voyages. Like Stuart Moffett he, too, had a fear of heights which he also overcame.

He recalls "On the ship I faced some of my own personal fears. The experience made me look differently at a lot of things within myself, and within the surroundings of my work and career. What the IFI has been doing not just on Wider Horizons but also with other programmes has been very important. People have come through a conflict of more

The late David Ervine – "The Jeanie Johnston offered young people the opportunity to talk to others they would never have had the chance to speak to".

than 30 years and they realise that it's time to move forward, even though there are those on either side who don't want to give it up. The likes of Springboard and the Wider Horizons Programme are breaking down barriers, and showing young people that although there are differences, these need not be a threat, and the shared challenges should help all. He's unemployed, just as much as I am unemployed. She's going through the same things that the wee girl from next door is going through. The Wider Horizons Programme actually did give me wider horizons, and the Jeanie Johnston was one of the bigger mind-openers, because I faced a lot of fears on it, and overcame them as well."[3]

One of the most eloquent comments about the value of the Jeanie Johnston project was made by the late David Ervine, a former Loyalist paramilitary who later became leader of the Progressive Unionist Party. He made a significant contribution to the peace process before his untimely death in 2007.

In a BBC television interview several years earlier he described the Jeanie Johnston as "a beautiful craft" and as "a lump of wood that's a vehicle for other people to get to know each other. People who came from diametrically-opposed positions on this island.... people from deprived backgrounds whether they be from the North or the South."

Ervine emphasised that "In the building of that ship, people experienced cultural shocks and when we got them back to Northern Ireland, the difference that made to them was quite substantial. So we've seen it in living colour, just with the sense of exposure that someone else can give you, and the benefit that you can achieve from it."

Later David watched the Jeanie Johnston sailing into Belfast harbour, and flying the Irish Tricolour. He said "It was received warmly, and I long for the day that not only is it back around Ireland's shores but it's in Belfast again. But where I want it to be most is on the high seas doing two things - showing the world the new Ireland and offering to young people the opportunity to capacity-build, and in doing so to be exposed to people who formerly they would never, ever have had the chance to speak to."

Some of the most important, and poignant, projects arose out of the Enniskillen explosion at the town's Cenotaph on 8 November 1987, prior to the annual Poppy Day Service of Remembrance. Eleven civilians died, and many others were badly injured, when a Provisional IRA bomb went off, without warning. Among the very seriously wounded was a student nurse Marie Wilson, and her father Gordon. In one of the most moving stories of the entire Troubles, he explained how he had held hands with his daughter under a mound of rubble.

Several years later he said "I shouted 'How are you Marie?' and she said 'I'm fine'. My heart skipped a beat, with relief. But then, suddenly and terribly, she screamed. I knew that there must be something awfully wrong for her to scream like that." Gordon shouted several times to Marie but "then suddenly, her voice changed. She sounded different. She held my hand tightly, and gripped me as hard as she could. She said 'Daddy, I love

Joan Wilson ... an ordinary heroine

Tomorrow marks the 20th anniversary of the Enniskillen bomb. Joan Wilson tells **Alf McCreary** why she'd still like the killers brought to justice

Joan Wilson, who lost her daughter, Marie, in the Enniskillen Poppy Day bombing of 1987, is not looking forward to the 20th anniversary which falls tomorrow.

She says: "I dread even the thought of it. The pain has not lessened in 20 years, and I think of Marie every day, often several times a day. I wonder what she would be like today if she were alive – would she still be nursing, would she be married with a family, all the what might-have-beens."

Joan Wilson talks matter-of-factly, and she is a strong woman with deep spiritual depths. Yet there is no mistaking the sadness that remains at the centre of her being. She reflects: "Time does not heal, as some people claim. It only helps you to cope better. I have talked to many who have lost loved ones, and most of them feel the same way about it as I do."

Marie Wilson, a trainee nurse, was one of 11 civilians who died when a no-warning Provisional IRA bomb went off near the Enniskillen Cenotaph as people were gathering for the annual Remembrance Day service. The deaths and widespread injuries sent shock waves across a province which had already suffered grievously. The atrocity was strongly condemned by the then Prime Minister Mrs Thatcher and by other leaders around the world.

The late Gordon Wilson, who was also badly injured by the bomb, spoke movingly about his daughter Marie, during a media interview later that night. He said: "I bear no ill-will. I don't have an answer, but I know there has to be a plan. It's part of a greater plan, and God is good. And we shall meet again."

His words brought him instant international recognition, and he became a tireless peace campaigner until his untimely death several years later.

Joan still remembers vividly the events of that awful day of the bombing, and she still deeply mourns Marie and Gordon, as well as her son, Peter, who was killed later in a car accident. Her remaining daughter, Julie-Anne, and her family live in Northern Ireland and they keep closely in touch.

She says: "I still see the pink dress and the jacket which Marie was wearing when she left the house on the day of the bomb. I asked her 'Have you got an umbrella?' and she replied 'Don't fuss, mum!' That was the last time I saw her, in our home. "Several hours later she died in the local hospital , from massive injuries suffered in the bomb."

Joan says: "I also miss Gordon greatly. He was a loving grandfather and I grieve that he is not seeing his five grandchildren grow up to be the great people they are. However, his presence is still about the house, and the others too. But you miss the physical presence, and you are always aware of the empty place at the table."

Joan's deep Christian faith gives her great re-assurance. "What keeps me going is the knowledge that I will see all of them on the other side. I love the Bible readings, and their promise of a better place."

'People ask me how to handle bereavement, and I tell them to ask God for the strength and grace to face each day'

Joan also lost her first son, Richard, at birth, so she has known immense loss throughout her life. "People ask me how to handle bereavement, and I tell them to ask God for the strength and grace to face each day. If you truly ask for His help, it will be given to you."

Joan Wilson, like her late husband, is an eloquent and thoughtful person but she has chosen to keep a low public profile. "I want to be with my family and friends and to lead my own life, but I have made a point of visiting many people who also have lost loved ones, and I try to bring them some comfort, from my own experience of bereavement. Sometimes people need much more than one visit, and I am happy to go on seeing

Some years ago she co-wrote a bereavement anthology called All Shall Be Well, and she has given many people a copy. She says: "I still get letters from people all over the United Kingdom, and also many from down South. I am always glad to hear from people, and to help where I can."

She is not bitter about those responsible for Marie's death, but she says: "I pity them, and I hope that they will come to realise what they have done, and ask for God's forgiveness." She would still like to see them being brought to justice. "I would like to meet them, and just ask them 'Why have you caused so much suffering to innocent people?' However it's perhaps better that I will never see them, because it would be a terrible ordeal for me. Even if they escape justice in this world, they will not escape the final judgement and justice of God."

Joan Wilson has lived in the same detached house in Enniskillen for the past 47 years. Though devoted to her wider family, she retains an independent life-style. She is a gifted musician and recently she celebrated 30 years as the organist in the Enniskillen Methodist Church. She was also a long-time choir mistress in the Church, but this role is now taken by her daughter-in-law Ingrid. She says: "I think we make a good team together!"

Tomorrow there will be a special 20th anniversary commemoration at the Enniskillen Cenotaph, but Joan will not be there. "I could not face it, because it would be too painful. However I will go to the local Presbyterian Church for a time of quiet reflection , until the others join us for a commemoration service there." It will be conducted by the Rev David Cupples, the Presbyterian minister who was also there on the day of the bombing, and in the evening there will be a service for all the relatives. The special speaker will be a former Presbyterian Moderator, the Rev Trevor Morrow. Joan says: "This is the same pattern as for the 10 year commemoration, and that gave me great strength."

On Sunday she will be playing the organ at the Methodist Church during the Remembrance Day service, just as she was doing 20 years ago when the news of the bomb began to filter through. "It will not be easy but I will be there. Life goes on."

Though Joan Wilson has suffered much, she is also very aware of the loss of other families and individuals. She adds: "I think of those on all sides who have lost loved ones. I used to think of this even before Marie died and I was always very sad for others. But you have no idea of how awful it is, unless you have gone through the experience yourself."

Despite all the bad times, Joan Wilson has always been a quiet heroine and an inspiring and gracious person whose inner strength and personal faith have carried her through. She says: "I am thankful for the years that I knew Marie, and also Gordon and Peter, and for all that we shared as a family. There is so much for which I am truly grateful, and even in the bad times that has been a great comfort for me. As Gordon said so long ago 'God is good, and we shall meet again'. And we will. I am convinced of that."

Joan Wilson at home beside the cherished photograph of her daughter, Marie, a victim of the Enniskillen Poppy Day bomb (inset above) and her late husband, Gordon

All Shall Be Well, Joan Wilson, with Alf McCreary, Marshall Pickering, £8.99

Joan Wilson meets the then Canadian Prime Minister Jean Chrétien at a reception in Hillsborough Castle. The Canadian Government has been a firm sponsor of the Wider Horizons Programme

Bronagh Lawson and George Briggs

you very much.' Those were her exact words, and those were the last words I ever heard her say."[3]

Marie died later in hospital that afternoon, with her mother Joan and sister Julie-Anne at her bedside. Gordon was lying elsewhere in the casualty department, in great pain with a badly dislocated shoulder. That night he was asked by a BBC radio reporter what he felt about the day's tragic events.

Spontaneously, Gordon said "I bear no ill-will, I bear no grudge. Dirty sort of talk is not going to bring her back to life.... I don't have a purpose. I don't have an answer. But I know that there has to be a plan. And it is part of a greater plan, and God is good. And we shall meet again."

The events of that day, and Gordon Wilson's dignity and forbearance in the midst of such tragedy, became one of the most iconic images of the Troubles. It seemed entirely fitting, therefore, that later on, the IFI Board helped to support the Marie Wilson Voyage of Hope project which sponsored hundreds of young people from both main communities in the North.

They travelled to Canada as part of the Wider Horizons Programme, where they learned more about what they had in common, and returned with a new perspective on their native land. Between 1998 and 2003, with the exception of 2001, the International Fund gave £67,000 towards the Voyage of Hope project. It was regarded by the International Fund as "a well-respected initiative." The Fund also supported the Spirit of Enniskillen Trust which developed an expertise in producing skilled young leaders for change in Northern Ireland.

Gordon and Joan Wilson were extremely supportive of this and other similar initiatives. After Gordon's sudden and untimely death in 1995, Joan remained closely in touch with the Marie Wilson Voyage of Hope and the Spirit of Enniskillen Trust. On the eve of the 25th anniversary of the Enniskillen bombing she talked about the awfulness of what had happened.

She said "People tell you that time will heal, but it doesn't. It only teaches you how to cope. You miss the physical presence, and you are always aware of the empty place at the table. You have no idea about how awful it is, unless you have gone through the experience yourself."[4]

Joan was appreciative of the work carried out by the International Fund, and others, in widening horizons. She says "The young people were well chosen to be sent out, and we were so proud of them. Gordon always said 'We'll have to work with the young people', and so the Marie Wilson Voyage of Hope, and the Spirit of Enniskillen, and all these things have helped to bring young people together and to widen their minds. Young people have gone all over the place, and my own grand-daughter went to Cyprus. She had her eyes opened, and she came to realise what goes on in other countries."

As the Wider Horizons Programme progressed, it was subject to systematic evaluation, and in 1990 the Board decided to concentrate on two main groups, namely young people – especially those attending community training workshops or the unemployed, and also managers and entrepreneurs, with a focus on small businesses.

'Spirit' bursary students look forward to work trips

Three students from Enniskillen who have been awarded the Spirit of Enniskillen bursaries this year (from left) Natalie Gilmore, Brendan McClave and Mandelle Noble.

Priority was given to projects from the disadvantaged areas of Northern Ireland and from the Southern border counties.

Significantly, a number of new projects were being opened up at training locations in the European Union, and especially in Denmark, France and Germany, as well as in the United States and Canada. By 30 September 2007 (the latest figures available) the Fund had provided a total of £110 millions for 1,068 projects in the USA and Canada, as well as in Europe and elsewhere.

Literally thousands of young people benefited from Wider Horizons courses in self-development and business expertise, and one of the most rewarding experiences was that of Bronagh Lawson, a talented textile designer from Co. Down who eventually ended up as a Training and Business Consultant.

Bronagh was brought up in the Strangford-Portaferry area, but she left the North at 18, because she did not want to go to college with the Troubles as a background, like many of her contemporaries. She was awarded a first-class honours degree in Textiles and Fashion at the Winchester School of Art, and took her skills abroad. She won a Fulbright Scholarship to New York, where she did well as a designer. However, the lure of her homeland pulled her back.

She says "I felt that I had got to the point where I was going to turn into one of those annoying people who say 'Oh isn't Ireland great, I just wanna have a wee cottage there, and everything's wonderful!' That was not the concept of Ireland which I knew, and had grown up with, and I felt that I was starting to romanticise it."[5]

She went to Strangford and then Belfast which, she admits, was "a bit of a culture shock," after New York. She was in her late twenties and single, and she had ideas of setting up a textile business back home. However, this was not as straightforward as she had thought, and she then went to Spain. She later returned to Belfast. She says "I believe that Irish people have been born with an elastic band attached to them, and no matter how far they go, they feel this wee tug to come back. There's a pull in Ireland that does not apply in other countries."

Back in the North she was introduced to a Wider Horizons Programme, and travelled to Thunder Bay in Ontario, Canada for additional training. She worked on two placements and recalls "The training in Canada was excellent. It was inter-active, and they got everyone involved. Someone explained to me recently that what I experienced on the course was a 'brainflip.' I had always seen myself as totally involved in textiles and fashion, but over there I began to realise that there were other things that I might be able to do.

She asked herself 'Do I actually have to produce an object like a jumper?' Maybe the world does not need another jumper, but it needs people with open minds who might have creative solutions for things." When she returned to Belfast from the placements she was asked by her tutor George Briggs what she had learned. She said later, with a twinkle in her eye, "I told George that I had learned so much what I wanted was his job! I realised that what I really wanted to do was the project management and the mentoring work, but I hadn't realised that I had been building up the skills that could be used for that."

Bronagh developed her career as a Training and Business Consultant, especially with community groups. She says "I seem to have empathy for that, and I try to take people from where they are at, and help them to move forward. I suppose that I try to look at things in a different way, and to bring to a situation another, different perspective. I particularly like to help them develop economic independence."

Bronagh Lawson settled in the North where her husband, who is French, works as a global marketing consultant with Telecom/IT firms. She sums up her experience in this way – "I reckon that if the IFI hadn't been in existence and hadn't been backing something like the Wider Horizons Programme, I wouldn't have stayed here in Northern Ireland. There seemed to be nothing that was suited for to me to do."

"I could never have fitted into, say, a Civil Service job, but the International Fund gave me an opportunity, and others who were with me on the placements felt the same. We were people who really didn't fit in with the traditional thinking back home, and we felt that we could not stay there because of that. It was 'doing our head in', but we have all stayed and we are making our living here. That – to my mind – is extremely important."[6]

George Briggs, who has helped thousands of trainees, sums up Bronagh Lawson's experience, which was shared in different ways by so many others. He said "When I think back to the original Programme, I believe that we really did give Bronagh and her colleagues a wider horizon. During those weeks in Canada they were effectively stopped in their tracks. They realised it was another world, and they returned as changed people."

That, in essence, was the whole point – and the continued success – of the Wider Horizons Programme.

Notes

1 In an Interview with the Author in Belfast, in July 2007.

2 Ibid

3 In an Interview with the Author in Belfast, in July 2007.

3 Marie - A Story From Enniskillen, by Gordon Wilson with Alf McCreary. Published by Marshall Pickering in 1990, Pages 33-34.

4 Interview with Alf McCreary Belfast Telegraph November 7, 2007.

5 In an Interview with the Author in Belfast, in March 2007.

6 Ibid.

CHAPTER NINE

Stewartstown

ONE OF THE MOST IMPORTANT initiatives of the International Fund was to provide help for organisations which were aiming to promote greater dialogue and to tackle divisions between different cultures and religions.

However it is important to note that many of the latter were basically "tribal" or "identity" divisions, which had little or nothing to do with theology and Christianity in its true sense.

This was a difficult area of operation, which required not only sensitivity and vision from the International Fund, but also courage from those at the grass-roots who were trying to implement these changes. The IFI was also pro-active in bringing forward projects which addressed needs and also gaps in provision which had not been filled by statutory or other bodies.

A good example of this work was the Suffolk-Lenadoon interface on the Stewartstown Road in West Belfast where Protestants and Catholics lived in an area of sporadic violence and misunderstanding.

The Suffolk Estate is a small Protestant enclave within predominantly Catholic outer West Belfast. Both places, according to an IFI briefing paper "were characterised by low self-esteem, high levels of poverty, high unemployment, poor health, low educational attainment and a general sense of hopelessness."

This mindset had solidified as a result of the Troubles which began in 1969. Originally, Suffolk had been a desirable green-site location for Protestant families, and some other Protestant families had moved into the mostly Catholic Lenadoon estate across the Stewartstown Road. However, in the major shift of population in West Belfast in the

Jean Brown (left) and Renee Crawford. pioneers for progress in West Belfast

early years of the Troubles, thousands of Catholics had been forced to flee from their homes and to take refuge in the Lenadoon area. This in turn had forced Protestants to move back from Lenadoon to Suffolk, and Catholics to flee from Suffolk altogether. Those who remained – only around 350 families – felt encircled and frightened. Nevertheless this made them even more determined not to be pushed out from Suffolk, which was seen very much as the Protestants' "last stand" in that part of West Belfast.

For years the deadlock remained, with no real contact between the two communities in an area characterised by continuous violence. Despite the unpromising situation, there was some ground for hope, because within both communities there were outstanding individuals and leaders who, with others, eventually engaged with each other across the divide.

Two such people were Jean Brown, from Suffolk, and Renee Crawford from Lenadoon. Jean, a Protestant who is married to a Catholic, lived on the Suffolk estate since it was built over 50 years ago, and became involved in a wide variety of community bridge-building initiatives for the past 25 years. She worked for 16 years as the manager of a 78-place ACE programme, and gained wide experience in finance, personnel, project-planning and management. She was Chairperson of the Suffolk Community Forum for two years, and she was later employed as a community development worker.

Renee Crawford, a Catholic, has lived in Lenadoon for over 30 years, and she is one of the founding members of the Lenadoon Community Forum, which was established in 1992. It was set up after a series of consultations concerning the social and physical regeneration of Lenadoon, and to build up capacity within the community. She worked in both a voluntary and a paid capacity for many years, and became the Strategic Development Co-Ordinator with the Lenadoon Community Forum.

This description of each woman is no more than a thumbnail sketch, but behind the scenes each has a story of courage and resilience in times of great trouble.

Jean Brown – "No matter how tough the going gets, hang on to your dream".

Jean remembers the early days when Suffolk was "almost an idyllic place to grow up, because it was like living in the countryside." The Protestant population increased and moved into Horn Drive in Lenadoon, where Catholics were living.

However Jean met her first Catholic, not in Lenadoon, but in the North Coast holiday resort of Portrush, some 60 miles away. She said "I got picked up in the dodgems by this Catholic fellow Tommy Brown from Rathcoole, and he asked me to marry him two weeks later, and I did eventually. I was only 17, and if my daughter came and told me that, I would have locked her up for her own safety!"[1]

Renee Crawford: "How can we make life better within our communities? It's not about winning wars. Its about winning small battles and small things. As someone once said 'If you look to the sun, you won't see the shadows'".

Their "mixed marriage", which was not easy in Northern Ireland in those days, worked extremely well and they settled down in Horn Drive, at a time of widespread community disruption when Protestants were leaving the Lenadoon estate.

Jean said "We watched the exodus coming closer and we knew it would soon be our turn. However, I was pig-headed and determined not to be forced out. I naively thought that being in a mixed marriage gave us some immunity, but we kept getting attacked. Every time I put out the baby in a pram she was pelted with eggs and stones. Our car was burned, the hedge was set on fire, the keyholes were blocked up, and the windows started getting put in."

The Army had a strong presence in the area, and Jean said that two soldiers stayed in her kitchen to help prevent attacks. She added "I later discovered that they were there to prevent Tommy and me from coming downstairs to see what was really going on, because in many cases it was soldiers who were breaking the windows."

"I later heard from a senior officer that it was a "managed evacuation" of Protestants, to prevent mass slaughter. My husband Tommy listened to media reports of the release of secret Government papers of 1983 and it was claimed that the Government had indeed stage-managed this evacuation."

By 1973 the situation for Jean and her family was so serious that they decided to leave. "My little girl was sitting at the table when the windows were put in, and she was showered with glass. So we had to go, and we moved to the Suffolk side of the Stewartstown Road. The place was riddled with empty houses, because people were leaving there as well."

Jean had a strong Christian faith, and she became involved with the local church, and with community development. By the 1990's, however, the Suffolk Estate was in deep trouble. Jean said "It was dying on its feet. Young people could not wait to get out. It was derelict, bleak, and shocking."

Jean and some of her colleagues approached the Housing Executive for help, and also the International Fund. "We didn't know much about the IFI, but we were desperate. There was a guy with them called Hugh McCloskey, and he was fantastic."

They asked for help to refurbish a derelict block of shops, and the International Fund did an economic appraisal. "They said that refurbishment would cost £1 million, which was a lot of money, and that it would be better to demolish the buildings and start from scratch. They also said that we were too small for such funding on our own, and the only way to get the money was to approach the people of Lenadoon and to work on a cross-community basis."

It was a tall order not only for those living in Suffolk, but also for the people of Lenadoon which had its own challenges and problems. Renee Crawford was brought up in West Belfast but in the aftermath of internment in1971, during one of the worst phases of the Troubles, she and her husband and young son were forced to flee to Lenadoon.

The pivotal development on the Stewartstown Road, before and after

Guy Crauser, second left, of the European Commission with Jean Brown, Chairman Willie McCarter and Renee Crawford

They found shelter in a house that was already vacant and damaged.

She said "I hated it from the day I went there, but it wasn't the fault of Lenadoon. This was happening at a time when people were being burned out and forced to move, and that was beyond the control of ordinary people like ourselves because the circumstances were not of our making. It was like being forced to play Russian roulette. You didn't want to be there, but you had no choice."[2]

The Crawford's home became part of an Army post when soldiers took over neighbouring houses as a base. Sadly, however, the Crawfords were only in the house six weeks when it was hit by a mortar bomb which had been aimed at the Army post.

Renee, who was pregnant, remembered lifting her son prior to the explosion and then being flung through a glass partition by the force of the blast. The baby was covered in blood, and after walking in and out of the house in shock, Renee lay on the settee with the child in her arms.

She recalled "There was hysteria, with everybody shouting and running. Then a man came in and took the baby. My aunt was outside and she brought him to her house. Our place had been blown to pieces – there was nothing left, no windows, no slates. I went up to my aunt's house to see the baby, and I remember her saying "Did you bring your purse, did you lock the front door. I said "No" because there was nothing left of the damn place."

After seeing the baby, Renee went back home again, and the soldiers ordered up an Army ambulance because a civilian vehicle was unable to get in to what was then a "no-go" area.

Renee described her sense of fear. She said "The vehicle set off at a fierce speed and I'm saying to myself "Please, somebody don't shoot at us because it's an Army vehicle. The driver was going so fast that he hit a roundabout, and I thought 'Oh God he's going to crash. I'm going to die in this ambulance' ".

However Renee did not die, and she was treated for her injuries in Lagan Valley Hospital. She later returned to her aunt's house, where her young son had also been cared for by a nurse, and he survived. Renee's unborn baby was also safe, though the birth of the little girl had to be induced later on. Unfortunately her son had suffered severe ear damage as a result of the blast, and his hearing has been severely affected ever since.

Amazingly, Renee and her family stayed put in their house beside the Army post. She said "Where else was there to go? My husband and I came from large, close-knit families. It wasn't an option for us to move. We were staying in Lenadoon, for better or for worse."

Jean Brown (centre) in discussion with Dr Hübner the European Commissioner for Regional Policy, with current Chairman Denis Rooney, at Stewartstown Road

The worst had happened, and it seemed that things could only improve. The Army eventually moved out of the area, the Crawford's house was fixed up.

Renee eventually became a founder-member of the Lenadoon Community Forum. She said "There is a standing joke in our family that I went out to a short meeting in 1992 and I haven't returned since!"

In those years Renee, along with others, set about trying to make Lenadoon a better place for everyone. She and Jean Brown met when representatives from Suffolk and Lenadoon came together for a joint meeting, and they stayed in touch. Even in the difficult times during the Drumcree stand-offs, when the situation in the Stewartstown interface (and all across Northern Ireland) was dangerous, both sides kept in touch, through a network of mobile phones.

Renee recalled "At the first joint meeting, people were totally honest. Some said 'I'm a Unionist, and others said "I'm a Republican.' There was no point in trying to ignore the elephant in the room, but we also realised that both communities had much in common, such as ill-health, poverty, lack of education, lack of jobs, and also contentious issues which would take a long time to resolve."

The community leaders also had to bring their own people with them, in order to pave the way for the ambitious inter-community project which the International Fund had offered to support, within certain conditions. This was not easy, because the legacy of long-held suspicions and mistrust could only be healed by patience, and by sensitive but determined leadership.

Fortunately, however, the difficulties were overcome slowly, despite the periodic setbacks. The Stewartstown Road Regeneration Committee, which was formed by representatives from Suffolk and Lenadoon, was given assistance to provide a Community Economic Resource Centre on the Stewartstown Road, which had been the notorious interface between the two communities. The main contact in the bad days was when people at the lower end of Lenadoon crossed the road, with a feeling of being under duress, to use the Post Office and Chemist's shop which were still part of the near-derelict block on the Suffolk side of the road.

The new project involved the demolition of the entire block, and the establishment of a new suite of buildings. These were to include retail units, and facilities for the development of cross-community relationships and community-based services. The idea was also to stimulate the social and economic regeneration of the area, and to improve the image of the place and the self-esteem of its people.

The new building was put up first, which allowed the Post Office and the local chemist to continue to provide their services to the

Jean Brown and Renee Crawford. "You need people who believe in you, and that belief came from the IFI and the Housing Executive".

community in the meantime from the old building. Once the new premises were ready they both moved in, and the old building was demolished.

The cost of the project was £1m, as mentioned earlier, and the International Fund provided £475,000 of this. The rest came from the Belfast European Partnership Board and the Belfast Regeneration Office. The Foundation Stone for the Centre was laid by Michel Barnier, the European Commissioner for Regional Policy in March 2001, and it was visited later by Dr Danuta Hübner, the EU Commissioner for Regional Policy.

The Board's Chairman William McCarter, welcomed Commissioner Barnier, and paid tribute to the support for the International Fund from Europe, and the other North American and Commonwealth donors. He also acknowledged the "pivotal role" of the Stewartstown Road Regeneration Committee and the Fund's Development Consultant Hugh McCloskey in bringing the project to fruition. He added "There were many obstacles to be overcome, at the various stages of planning and implementation, but everyone is pleased with the outcome." The Northern Ireland Housing Executive also played an important role in transferring the old building to the Committee, and in providing on-going support.

The project proved to be a remarkable success, with a significant decrease in violence and crime since the new Centre was established, as well as a sustained improvement in inter-community relationships and co-operation. Nevertheless, community leaders on both sides remained aware of the need for constant vigilance to make sure that the mutual trust was not eroded, and that the fragile peace was nurtured for as long as was necessary, to a point where it could withstand even the most determined assaults from those who might have wished to turn back the clock.

In 2004, the Stewartstown Road Regeneration Project was granted another £400,000 by the International Fund to develop an adjacent site for the provision of more retail units, office accommodation, and a new purpose-built 50-place child-care facility. The new project was also to create some 25 new jobs.

The Stewartstown Road story is a remarkable example of courage and initiative from the residents of both communities, and the faith shown by the International Fund and other supporters. Chris O'Halloran, Director of the Belfast Interface Project, who had done much himself to make the venture a success, noted "This project is an object lesson in self-preservation. People had their backs to the wall here, as in other interface areas, and they had to be really creative in how they got themselves out of the situation they found themselves in, and they have been creative, hugely creative."[3]

Jean Brown and Renee Crawford were full of praise for the IFI's involvement. Renee said "The building was not just shops and offices. It was symbolic, and we needed a champion when we were doing something like that. You need people who believe in you, and that belief came from the IFI, and also the support of the Housing Executive."

Incidents of sectarian nature on Suffolk/Lenadoon interface (Police Service of Northern Ireland)

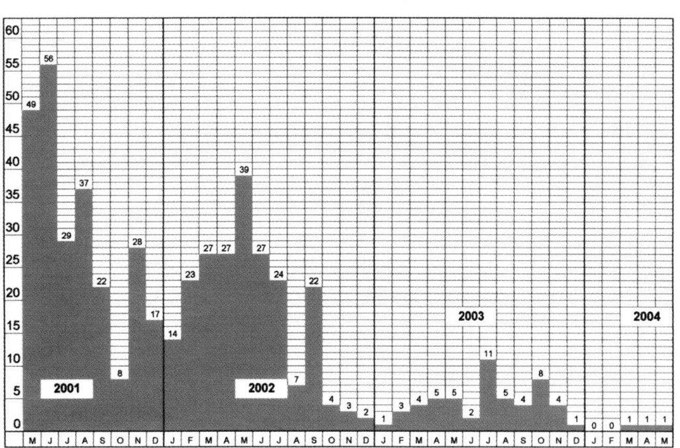

This chart illustrates the dramatic drop in number of incidents recorded since the completion of the project

Jean said "Without the IFI and the Housing Executive and the Belfast Interface Project, none of this would have happened. They were absolutely brilliant, and they believed in it from the beginning. Other agencies laughed at us and said it would never work. It was so important that other people had faith in us, and that was one of the factors which helped us to keep going."

It was also important that this support was expressed in practical terms, as well as in moral support, and right from the early days when others remained sceptical about the outcome of such a project.

Jean said "The IFI gave us a letter up front for a large sum of money and they allowed us to hold it there for as long as we took to raise the rest. That letter of offer must have been there for three or four years, and I don't believe that any other funder would have allowed that money to lie there on the table for so long. Eventually, we were able to take up that IFI offer and to say to others 'Here's a funder who believes in us, and we need you to believe in us as well."

The two women, despite their individual and collective achievements, remain modest, but their matter-of-fact courage and quiet heroism from the darkest of days remains impressive - and their underlying philosophies tell much about the eventual success of the project.

Renee said "We have learned that we are all trying to find the same solutions to the same things. How can we make life better for our children and grandchildren? How can we make life better within our communities? It's not about winning wars. It's about winning small battles and small things. As someone once said 'If you look to the sun, you won't see the shadows.' "

Jean summed up "Thirty years ago, I believed that God was giving me a wee glimpse of a vision, and people laughed at us, and what we were trying to do. I know now that I'm very privileged to have seen that vision become a reality, and not many people get to do that. My motto is this 'No matter how tough the going gets, believe in what you are doing, and hang on to your dream.' And we did that."

They did, indeed.

Notes

1 In an Interview with the Author in West Belfast in 2007.
2 In an Interview with the Author in 2007.
3 Building Bridges at the Grassroots, compiled by Michael Hall and Published by Island Pamphlets, Page 35.

CHAPTER TEN

from Horror *to* Hope

THROUGHOUT THE TROUBLES there were major atrocities on both sides which traumatised the victims and their families, and which were not confined to tense urban areas alone.

Two of the most horrifying of these took place in quiet villages which had no previous history of violence. Greysteel on the North Derry coast and Poyntzpass in South Armagh were far apart geographically, but what they had in common was an experience of tragedy, but also of hope and of new, shared structures rising from the despair of death and injuries.

On 30 October 1993, two Loyalist paramilitary gunmen burst in to the Rising Sun Lounge and Restaurant at Greysteel in Co. Londonderry and fired indiscriminately into the crowd. Seven people died almost instantly and an eighth died later. Six of the dead were Catholics, and the other two victims were Protestants. Many people were badly injured, and the place was covered in blood.

The scene was graphically described thus " The door opened and in came two men, wearing boiler suits and balaclavas and carrying an AK-47 rifle and a Browning 9mm automatic pistol. One of them called out 'Trick or Treat' "

"A woman, thinking it was a Halloween prank, turned and said 'That's not funny.' The man with the AK-47 shot her first, then walked through the lounge, firing as he went. The other gunman's pistol jammed after one shot, and he cursed as he tried to clear it. In all, 45 shots were fired in the attack. The man with the rifle emptied one clip of ammunition, reloaded and resumed firing. When they left, the walls and floors were splashed with blood...."[1] One of the most poignant deaths was that of a man who had thrown his wife to the ground when the gunman came in, and was shot dead protecting her.

The attack was in retaliation for the killing of Protestants by a Provisional IRA bomb on the Shankill Road, Belfast a week earlier. The Loyalist paramilitary group the UFF issued a statement saying that "This is the continuation of our threats against the Nationalist electorate that they would pay a heavy price for last Saturday night's slaughter of nine Protestants."[2]

The atrocity sent shock waves across the entire community. There was also deep fear and pessimism that the situation in Northern Ireland could spiral out of control, given that so many people had been murdered within a week. It was one of the

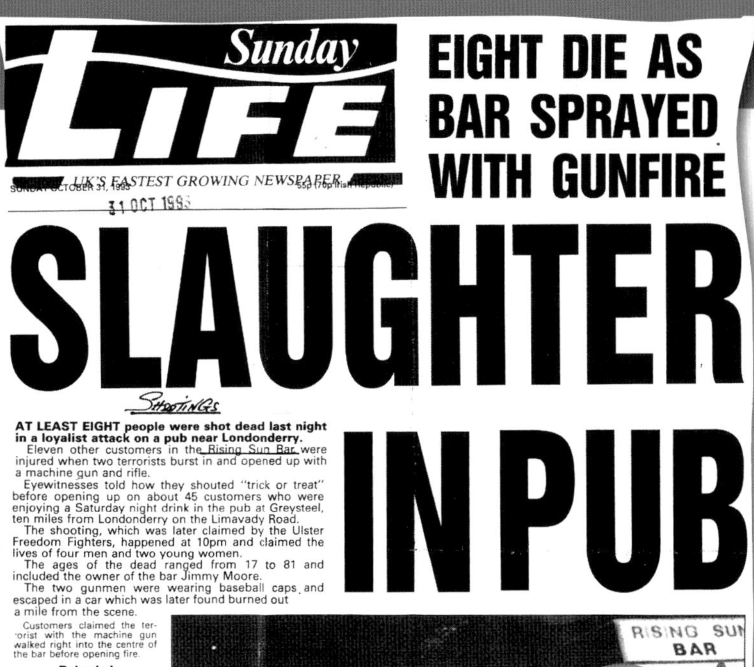

Sunday LIFE

UK'S FASTEST GROWING NEWSPAPER

31 OCT 1993

EIGHT DIE AS BAR SPRAYED WITH GUNFIRE

SLAUGHTER IN PUB

Shootings

AT LEAST EIGHT people were shot dead last night in a loyalist attack on a pub near Londonderry.

Eleven other customers in the Rising Sun Bar were injured when two terrorists burst in and opened up with a machine gun and rifle.

Eyewitnesses told how they shouted "trick or treat" before opening up on about 45 customers who were enjoying a Saturday night drink in the pub at Greysteel, ten miles from Londonderry on the Limavady Road.

The shooting, which was later claimed by the Ulster Freedom Fighters, happened at 10pm and claimed the lives of four men and two young women.

The ages of the dead ranged from 17 to 81 and included the owner of the bar Jimmy Moore.

The two gunmen were wearing baseball caps and escaped in a car which was later found burned out a mile from the scene.

Customers claimed the terrorist with the machine gun walked right into the centre of the bar before opening fire.

Reloaded

most sustained periods of serious violence since 1976.

The funerals of the victims on both sides emphasised the tragedy and loss which so many people were feeling, and at one of these funerals for a victim of the Greysteel atrocity. John Hume - who had done so much to bring peace - was visibly moved, to the point of despair. It seemed that nothing good could come from such evil, but the atrocity made the people of Greysteel and its neighbouring village Eglinton more determined than ever that violence would not separate them.

People of both villages held a joint march to show their solidarity, as key members of both communities remained determined to find a way forward for all. One of these was Hugh Nicholl, a Greysteel businessman, whose elderly father-in-law James Moore had died in the attack on the bar, which was owned by his brother-in-law Jim Moore.

He said "There was a feeling of numbness and shock. The whole of Northern Ireland had been on tenter-hooks after the Shankill bombing, but little did Greysteel know that its people would be suffering as well. After that happened, there was a feeling that we were on the brink. People had to make up their mind - was this going to be a full civil war? It was a crucial time for Northern Ireland, and thank God, we were able to move back from that brink."[3]

Shortly after the Greysteel killings and injuries, an IFI representative contacted Hugh Nicholl and asked what the Fund could do to help both communities. From this, the idea developed to form a cross-community committee to represent Greysteel and Eglinton. In the peculiar nomenclature of Northern Ireland, Greysteel was perceived to be "mostly Catholic" and Eglinton "mostly Protestant", though both were mixed, and relations in the area had always been good.

Hugh Nicholl – "We wanted a positive memorial to the people who had lost their lives."

A committee of Catholics and Protestants was set up, and chaired by Hugh Nicholl. He said "We wanted a positive memorial to the people who had lost their lives, and we chose to do this on a cross-community basis. The atrocity had been meant to divide us, but in fact it brought us closer together."

The Committee, which contained businessmen, farmers and church and community representatives, had a welcome sense of realism, and with advice from consultants, it looked to a project that would be self-sustaining economically.

They acquired 16 acres from a local farmer on a site below the main road, which overlooked a beautiful landscape of sea and coastline. It seemed to be a world away from the grim memories of the Rising Sun which was situated not far away on the other side of the main road.

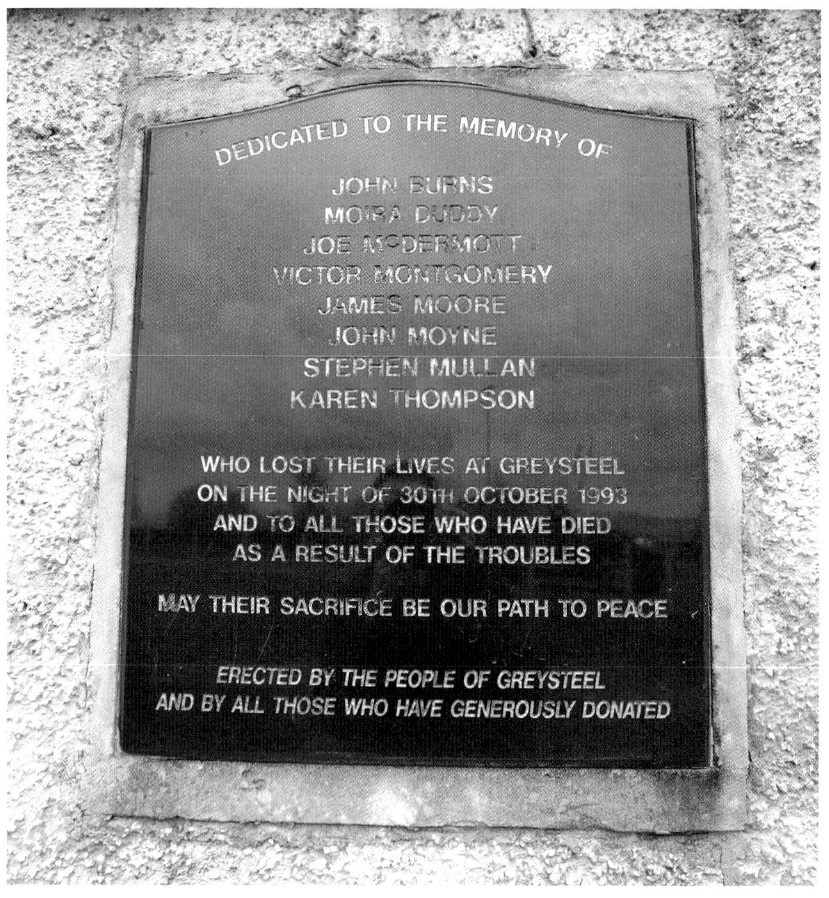

The Committee established a company called Greysteel Community Enterprises and set about the construction of a Community Centre, with recreational and sporting facilities. Crucially, there would also be industrial and workspace units which would help to sustain the economic base of the project.

Hugh Nicholl said "The whole plan was that the rental income from our commercial side would provide sustainability for the social aspect of our work. In other words we were moving forward on a solid, commercial basis, and not just on an emotional one, though that too was extremely important."

The International Fund contributed £200,000, which was around 29% of the £700,000 cost of Phase One of the project. This was to build retail and workspace units. The rest of the funding came from local councils, as well as the Northern Ireland Rural Development Agency, the Rowntree Foundation, and others. Significantly, the Greysteel-Eglinton people themselves raised funds locally.

Hugh Nicholl paid tribute to the work of the IFI, and the others. He said "To be honest, it would have been a huge challenge without the IFI. Hindsight is a wonderful thing, but I believe that the Fund was the catalyst. It opened the door by putting the money up front, and the others came in." Mr Nicholl also paid tribute to the politicians from all parties for their support, as well as Church and community leaders, and all his fellow Directors without whose help, hard work and dedication the project would not have been possible.

On a bright autumn day in 2007, Hugh Nicholl took me on a tour of the new facilities which by then included a range of meeting-rooms, and a large function hall which is used by groups as varied as a Presbyterian Church Badminton Club and the GAA. He also showed me impressive facilities for the daytime provision for the elderly and the disabled, and an industrial workshop for people with handicaps.

One of the industrial units was being rented to a bakery to make bread for the increasing Polish community – another sign of the changes that have been taking place in the Province. The International Fund has remained supportive of Greysteel Community Enterprises throughout the company's existence. The Fund approved another £84,000 in 1999 for the construction of industrial workspace accommodation, and in 2003 it provided another £249,000 for the same purpose.

The entire project, which was meant to be a living memorial to the people who died at Greysteel, is indeed that. Near the Rising Sun there is a dignified memorial, with the names of the dead inscribed upon it, but the vibrancy and sense of purpose at the Centre across the road is impressive and also moving. As I stood, incognito, watching what was going on, dozens of busy young people, some of whom who weren't even born when the Greysteel atrocity took place, rushed passed me on the way to or from their latest shared activity. This was indeed a living memorial, which was eminently worthy of note.

Patrick and Breda McGinnis of Greysteel, who are pictured at a memorial to the victims which was created by Breda. Titled "New Dawn", it is made from Irish linen, and the acorn leaves symbolise newness and the cycle of life. Patrick is a founder-member of the Board of Greysteel Community Enterprises, and Breda is a former member of the Greysteel Community Association and a founder-member of the Faughanvale Womens' Activity Group. They said "There has been a totally positive transformation in the area. There is a new confidence, and a more relaxed sense of community in the village and the entire district".

Hugh Nicholl summed up "Greysteel happened to be an easy target for those who felt that they were doing something for their cause, but our record of good community relations has withstood the test of that tragedy. The atrocity was meant to tear us apart, but the opposite has happened. Out of the midst of evil has come great good."

After so much suffering, it is impressive to witness a community like the people of Greysteel and Eglinton which, with the help of the International Fund and other agencies, has had the courage and the initiative to move on from tragedy and to build a new perspective for the entire area.

The same applies to Poyntzpass which suffered one of the most appalling atrocities of the Troubles when, on 3 March 1998, two friends – one Catholic and the other a Protestant - were shot dead by two Loyalist gunmen who burst into the Railway Bar and ordered six customers inside to lie on the floor. They opened fire with handguns, and seriously injured four people including Philip Allen, a Protestant, and his friend Damien Trainor, a Catholic.

The bar's owner said later "Two men came in through the front door of the bar and they shouted in very rude terms for everybody in the bar to lie down, and everybody just lay down. They did not ask for denominations or anything, they just opened fire on the fellas that were on the ground."[4]

Philip had recently asked Damien to be best man at his wedding. Roughly an hour after the shooting they both died in the Daisy Hill

Hospital in Newry. The Independent newspaper described their funerals thus; "They lived not far away from each other, socialised together, and this week they died together, shot when the balaclavaed gunmen burst into their local bar. Buried in cemeteries just around the corner from each other, they will never again be far apart."[5]

As with Greysteel, the shock-waves from Poyntzpass traumatised the village and spread all over the island of Ireland, and much further afield. It was not only the brutal nature of the Poynztpass killings that sickened people, but also the fact that two young men who had been so united in life, were suddenly and inexplicably united in death.

There was also a sense of puzzlement that a small village like Poyntzpass, which had no history of violence, had become the centre of such random horror. The then Secretary of State, Mo Mowlam accurately described the killings as "soul destroying."

They came at a time when the situation in Northern Ireland had been improving, after the carnage of earlier years, but the killings in Poyntzpass were a reminder that a small number of dangerously misguided people were still choosing violence rather than politics, and that death could strike in even the most innocent of places like Poyntzpass at any time.

The village was traumatised by the brutal murders. Though the village was predominantly Catholic, the surrounding countryside had a majority of Protestants. The local bars were Catholic-owned but they had a mixed clientele. Poyntzpass had been a living example of what the vast majority of the people of Northern Ireland, and the politicians, were aspiring to - namely a mixed community where people lived in harmony and peace.

John Waddell, secretary of the Poyntzpass Regeneration Company

The burden of Poyntzpass was not just the killings, but also the shadow over community relations, yet – as in Greysteel – there was hope of recovery from such horror. This hope would manifest itself in the continuing good sense and dignity of the people, and in their determination to continue to work together, with help and funding from outside.

The IFI provided £300,000 to the newly-formed Poyntzpass Community Regeneration Company for a £650,200 development scheme in the main street of the village. This was to build a 3-story

A VILLAGE IN MOURNING

6 MAR 1998

Tears on streets as community bids farewell

SHOOTINGS

By Julie O'Connor and Jason Johnson

THE village of Poyntzpass came to a standstill today as its community united to say farewell to two friends who died together.

A single candle glowed among bunches of flowers on the rain-soaked doorstep of The Railway Bar, scene of the killings.

Philip Allen's three brothers helped carry the coffin of his friend Damien Trainor. Local MP Seamus Mallon was among hundreds of mourners for the service at St Joseph's Catholic Church in the village.

Crowds followed the coffin of the 25-year-old — later they made the same sad journey for his best friend, Philip Allen (34).

In heavy rain hundreds of mourners, led by Damien's parents Ann and Sean, walked slowly from their home in the tiny village of Poyntzpass to the Catholic chapel across the road.

The murdered man's mother clutched a tiny bouquet.

And at the funerals people were urged to continue the quest for peace as a testament to the two friends, and a call was made for the community not to shield the killers.

The two pals, one a Catholic and one a Protestant, were gunned down and left dying on the floor of a local bar.

Two other men injured in the shooting are "in a satisfactory condition".

At the funeral of Mr Allen the Presbyterian Moderator Dr Sam Hutchinson said: "However little support these gunmen have, they will surely have less now. How can anyone shield or help them?

"If they have relatives or colleagues who have any influence over them, will they not now use that influence to restrain them?"

Catholic Archbishop Sean Brady told mourners at Mr Trainor's funeral that two men were united in life by friendship and mutual respect.

"The friendship of Philip and Damien was built on the equality of their dignity as human beings.

"Those killers came in the dark of night, their faces masked lest anyone should recognise them and their evil intentions.

"Their mouths filled with obscenities, their hearts were filled with hatred and their hands filled with weapons of destruction and now two families are united in shock, horror and devastation.

"The whole community is united in disbelief, horror and revulsion. Hopefully we will all be equally united in our determination to find and accept a settlement that will put an end, once and for all, to atrocities like this."

Mr Allen was due to marry fiancee Carol Magill in the summer and Mr Trainor was to be his best man.

Miss Magill was said to be distraught today. Her friend Gabrielle Jordan said: "Everything looked so bright for her but now there is nothing ahead but grief and memories."

No paramilitary organisation has admitted the killings but security sources are pointing the finger at the Loyalist Volunteer Force.

Four men, believed to be from the Banbridge area, are still being questioned by police today.

Detectives investigating the Poyntzpass murders today issued an appeal for information about a second car believed to have been used in the killings.

An RUC spokeswoman said police wanted to speak to anyone who saw a white Nova in the Dromore, Scarva, Poyntzpass, Banbridge area between 12.30pm and 9.30pm on Tuesday, the day of the bar shootings.

● Viewpoint: page 10

Final farewell: Damien Trainor's parents, left, and mourners at the funeral today. Top, Damien Trainor, above, Philip Allen.

development for community use on the site of a derelict garage.

John Waddell, the secretary of the Poyntzpass Committee, knew personally the two men who were murdered, and he recalled the community's shock at what had happened.

He spoke to me on a cold winter night in the new Community Centre in January 2008, several years after the killings, but his memories were still vivid. He said "There was immense shock that such a thing could happen in a village where there never had been any trouble.

"It was devastating, and the fact that the two boys had been such close friends from different sides of the community, made it all the worse. The funerals were massive, and it was an utterly miserable time, with the grief and the sorrow, and the rain lashing down all day long."

However, the atrocity - far from alienating people - drew them closer together, as had happened at Greysteel. John said "There always

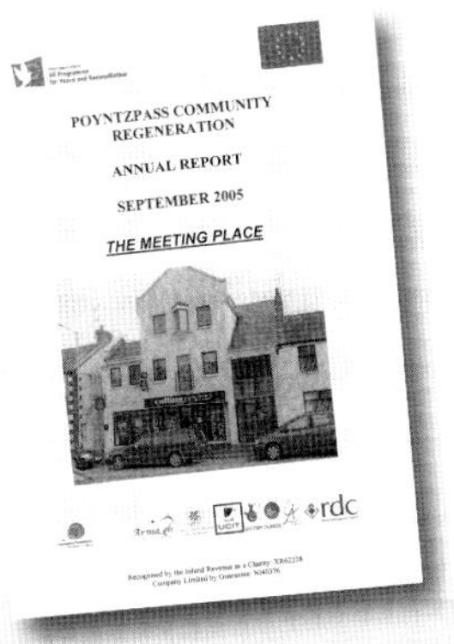
POYNTZPASS COMMUNITY REGENERATION

ANNUAL REPORT

SEPTEMBER 2005

THE MEETING PLACE

Poyntzpass – the 'Meeting Place', and a symbol of togetherness

had been a desire on the part of people to do their best for Poyntzpass and for each other. There was also a strong feeling that we wanted to do something to remember Philip and Damien".

As in Greysteel, the aim was to provide a living memorial, and the catalyst was the International Fund which invited people in Poyntzpass and the surrounding area to attend a meeting in the village. John Waddell recalled "The IFI indicated that funding might be available for the right kind of project, but they advised us to form a group and to find out what the village needed."

A cross-community committee was duly formed, and after consulting the local people, it was decided to build a Community Centre on the site of derelict property in the main street. One important motive was to provide accommodation for an inter-community play group that was already in existence.

It was felt that part of the good community relations in the village was due to the excellent co-operation between the Catholic and Protestant primary schools, many of whose pupils had attended the playgroup. It was important that the accommodation for the playgroup would be self-contained.

John Waddell said "We were also conscious that the project needed to be self-financing, so part of the building would be rented by commercial tenants to help provide regular income." The IFI provided substantial funding, as had been noted earlier, and the remainder was raised by other funders and by the organising committee which also took out a loan at a favourable rate from the Ulster Community Investment Trust.

The project took some four years and nine months to complete, and the new building - simply titled "The Meeting Place" - was opened

The different stages of development of the Community Centre in Greysteel

officially by President Mary McAleese in September 2004. John Waddell said "It was a fantastic day, partly because it was the first time, to my knowledge, that we had a President of Ireland at an official function in Poyntzpass. It was also totally opposite to the day of the funerals which had been so dismal, because the sun was splitting the trees and there was a great atmosphere of hope about the place."

Since its official opening, the Community Centre has been a success. A rental income has been provided by two commercial tenants, and the rest of the building is meeting a wide range of needs for the community. These include inter-denominational Carol Services and other events, and the hall is a suitable venue for everything from Set Dancing and meetings of the local Historical Society, to English classes for Polish immigrants, and meetings for senior citizens.

John Waddell said "We were keen to provide the kind of things which people needed, and I hope that what we have done is a proper tribute to the memory of Philip and Damien. We wanted a living memorial, and that's what keeps the memory going and not just a plaque on a wall somewhere."

Significantly, however, there is a plaque to the two dead men - not on a wall of the building but on a bench outside in the Memorial Garden, which has been created and dedicated to them. This once overgrown area had been a playground, and with funds from the Conservation Volunteers, the members from the community group and others from the village cleared the ground and built an attractive garden.

John Waddell said "They did it by the sweat of their brows, and none more so than John McVeigh and our chairman John Morrow. When you are running something like this you need a range of skills, and we have been very fortunate in that respect."

The memorial garden was opened, in the presence of the families of the dead men, in August 2005 and it continues to provide a fitting space for quiet reflection. The dedication on the bench is simply "In Memory of Two Friends" and it symbolises the long journey from horror to hope, in that previously trouble-free village.

Would all this have happened without the terrible spur provided by the atrocity? John Waddell believes that there were enough community-minded people in the village who had continued to do their best for Poyntzpass, but one of the perpetual problems was funding.

He said "Poyntzpass had been so peaceful and trouble-free that it was not on anyone's list of priorities. However we were very grateful to everyone, including the IFI, who helped us with the project, but it was not just the money. The International Fund also supplied the knowledge, and the networking skills to help us. We would never have been able to do it on our own."

President Mary McAleese visiting Poyntzpass

John Waddell, like the others involved, saw the project as a means of putting something back into the community. He said "Poyntzpass has been my home for more than 50 years and you want to give something back to what helped to form you as a person. This Community Centre, hopefully, will still be here to provide a service when people like me have long gone. However it's not the building itself, but what takes places within it, which will continue to be the best testament of all to Philip and Damien who were so much a part of the life of this village."

The stories of Poyntzpass and Greysteel are inextricably linked – not only through the numbing horror of past events but also because of the patient hard work and courage which, with the help of outside funders like the IFI and others, has brought hope to a once-dark horizon.

To visit Poyntzpass and Greysteel and other places where people were killed or injured during the Troubles, as this writer has done, is to be appalled by the depths of suffering which human beings can inflict on one another, but it is also to be deeply moved by the nobility and strength of the human spirit. Greysteel, Poyntzpass and their people have known the worst of times, but they have also demonstrated the best of human behaviour, and that will remain truly inspiring not only for the present time, but for generations to come.

Notes

1 Lost Lives Op. Cit. Pages 1335-6 which also quotes from the book "The Fight For Peace".
2 Ibid Page 1336.
3 In an Interview with the Author in Greysteel, in the autumn of 2007.
4 Lost Lives Pages 1428-9.
5 Ibid Page 429.

CHAPTER ELEVEN

a River runs Through it

ONE OF THE MOST DEPRESSING aspects of the Troubles in Northern Ireland was the misnamed "Peace Line" which was built basically to keep people apart.

Townsend
Where Business Begins

1987 - 2002

Fifteen Years of Community Development

Welcome to Townsend Enterprise Park. 2002 represents an important milestone in our history. Founded in 1987, the company's remit was originally to establish an enterprise culture in it's inner city hinterland, to encourage economic regeneration and to support the establishment of new businesses.

These first 15 years have witnessed the establishment of 65,000 sq feet of commercial space in a purpose-built enterprise environment where business accommodation is continuously in demand. In the early 80's, the present site was comparatively small and unoccupied with only a handful of deteriorating units available to let. Today, this site is home to almost 40 businesses employing over 300 people in a diverse range of business activities. Since acquiring the site in 1986, over 50,000 sq feet of business space has been added, together with a range of small business support services, and a network of business advisory structures.

In the early years of the company, the Board (comprised of voluntary directors) concentrated on establishing the company as a sound, sustainable business and more recently, the emphasis has been on consolidation. Having fulfilled its original remit and now with the advent of it's 15th Anniversary, the company feels confident in it's role to encourage further economic development at community level.

Today's economic environment is decidedly different with the prevailing circumstances in 1987 and without the active support of our dedicated staff, our voluntary Board of Directors and the local community, Townsend Enterprise Park could never have survived. We look to the future with confidence and our place as a means of promoting community based economic development is assured.

Best wishes,

Alphy Maginness
Chairman & Board Members of Townsend Enterprise Park

The ugly barrier was first erected by the British Army in 1969 and was situated mainly between the Protestant Shankill and the Catholic Falls Road. It was built initially in the wake of serious rioting in the area during the summer of 1969 when rival groups would attack one another or the security forces, or sometimes both, and then retreat into the relative safety of their own areas.

No doubt some people fondly hoped that the Peace Line would be only a temporary structure, but as the Troubles increased - rather than lessened - in intensity, the structure became more permanent. The division symbolised by barbed-wire was solidified into brick walls and other solid barriers, not only in the Shankill-Falls area but also in other interface parts of the city.

In some places these structures were virtually impregnable, though in others there were gateways and barriers which could be opened or closed according to the prevailing state of peace or unrest in the area. The Peace Line was obviously well-known to the locals who accepted it as part of their basic geography which required patience, uncommon common sense and navigational skills.

On occasions, however, unwary motorists and other strangers would find themselves in what seemed to be the wrong place at the wrong time, and a feeling of panic could engulf the traveller. In practice this meant that most people from outside would avoid these "no-go" areas. However, these areas were home to the people who lived in them.

At time of writing, in the afterglow of the peace process, some of the structures of the Peace Line are still visible, as a reminder of a tortuous past. No doubt the Peace Line helped to save lives and also to prevent injuries, but it stood as a baleful reminder of the inability of the two main communities to live together in peace.

Despite this broad picture of gloom and confrontation, however, there were shafts of light - not least in the development of the Townsend Industrial Park and the Farset Enterprise Park and International Hostel which were both situated on or near the Peace Line. Incidentally the city of Belfast, takes its name from River Farset, which runs nearby - though mostly underground.
The city was originally called "Beal Feirste", literally the Gaelic for "sandy ford at the river mouth", which is now the modern "Belfast."

The Townsend Enterprise Park, which became a prototype for many others assisted by the International Fund, had its own distinct character and origin, like its location. The history of Townsend Street dates back to the mid-18th century when

Pictured L-R Jim Dougal, Head of Representation European Commission; George Briggs, Townsend Enterprise Park; Neil Kinnock, EU Commissioner; Chairman Willie McCarter and Joe McCormack Townsend Enterprise Park

it was founded by the McAdam family, whose name was associated with the invention of "tarmacadam", which revolutionised transport throughout the world.

The Townsend Enterprise Park was established in the Lower Shankill and Falls area of West Belfast, alongside the Peace Line.
It eventually provided some 63,000 square feet of work-space accommodation for a range of small businesses where some 300 people have been employed in manufacturing services and youth experience schemes.

In the early days the project developed from a job-creating initiative of a group comprising well-known local business people and clergy. This had been established in an area of low employment even before the Troubles started. Not surprisingly, the recurring violence, and the pitched battles between both sides near Townsend Street continually threatened the existence of the fledgling business enterprise.

However, it survived through the courage and persistence of people from both sides in helping to make it work, and with not a little luck.

George Briggs, a qualified textile technologist, later became an academic and then a business consultant. He had worked with the Local Enterprise Development Unit and, among other things, he was involved in setting up the enterprise network in Northern Ireland.

The Townsend Enterprise Park was formally established in 1987, and George became manager ten years later, following the death of the previous manager. Before that, he had worked closely with the three previous managers on a range of training programmes.

He recalled "Around the time I arrived it was literally a war zone, and the young and not so young people from the Lower Shankill and the Lower Falls used the area to fight their own regular battles. Townsend Street itself was used as a getaway if the Falls people were gunning for the Shankill and vice versa.

"Eventually we put up a barrier with a gate that was locked at certain hours. That meant that the assailants could not nip through as others had done in the past, and were forced to take a mile-long detour to escape. So the barrier and the gate certainly quietened things down."

During the daytime, the Enterprise Park had more than the trappings of a normal Business Park. Briggs said "We were seen by the people of the area as being in neutral territory. Once they came in through the gate, it didn't matter whether they were Catholic or Protestant, and we didn't ask.

"Many politicians asked me how many Catholics or Protestants we employed, and I told them that this was not part of our remit. It was very encouraging to see people coming in though the gate each morning from the direction of the Shankill or the Falls and of simply going about their business as normal."

The Townsend Enterprise Park provided a safe locality for a wide variety of small businesses, including clothing, craft work and a bakery where people started work at 4am. Many of them learned new business skills and moved on to other things. The Enterprise Park was also used as a base for a large number of youth training programmes, including the Wider Horizons Programme of the International Fund.

George Briggs said "The experiences of people at Townsend help in many cases to change their lives. Overall the Enterprise Park helped to provide a way for two communities to live together. It also provided a safe environment, and people who came

Neil Kinnock "hands on" at Townsend Enterprise Park

here had a vested interest in securing economic viability and in working with their neighbour from the opposite community. That has been the essence of Townsend Enterprise Park and it has been replicated to a greater or lesser extent across our whole enterprise network in Northern Ireland."

The International Fund helped with the establishment and upgrading of Townsend, and to date it has given a total of nearly £1 million in funding.

George Briggs said "The IFI were most helpful because they could see the tremendous need. They were not the only funders, of course, but at the very start they gave us the assistance to do what had to be done, and when we asked for a second 'tranche' we had something to show for our efforts. Without the

IFI we would certainly have had to move more slowly, and we might have been less ambitious, but in the end it has all worked out well.

"We have people and managers here who are second to none. There are always challenges, but I am a positive person who always sees the cup as half full. I don't think that I would have spent so many years at the Townsend Enterprise Park if I had not found it to be a very fulfilling role."

Another important example of how a run-down and dangerous interface area can be transformed is the Farset project. This scheme was set up in 1982, and was built upon a series of Youth and Community initiatives which were administered by the Ainsworth Community Association, dating from 1974. Farset was based on the Springfield Road in West Belfast, adjacent to the sectarian interfaces of Clonard-Shankill and Highfield-Ballymurphy.

In a series of imaginative projects, ranging from voluntary work to training, the idea was to improve the skills and employment prospects of young people on a cross-community basis and also to give them confidence in themselves and a pride in their area. It was difficult, but rewarding, work in what outsiders would have regarded as a "no-go" area.

Barney McCaughey. "The IFI saw that we could create something different".

Over the years, Farset developed a large number of contacts and working relationships in greater Belfast and further afield, and its work attracted visitors from a wide area. One of the major problems, however, was a lack of overnight and conference accommodation. Given the history of that area, with its record of interface conflict, it is hardly surprising that public or private entrepreneurs were not queuing up to build a hotel or hostel on what was generally perceived to be a "twilight zone."

However, members of the Farset Youth and Community Development Project thought differently. They could see the need, but the problem was in persuading people not only to share that vision but also to put their money on the table. Barney McCaughey, a management consultant, was also a board member of Farset, and he played a leading role, with Anne Brown, Jackie Hewitt and others, in the process of turning the idea of a hostel into a reality.

He recalled "We had developed the Enterprise Park further up the Springfield Road and we proved that we could work with people from both sides of the divide to train together, to establish businesses in close proximity to one another, and to use common resources provided by Farset."

always clear, and you got an answer quickly, even if it was sometimes 'no.'

"They also seemed to be able to move things up front, and to make money available quickly. That provided leverage to ask for help from others, whereas some funders work in a way that, because of the regulations, the money arrives late or in dribs and drabs, and you always seem to be on the back foot."

Barney McCaughey expressed well his sense of frustration, and that of others, in such a situation. He said "I met this guy one day and said to him 'For once will you please say to people that they should really be looking for better chairs, decent windows and doing a good job on the cladding – because all I ever hear from you is 'Cut back, cut back." If you are going to fund a project, fund it well'. They were treating people as if they didn't deserve good quality."

In the event, the International Fund put up £652,000 of a £2.273 million project for a high-quality hostel, with 38 twin beds, a conference centre, a restaurant and a snack bar. Other funding came from the Northern Ireland Tourist Board, the Belfast Regeneration Office, the Belfast Enterprise Partnership Board and the City Council.

Jackie Hewitt. "The IFI were solid. It wasn't just the money, they also gave us moral support".

The first phase opened in 1990 as a Local Enterprise Agency, providing 26 units for business-start-ups and also training and administrative facilities. By 1992, the Park had hired out some 95% of the available space and had created around 70 jobs.

This success was followed by a second phase. Adjoining land was purchased to provide a further 14 units, with an administration centre. Both phases were supported by a range of funders, including the IFI which provided £180,000 for Phase I and £140,00 for Phase II.

Raising money for a hostel project was rather more difficult. McCaughey said "There was no hotel or hostel facility to serve the area, right from the Antrim Road to Black's Road in West Belfast, and that's one heck of a distance.

Some of the agencies we approached seemed to be there almost to identify problems and to leave you with them, or to use them as a reason for slowing the project down."

The IFI, he said, was different. He added "They saw that we could create something different on this interface, and if we succeeded in this, it would encourage people in both communities around here. There was a quality about the IFI development workers who seemed to identify with the vision for the place, and who were positive about overcoming the problems. The International Fund people were

Jackie Hewitt and Barney McCaughey, "This whole place has been changed for the better".

The Farset International Hostel, on a site with panoramic views over Belfast and the outlying suburbs, has been a remarkable success, and has exceeded all expectations.

The official opening ceremony, on 11 December 2003, was a joyful event, and the Hostel was made open to all. Barney McCaughey said "We encouraged local people from both communities, as well as others from education, health and the business sector, to come and see us here. We have been doing a great deal of cross-border exchange work, and we also attract a large range of tourists at the budget end of the market. It really has been a great success."

Jackie Hewitt, a board member of Farset – and now also a Board Member of the IFI – recalled some of the pain of the gestation period. He said "I just had a gut feeling that something like this would work, but there was nothing you could write down to say that these things could be planned in advance. How could you predict the number of tourists, right then in the middle of the Troubles. But we could see some light on the horizon, and we needed help".

"The IFI was solid, and it wasn't just the money. They also gave us a great deal of moral support, and that was very important. We would also acknowledge our gratitude to Felix Mooney for his guidance and support as we struggled from the first idea through all the problems of planning and development, until we were up and running."

The success of the Farset Enterprise Park and the Hostel had far-reaching effects. Hewitt said "It created not only a neutral space but it opened up the whole area. It had been a dangerous interface where nobody would walk at night. Now there are French people and Germans and Americans along that road and going into the local bars for a drink."

"It used to be a 'no-go' area but now it's a melting-pot. This whole place has been transformed for the better, and the footprints of the IFI are all over it. They came here on visits, they asked questions, they looked for updates, and they were reassuring in the difficult times. It simply would not have worked without them."

CHAPTER TWELVE

Staying on Track

THE IFI HAS GIVEN ASSISTANCE TO MORE THAN 5,700 projects since its establishment, and one of the most distinctive is the little Steam Train on the North Antrim coast at Bushmills which the Fund helped to keep on track in the early days.

The train still continues its journey in clouds of smoke, and regularly passes by the small and beautiful Bushfoot Golf Course on its way to and from Bushmills to its destination near the Giant's Causeway. In doing so it maintains a unique service for tourists and day-trippers, and adds to the attractions of the area – which was one of the reasons for the IFI funding in the first place.

Over the past 21 years and more, the Fund itself has stayed on track, despite its many challenges and the changing political, economic and commercial contexts within which it has had to operate. During this time there have been considerable successes, as has been noted elsewhere in this publication, and some that were controversial.

Part of the success story has been the way in which the IFI chose the projects which it helped to fund. It instituted a process of searching out proposals through its Development Consultants on the ground in urban and rural areas. They kept closely in touch with community groups and other organisations - many of which produced fledgling, or more developed, proposals which were in line with the IFI's objectives and strategies. In many cases the Fund's agents helped to re-shape the project to produce a submission to the Board for a project that appeared worthwhile, affordable and justified within the IFI remit.

The Causeway Steam Train – Staying On Track

In turn the project teams working within specialist areas such as Community Bridges, Disadvantaged Areas and others, studied the submissions and looked for potential weaknesses and conflicts of interest, and also whether the same kind of project was being carried out by somebody else.

Following this process, those Members of the Board with specialist expertise would further examine the proposals and, if necessary, refer any further queries back to the project team. Finally the project would be submitted to the full Board, where it would be considered for the first time by those Members who had not been involved already, and by an experienced group of international observers - thus guarding against any rubber-stamping.

In practice relatively few of the projects were rejected, particularly those which had been developed in association with the Board's agents at ground level. However, a number of projects from individuals and others did not receive approval, though the proposals went all the way to the stage of consideration by the Board.

Some of the major projects could be judged a success, though their subsequent development was not as successful as had been hoped initially. They included the Navan Centre, a project under the Flagship Programme which reflected the ancient history of the area around modern Armagh, and the St. Patrick's Centre, another Flagship Centre in Downpatrick, where Ireland's Patron Saint is reputedly buried outside the local Church of Ireland Cathedral. (Whether he was actually buried there or not is immaterial, because tradition has subsumed the facts into virtual reality – and why let the facts spoil a good story!)

St Patrick's Centre in Downpatrick

Both Flagship projects were visionary in their own way, but each experienced financial challenges later on, which hopefully will be finally overcome. As to the need for the Fund to lead on these projects, Sandy Smith, the Joint Director General of the Fund in Belfast, explained part of the background. "We were aware that if the Troubles were over, Northern Ireland could become awash with visitors, but apart from superb scenery and hospitality, we had very little to occupy tourists in terms of what people expect today.

"No-one could see any real economic return in helping to establish the St. Patrick's Centre, but the people in Downpatrick were aware that the Patron Saint of Ireland was a world icon. There was a risk that no-body would put money into this because they could not at that stage guarantee visitor numbers. So the International Fund stepped in, with the local authority and the Tourist Board to help make it happen."

The same thinking lay behind the decision to develop the Navan Centre. Smith said "Unless somebody puts in the investment and gives other people the challenge of making it work, it isn't going to happen anyway. On the other hand, take the example of the Foyle Ferry. The received wisdom was that nobody travelled from Magilligan to Greencastle, but once the Ferry began to operate, then everybody wanted to use it. So it's sometimes a fine judgement call whether or not you put the money into a project. There's always been a number of these that needed investment, even if we did not know how exactly they might work out in practice."

Occasionally there were embarrassments, and poor publicity. In the early days, the Board approved a grant to a family hotel in a rural area to help upgrade its accommodation. Money was made available to create jobs for ground staff at an adjacent golf course, which was part of the tourist attractions in the area.

It was essentially a job-creation scheme, where the golf club was the employer, but this was represented by the media in the USA and elsewhere as tax-payers' money being used by the International Fund to help support an elitist sport for people who were already well off.

The IFI Board and staff were taken aback by such headlines, and although the Fund's supporters in the USA eventually understood and accepted that its actions had been consistent with IFI policy on job creation, the damage had been done in terms of bad publicity from coast to coast.

Another embarrassment, later on, was the adverse publicity over the funding given by the IFI to the Northern Ireland Tourist Board to help promote a "World Toilet Summit" in Belfast. The mind boggles at the infinite possibilities of headline-writers having fun at the IFI's expense, and one of the least inventive twists was "Fund Money goes down the Tubes!" – but the reality was rather more mundane.

The main purpose of such funding in general was to encourage major International conferences to come to Northern Ireland, and this was signally successful in helping to put the Province back on the conference map.

For example, one of the most successful was that of a major US ice-cream chain which held its annual conference in Londonderry and which, by all accounts, was better attended than any of the organisation's annual conferences in the USA.

Ironically, while the furore continued over the "World Toilet Summit" in Belfast, cities in the United States were bidding to stage the same conference in America the following year. In the longer-term, however, Belfast did attain its rightful place in the world conference arena and continued to attract high-profile and prestigious business – as well as becoming a popular city for weekend breaks.

The fact that the IFI attracted some adverse publicity – apart from the opposition from Unionists and others

Senator Patrick Leahy, who helped to steer the US contribution through to the International Fund

at its inception – underlined that it was an organisation run by human beings and therefore fallible. However, given the range of projects and the wide variation in funding, it is noteworthy that there was so little "bad" publicity. This was due, in no small measure, to the solid structure of the project development mechanism, the expertise within the Fund at various levels, and the backing of its supporters in the USA and Europe, as well as in Australia, Canada and New Zealand.

The American support was particularly important, with significant funding from Washington on an all-party basis. The long-standing support of Senator Edward Kennedy and Senator Mitch McConnel has been mentioned already. Senator Pat Leahy was, at crucial moments, a particularly strong supporter helping to steer the US contribution through to adoption in the Senate. Another long-time supporter of the Fund was Congressman Richie Neal, currently

Chairman of the Friends of Ireland Group in Congress, who told me "I thought that it was not enough to spend time just criticising one tradition over there. I felt that as part of the way forward we had to demonstrate that we needed to put behind us some of the ancient antagonisms, and one of the ways to do that was to embrace co-operation and the idea of economic growth."[1]

One of the problems, of course, was to convince the Unionists. Neal said "We tried very hard to demonstrate to them that we represented no threat to their heritage, and that we just wanted to move things forward. However, they had the longest walk of all to make."

The Reverend Dr. Ian Paisley, who became First Minister in the historic power-sharing administration with Sinn Fein and the other political parties, was a pivotal figure. Neal recalled "I met him at Stormont, and we knew each other, as I used to meet him when he came over here. We disagreed, as you might expect, about where the sun would rise and where the sun would set. His greeting to me at Stormont was 'I see you're still living!', but there was laughter and a firm handshake."

"As I got into the discussion I realised the depth of the Unionist community's pride in their contribution to America, and deservedly so. The two founders of my political party are Thomas Jefferson and Andrew Jackson, and Jackson's roots were in Co. Tyrone. I know that the Unionist community takes great pride in that."

Neal maintained an even-handed attitude to both traditions in Northern Ireland and also to their political parties, including Sinn Fein. He also told me the story of Fr Alex Reid and the Rev Harold Good, the two Northern Ireland clerics who verified the Provisional IRA arms decommissioning which helped to unblock many of the remaining barriers to a political settlement.

He said "One night I was at a meeting which was being addressed by the two men, and a young woman asked the Rev Good 'Isn't there going to be continued conflict between the two communities in Northern Ireland?' He replied 'Excuse me, but we don't have two communities, we have one community with two traditions.' You couldn't have paid somebody on New York's Madison Avenue to come up with a better statement of principle."

"I believe that the International Fund speaks to the future of what things can be like. It has taught me about reconciliation, and one of the great problems has always been the fact

Congressman Richie Neal who maintained an even-handed attitude to both traditions in Northern Ireland

that if you don't know people, it's hard to figure out if you are going to like them. I believe that the breaking down of barriers has been one of the great success stories of the IFI. It certainly lessened the suspicion that America was not trying to be an even-handed broker. That suspicion was eliminated because as time passed, people saw the Fund as an act of good will, and it also brought together those who might not have otherwise come in contact with one another. It encouraged them to work shoulder to shoulder."

Jim Walsh, a Republican Congressman, was Chairman of the influential Friends of Ireland for 12 years and also a strong supporter of the International Fund. He told me "There is some idealism left around the globe, and there was a lot of that in supporting the Fund, but there was politics in it as well. There's a tremendous number of

International Fund Chairman Willie McCarter with, from left to right, Congressman Jim Walsh, John Hume MP MEP, the former US Speaker Newt Gingrich, and the then Mayor of Derry, Joe Millan, at the Calgach Centre in Derry

Irish-American politicians in the Congress and in the States in general, so supporting Ireland, which at that time was a poor place economically, was a popular thing to do. It's a great political connection to show your support for the people of Ireland in the dialogue between the Irish and the Americans."[2]

Walsh worked closely with the then Chairman Willie McCarter and visited a number of projects in Ireland. He said "I saw developments in the Shankill area of Belfast and in Ballymurphy and the Falls, in Newry and the border counties, and in other places. People were being brought together, and it seemed to me to be a really good idea."

Walsh also worked with Ben Gilman and other supporters of the Fund in Congress. He said "Ben was Chairman of the Appropriations Committee, and was always very close to the Irish. So this was probably why it was relatively easy to bed the Fund down with the Republican majority."

There were challenges, however, in the Mid-Nineties when the "Celtic Tiger" began to change the economic face of Ireland, and some in Washington were asking how economic aid from the US could any longer be justified for Ireland.

Walsh recalled "It was a good question, but my argument was not so much about bedding down the Irish economy, which was doing very well, as of bedding down the peace process. It was all about continuing an American role which had been very constructive in getting two diametrically-opposed sides to work together."

Despite such challenges, the International Fund continued to receive solid backing from Washington, and Walsh believes that it was "one of the real success stories for American foreign policy, and we haven't had a lot of them of

Chairman with Senator Tom Foley

late. I really believe in the exchange of ideas and people, and in this case providing money to lever other money, and to create opportunities for people. It's like planting seeds and seeing them bear fruit."

Walsh recalled the day when he visited a factory in Belfast with President Bill Clinton, during his historic visit to Northern Ireland in 1995. He said "The President told the large audience 'It's time to forgive', and a voice from the back of the room said 'Never, never!' That told me volumes about the problem, but I'm an optimist. I always believed that they would get an agreement."

"Working with the International Fund has been one of the most important things I've been able to do, and truly it has been a labour of love. I started out not knowing anything about Ireland, but since then I have read everything I could about it. My visits to Ireland were all memorable, and one of the most impressive projects I visited was at Glencree. To take something that was historically one of those dark, evil places and create a place where young people could interact and create hope for the future is what I call 'making lemonade out of lemons."

On the day that both Congressmen spoke to me in Washington DC, they were on call for an important debate on Capitol Hill about the war in Iraq. The Northern Ireland Troubles seemed so far away, both in time and in scale, yet I could not fail to be impressed by the goodwill expressed by these two men - and many others - for the successful outcome of the peace process in Northern Ireland. The symbolism of that profound change was illustrated to me by an event which would not have seemed possible several years earlier.

In mid-July 2007, I was visiting a Northern Ireland exhibition in The Mall in Washington, in association with the Smithsonian Institute. After talking to members of the Gaelic Athletic Association in their promotional marquee at The Mall, I walked round the corner and met members of the Orange Order in their own marquee.

Later as I sat in the warm sunshine reflecting on the amazing changes in my homeland, I heard the distinctive thud of a Lambeg drum being played, and its sound resonating across the multi-cultural exhibition at The Mall. The unbelievable was happening. The sense of goodwill all around was palpable.

That was underlined by my recollection of Congressman Neal's earlier comment to me that the establishment and work of the

Chairman Willie McCarter with IFI Supporter, Senator Ben Gilman, in Belfast

International Fund was itself "an act of goodwill." It was, literally, a "Fund of Goodwill", which was established at a time when the outcome was still bleak, but which developed as time passed and which itself made a significant contribution to the peace process.

The special relationship with America was outlined eloquently by the former Taoiseach Bertie Ahern in his historic address to the United States' Joint Houses of Congress in Washington on 30 April 2008.

In one of his last public statements as Taoiseach, he talked of the American contribution to the peace process in general, but his comments could have applied to the International Fund in particular. He said "When we needed true champions of peace, when we

Irish Independent

IRELAND'S BEST-SELLING DAILY NEWSPAPER METRO EDITION

STORE WARS HIGH STREET GIANTS FIGHT FOR CUSTOMERS IN YOUR 20-PAGE BUSINESS SUPPLEMENT

RED ALERT UNITED FANS IN MOSCOW RIP-OFF SEE SPORT

WWW.INDEPENDENT.IE Thursday 1 May 2008 UK price £1 Europe price €3.75

'Ireland is at peace'

Ahern delivers historic message on highest stage

INSIDE The best writers on Bertie Ahern's historic address

●Lise Hand On the performance of a lifetime P3

●The speech – what he said P4-5

●Senan Molony Drama at Taoiseach's hotel P6

●James Downey Analyses Mr Ahern's speech P7

●Editorial Comment P40

Senan Molony
Deputy Political Editor in Washington

IRELAND is at peace. With those four words, Bertie Ahern ended his political career on the highest stage and signalled the hour of his country's coming of age.

Yesterday he followed in the footsteps of three former taoisigh, Garret FitzGerald, John Bruton and Liam Cosgrave, along with two former presidents, Eamon de Valera and Sean T O Ceallaigh, in addressing the US Joint Houses of Congress.

The Taoiseach received a standing ovation as he delivered a message that had eluded them all.

The short sentence brought the assembled leaders of the most powerful country on the planet to their feet.

The Taoiseach's historic address, delivered with dignity, resonated both politically and emotionally with his final audience. They heard Mr Ahern state for the record that Ireland had finally ended centuries of distrust and division.

"On St Patrick's Day, 2008, a few short weeks ago, I came here to Washington. I came with a simple and extraordinary message," he said.

"That great day of hope has dawned. Our prayer has been answered. Our faith has been rewarded."

Turning to Nancy Pelosi, the speaker of the US House of Representatives, Mr Ahern added: "I am so proud, Madam Speaker, to be the first Irish leader to inform the United States' Congress – Ireland is at peace."

Mr Ahern will step down as Taoiseach next week after over a decade in power.

On Tuesday, May 6, he will hand his letter of resignation as Taoiseach to President Mary McAleese at Aras An Uachtarain – but only after officially drawing the veil over centuries of bitter conflict, during a visit to the site of the Battle of the Boyne with the North's First Minister, Ian Paisley.

Mr Ahern's landmark speech in Washington was also a speech about beginnings, about age-old ideals and new opportunities. On a day suffused with a

Continued on page 2

Outgoing Taoiseach Bertie Ahern acknowledges the applause after concluding his address to the Joint Houses of Congress in Washington, with House Speaker Nancy Pelosi and Senate President Robert Byrd in the background.

Vol. 117 No. 104

●FEATURES

●LIFESTYLE The quick way to a bikini bod P49

●COMMENT Martina Devlin on pampered brats P41

An historic front page story in the Irish Independent on 1 May, 2008

needed true friends, when we needed inspiration, we found them here. We found them among you."

Bertie Ahern noted that in 1981 the Friends of Ireland had placed on record a Congressional statement during a session chaired by Speaker Tip O'Neill, one of the early champions of a process which led to the establishment of the IFI. Their statement had expressed the hope that they could look forward, at some time, to a St. Patrick's Day when peace could finally come and that people from all over the island could hail that peace, and welcome "a new dawn for Ireland."

The former Taoiseach dramatically reminded his listeners that on St. Patrick's Day in 2008 he had come to Washington "with a simple and extraordinary message; that day of hope has dawned. Our prayer has been answered. Our faith has been renewed. After so many decades of conflict I am so proud.... to be the first Irish leader to inform the United States Congress: 'Ireland is at Peace.'"

He added "Look to the hope and confidence that we now feel on our island. The healing of history. Look and be glad. It was a pivotal moment in the history of US-Irish relations, and an acknowledgment of the hard work that had gone in to the long peace process, including the establishment and work of the International Fund.

However, another important factor in the continued success of the International Fund was the immense support given by Europe (which is outlined in the next chapter) and also by the Commonwealth countries of Australia, Canada and New Zealand, as mentioned earlier. They provided funding when it was needed, and also a steady supply of official observers who made an important contribution – individually and collectively – to the work of the Board.

Tom Quinn, the brother of Paul Quinn, and also a well-connected figure in Washington was the American Observer on the IFI Board for several years. He emphasised to me one of the most important aspects of the Fund, and said "The significance of the International Fund wasn't just the money that was involved, but the perception that somebody else wanted to help the people of Northern Ireland. Both sides needed outsiders who would be honest brokers."

The 2002 Annual Report underlined the contribution of the outside Observers, including the Hon Russell Marshall from New Zealand. He wrote "As a member of the Irish diaspora, New Zealand was delighted to be invited to join the Fund, and to lend its weight to the search for a permanent peace

The then First Minister, the Rev Dr Ian Paisley, and Deputy First Minister Martin McGuinness on a promotional visit to the USA

between the communities of the North, which had given so much to New Zealand's early history.

"The Fund proved to be a very impressive organisation. It was the right thing to do at the right time. It brought the outside world into the problem."

The Australian Observer, HE Ambassador Bob Halverson, noted that notwithstanding the difficulties, the Fund was doing "incredibly well." He wrote it has "brought disparate people with disparate views together, and has lowered, if not yet eliminated, barriers. It has a unique role, and other areas of the world which could do with a similar organisation, such as the former Yugoslavia or the Middle East, could learn from the Fund."

The Canadian representative Ted McConnell, and one of the longest-serving observers in 2002 was, at that stage, the only one born in Northern Ireland. He was brought up on the Falls Road in Belfast and moved to Canada after reading Law at Queen's University. In Canada he had a successful career as an investment consultant.

He noted, in the 2002 Annual Report, that Canada had made its first contribution to the Fund in 1987, and that its job was "to go beyond what a Government can or will do, and this role it performs courageously across a multitude of activities for which I have a high regard."

McConnell underlined his special affection for the Wider Horizons Programme, which was a special interest of the Canadian Government. He referred to his experience of observing closely the work of the Programme when a group of young people from Tallaght in Dublin and from the Falls and Shankill areas of Belfast came to Toronto on a shared project.

McConnell noted "The way the young people intermingled was tremendous. In this instance they were being taught to create web-sites, but what they were really learning about was self-esteem."

He also stressed (as did others) the importance of the Fund in obtaining leverage. He wrote "In this, I believe that the Fund has been both an example and a springboard. We put up the money first and invite others to contribute - and they do. The Fund blazes a trail for everybody else. It is often forgotten that the Fund is the first to set the stage, and it doesn't often enough get the credit. The whole field of North-South co-operation is so very important. In that we punch more than our weight."

Those words were written in 2002 when the peace process seemed far from secure. However, history will almost certainly regard favourably the work of the International Fund, and others, in helping to form a base on which a lasting peace could be established. The IFI had faced many challenges since its establishment in 1986, but despite these, it remained on track to finish the job it had been given to do, and which it did in its own way.

Notes

1 In Conversation with the Author in Washington in July 2007.

2 In conversation with the Author in Washington in July 2007.

CHAPTER THIRTEEN

The European Dimension

IRELAND'S RELATIONSHIP WITH EUROPE EXTENDS OVER the millennia. In medieval times, when the Dark Ages fell over much of the continent, Ireland remained a bastion of Christianity. After the Anglo-Norman invasion in the 12th century, the European dimension was a major factor in Ireland's history during the centuries of England's conflicts with the Spanish, the French and others.

For England, Ireland remained a dangerous back door through which European nations at various times in history might mount an attack – which explains partly the ferocity with which the English dealt with any insurrection in Ireland or to prevent any incursion upon her exposed western flank.

Europe continued to play a crucial role in Irish affairs up to and including modern times, and not least in the economic support which helped to produce the "Celtic Tiger." This, however, was not a one-way traffic, and the Irish themselves have made a significant contribution to the enrichment of Europe.

Membership of the European Union by both the United Kingdom and Ireland had an important effect on Northern Ireland. For many people in the North, however, the attitude was that of being at some distance removed from Brussels.

Though the three long-serving MEP's – Ian Paisley, John Hume and John Taylor – and their successors lobbied in Brussels and Strasbourg on behalf of Northern Ireland, there was an attitude among the people in the Province that most of the important decisions about Europe were made in London.

However there were no such inhibitions in the South which had a much more direct political, economic and indeed social connection to Europe. This was witnessed not only in the increased wealth of the "Celtic Tiger" arising in part from European support, but the direct link was reinforced in recent years by a massive flow of East European immigrants to the Republic - although this was paralleled to a lesser degree in the North, where a more visible number of Eastern Europeans followed in the wake of the developing peace process.

The Roman Catholic Primate Archbishop Sean Brady

The close historical and modern connections between Ireland and the wider Europe were summarised by the Catholic Primate of All-Ireland Cardinal Sean Brady at a special Mass in Rome on 13 April 2008 to commemorate the Flight of the Earls to Europe in 1607.

He said "The departure of the Earls was one of our history's milestones. It has been described as perhaps the most significant event since the coming of St. Patrick in terms of its impact on our country's destiny." It was, he said, "a time of tumultuous change and uncertainty in Irish affairs" and also "the beginning of four centuries of unhappy, bitter and sometimes acrimonious Anglo-Irish relations."

He went on, however, "Happily, today, Britain and Ireland enjoy a very different relationship... which has never been more interdependent, and more characterised by respect and solidarity than it is today. Our geographical and historic proximity is a gift and an opportunity... indeed the transformation of the relationship between Ireland and Britain generally, and the Northern Ireland peace process in particular, is one of the most tangible manifestations of the founding aims of the European Union."

In an equally important address, given almost a year earlier, the former Taoiseach Bertie Ahern also underlined the vastly improved relationships between Britain and Ireland during his historic speech to the Joint Houses of Parliament at Westminster on 15 May 2007.

He said "The intertwined history of Ireland and Britain was - let us not deny the truth - in large measure a story of division and conflict, of conquest, suppression and resistance. But, of course, there are episodes in that story which are a source of pride – just as there are others that are rightly a source of regret and anguish."

Mr Ahern underlined "a groundbreaking act of recognition in our shared journey", when in 1998 Queen Elizabeth II and President Mary McAleese jointly opened the Memorial Peace Park at Messines – a requiem to the 200,000 young men from across the island of Ireland, Catholic and Protestant, North and South, who fought in the First World War, side by side. Some 50,000 did not return.

Former Taoiseach Bertie Ahern TD

Given such manifest and poignant connections between Europe and the island of Ireland, so well outlined by Cardinal Brady and Bertie Ahern, it seemed obvious that within such a wider historical and political context the EC would wish to play a role in the development of the International Fund, as well as providing significant amounts to Northern Ireland in the various stages of the peace process.

The European Union, however, only became officially involved with the Fund more than two years after America, Australia, Canada and New Zealand. One of the major reasons for this was outlined to me by the former Taoiseach Dr Garret Fitzgerald.[1]

President Mary McAleese inaugurated the Peace Tower at the Peace Park in Messines (Mesen) in Belgium on 11 November 1998 in the presence of King Albert II and Queen Paola and Queen Elizabeth II.

The Peace Tower is dedicated to the memory of those from the island of Ireland who fought and died in the First World War. It is erected at the site of the Messines Ridge Battlefield, the only location in that conflict where the 36th Ulster Division and the 16th Irish Division fought side by side. The Memorial not only recalls the sacrifices of those from the island of Ireland from all political and religious traditions who fought and died in the war but it also serves as a powerful symbol of reconciliation in the present day.

The construction of the Peace Tower was made possible by funding from the Irish and British Governments as well as by sponsorship from the private sector.

The IFI, under the Wider Horizons Programme, provided funding which enabled young people to complete a major job of landscaping and further developing the Peace Park.

He said that in the run-up to the establishment of the IFI and the announcement of economic aid from America, he had been working hard for similar funding from Europe. He added "I talked to all the heads of government in Europe individually and on different occasions about this. The only exception was the Danish Prime Minister, because it just wasn't possible to contact him.

"I spent my time lobbying the others, even to the point – on occasions – of dashing round to speak to some of them in the car-park after a European Council meeting. All those to whom I talked agreed to help, and the idea was to announce just after the signing of the Anglo-Irish Agreement some significant funding for the IFI which would be in parallel to the support from America."

However, there was a major hitch. Dr Fitzgerald said that directly after the signing of the Hillsborough Agreement, he told Mrs Thatcher about the proposed money from Europe. He recalled "She said to me 'What, money for these people? Look at their roads, look at their schools, I need it for MY people' and she cancelled the whole thing! It took us two years to get it back on course. Geoffrey Howe worked hard at it, and we managed to get some funding, but the scale was far less than it would have been."

Geoffrey Martin

Geoffrey Martin, the first European Commission Representative to be based in Belfast, from December 1979 until January 1985, kept closely in touch with his colleagues in London, Dublin and Brussels. He was well aware of the implications of a possible European intervention in Northern Ireland, in support of the International Fund.

He suggested to me, during a meeting in London on 2 May 2008, that one of the reasons for the delay in European support for the International Fund was the reluctance of Mrs Thatcher to countenance such a move. He said "It was one thing to accept help from America and from several Commonwealth countries, but a very different matter for her to

Dr Garret Fitzgerald.
"Mrs Thatcher said 'No'."

countenance direct funding for the IFI from Europe, even though the United Kingdom was a Member State."

Martin believes that European intervention was a top-down decision which was driven by the then President of the Commission Jacques Delors. He said "I served under Delors, who was a strong character. He knew about the situation in Northern Ireland, and he wanted to give a lead. It was an unusual step for Europe to hand over funds to an independent body like the International Fund, but I believe that it was the right thing to do."

"I was brought up in the village of Bessbrook in South Armagh, so I fully understood the attitudes of both communities in the border areas. The IFI had the potential to encourage people to work together, even if at the most basic level they did so because everyone could benefit economically."

"Certainly, the IFI could make a practical contribution on the ground, and the small relative scale of the funding would be more than off-set by what it could be used to achieve, by getting people who were sworn enemies to sit down together for the first time since 1922, when Ireland was partitioned. I think that Jacques Delors and others realised that, so there was a strong argument for European intervention, even if it did take some time to materialise."

Eventually, in 1989, following an earlier announcement, the European Commission confirmed a contribution of 15 million ECU – with similar amounts proposed for the next two years. The then IFI Chairman John B McGuckian underlined that he and his Board

Jacques Delors, the former European Commission President, who was strongly supportive of the IFI initiative

were "greatly encouraged" by this European intervention, which was unique in the history of funding from Europe. In fact the former Secretary-General of the European Commission, Carlo Trojan, who was also for several years the European Observer on the Board of the IFI, told me that he regarded it as "a very peculiar arrangement." He said "We were giving money without having any responsibility for spending that money, apart from having a European Observer on the Board. It was a very peculiar way of carrying out structural policy. However, the nice thing about the International Fund was the fact that by working through projects, you were trying to get people to work together and to understand one another across the communities."[2]

Over the years, the European Union has given significant backing to the International Fund, not only financially but also through the continued support of its officials at all levels. This was underlined in the 2002 IFI Annual Report by the EU

Former European Observer Carlo Trojan (centre), with The Fund's South Joint Director General Eamon Hickey (left), and the North's Joint Director General Alexander Smith

John Hume and EU representative Jim Dougal in building mode

Board Observer Guy Crauser from Luxembourg who was the then Director-General for Regional Policy.

He noted that the EC contribution to the International Fund in 2002 represented more than 37% of all donors' contributions. He also emphasised that when compared cumulatively from the time when the EC began to contribute to the Fund in 1989, the EC share was – in 2002 – more than 39%.

He stated "The work of the International Fund is essential in maintaining the momentum for peace and reconciliation in Northern Ireland, not only for the benefit of the region most affected, but also for the benefit of the wider European Union as a whole."

In reflecting the political uncertainty which prevailed in 2002 he wrote "It is in times.... like now – with the suspension of the devolved institutions – that it is most crucial for bodies like the Fund to continue to build confidence and bring wealth in support of peace and reconciliation.

"This continuous support for cross-community and cross-border activities is all the more important as it sets an example – and an incentive – for the top political leaders to overcome their difficulties and bring about rapprochement from each end of the political spectrum."[3]

Crauser also emphasised that it was the model of the IFI which inspired the first EU PEACE Programme in Northern Ireland from 1995-99. He noted, significantly, that the model "with some adaptations" could be "transposed to other parts of the world – as unfortunately regions of conflict or post-conflict are numerous."

He added "In a way the European Commission is also learning from this experience in Northern Ireland, and we may in the future help to set up similar types of interventions in other parts. The Commission considers that, overall, the International Fund is doing a very good job, and that it maximises its impact best by co-operating closely with the new EU Programmes in the region."

Several years later Dr Danuta Hübner, Commissioner for Regional Policy, reflected upon the European contribution to the International Fund, during a conversation with me in her Brussels office in November 2007. She said "It was very different from a lot of the funding we have in our EU system, but it was right for us, back in 1989, when we first made our contribution."

www.belfast

BELFAST TE

Ian Paisley smiles as he addresses the media together with EU Commission President Jose Manuel Barroso in Brussels

Ulster leaders' thanks as EU money pours in

BY GEOFF MEADE

"It seemed an obvious thing to do, and the decision came naturally that we should be involved because it is important for we Europeans to know what it means to emerge from the ashes of a conflict. From day one it was for us a political challenge, as well as a financial contribution."

She added "It was unique, and different, and also an inspiration. We understood the interest of the international community in contributing to the process of bringing peace to this part of the European Union, with the emphasis on flexibility, going to the level where the problem is, and working towards the development of ownership on the ground. So there is a lot of similarity between the IFI's approach and the Union's instruments."

The overall financial contribution from Europe was considerable. Up to December 2007, the IFI received Euros 274 millions (£192 millions), and taking into account the pledges for 2006-2010, the total figure amounted to Euros 349 millions (£250 millions). These sums, as the father of the former IFI Chairman Willie McCarter would have observed, were not "inconsiderable" amounts.

Naturally, however, the Europeans kept a check on progress on the work of the International Fund and its agencies, and various senior Commission members like Dr Hübner, and her predecessors, visited some of the projects in Northern Ireland, including the impressive Stewartstown Road project.

She told me "It was important that we could show the involvement of Europeans in helping the people of Northern Ireland, and that Europe wanted to be involved. I had meetings with people from both communities who ran projects, and I recognised a positive feeling about the involvement of the Union."

"It's also good that people keep the photographs of how it actually was, because new generations don't remember the bad times, and it is important to realise that nothing can be taken for granted, even if you have peace."

"You have to care for it, and you have to nurture it, and you have to work together. I also think that women play and have played an important role. Well-educated and understanding women are the most important instruments to get real change in a society. The involvement of the ordinary people is so important, because they know the price of conflict and the lack of peace, and often they have to pay that price daily."

Dr Hübner, who is Polish, admitted to having an "inherited sympathy for the Irish." She said "I have a lot of Irish friends, from North and South,

Dr Hübner. "It is important for Europeans to know what it means to emerge from the ashes of a conflict".

The then First Minister the Rev Dr Ian Paisley and Deputy First Minister Martin McGuinness in Europe

and I have an understanding which comes from our own Polish history which is full of conflict, a lack of independence and being on the battle field."

"So there is a certain something in Polish society which allows us to understand the Irish better. So many Polish people went over there when the borders were opened, so it is maybe easier for me to understand the challenges there, and the feelings of the people, than maybe someone coming from a different history and background."

The challenge remains to maintain the peace in Northern Ireland which could be an example for others, even though no two situations of conflict are the same. Dr Hübner said "There is a challenge of changing the image of Northern Ireland in the eyes of the world, and making it a place where people can come and invest. The real challenge facing the European Union is not only investment where we have been mostly opening roads over the last decade, but also opening minds, because we have to change the way people think."

"I do not know how this period will go into the history books on Northern Ireland, but it is important to show that the people, with a little bit of help from outside, finally did it. Let's hope it is a lasting solution. In the context of the work of the International Fund, I don't think it is important to quantify how much the Canadians or New Zealanders or the Americans or the Australians or the Europeans contributed. This can be measured in percentages, but we all did as much as we could. I believe that the settlement of May 2007 would not have happened without all those years of work with the local communities."

Undoubtedly there was great appreciation in Northern Ireland for the help given by the Europeans. In January 2008 the then First Minister, the Reverend Dr Paisley and the Deputy First Minister Martin McGuinness visited Brussels and at a Press Conference with EU President José Manuel Barroso and Dr Hübner they expressed their thanks for the help from Europe.

Dr Paisley said "We are in Europe, we want to be part of the European experience. We believe that we have a contribution to make and that there is room for innovation and growth in Northern Ireland. We are very grateful for the continued support we get from the Commission."

Mr McGuinness was equally fulsome and said "We appreciate the tremendous support and encouragement we have been getting from the Commission. We have had a wide-range of discussions about the need for regeneration in Northern Ireland and the need for support for small businesses, and we will do our bit on our side."

Tony Blair and Bertie Ahern. "It is time to pray that the lessons of peace and reconciliation of Northern Ireland can be learned the world over".

Dr Hübner underlined the good relationship between Brussels and Belfast and said that everything possible was being done to support the Province and that this could only increase the attractiveness of the region.

These were not merely polite words from both sides, but a confirmation of a durable relationship with Europe that had survived some of the dark days of the Troubles and had helped to pave the way for peace. How fitting it would be if the example of Northern Ireland could help other troubled areas in Europe, and elsewhere.

A similar point was made by former British Prime Minister Tony Blair, writing for the Irish Times (4 April 2008) on the 10th anniversary of the Good Friday Agreement. He stated "As I travel to different parts of the world, what has happened in Northern Ireland is something that immediately connects with people. They see it as a real beacon of hope for other such conflicts, they think it is amazing and that it has lasted."

He underlined that the settlement in Northern Ireland is "really a great symbol of how the 21st century, as it changes so fast, will throw up opportunities to settle conflicts that seemed previously to be irresolvable."

"So, ten years on, it is a time for remembrance of the past, and hope and confidence for all of Ireland's future. It is a time too, to pray that the lessons of peace and reconciliation in Northern Ireland can be learned in other parts of the world."

Few people would quarrel with that.

Notes

1 During an Interview in his home in Dublin in February 2008.

2 During an Interview with Carlo Trojan at his home in The Hague on 21 February 2008.

3 Op. Cit. Pages 9-10.

CHAPTER FOURTEEN

Businesslike Approach

ONE OF THE KEY AIMS OF THE INTERNATIONAL FUND, from the beginning, was to stimulate economic development in disadvantaged areas, and this was carried out in a number of different ways.

The Business Enterprise Programme was developed to create conditions within which local initiative could be helped to develop a sense of enterprise and to create self-employment and job opportunities. The Programme also encouraged local businesses to seek new markets for their products.

Significantly, the Fund also developed a close working relationship with local enterprise groups from North and South. Continual emphasis was maintained on helping disadvantaged areas, and a large proportion of the funds went to projects in these locations.

The basic philosophy in the interface areas was straightforward, though at times it was difficult to implement. Instead of fortifying the so-called "Peace Walls" to keep the communities apart, the idea was to develop areas with literally four walls and a roof where people could work together.

One of the most successful of these was the Townsend Enterprise Park on the interface of the Lower Shankill and the Lower Falls in Belfast.[1] Another successful project was developed in the Limestone Road area of North Belfast, which had been the scene of regular pitched battles between the two communities.

However with the establishment of the successful Enterprise Park, and the general improvement in the political and security situation, the local businesses were able to operate in an atmosphere of relative calm, and thrived in the process. The success of the Programme was such that some forty successful Enterprise Units were established across Northern Ireland and the border counties. The Business Enterprise Programme was administered in Northern Ireland on behalf of the IFI by the Department of Economic Development, and in the South the Central Development Unit of the Department of Finance acted as the Fund's primary agent.

The Lurgan shirt making company Ben Sherman Ltd

Another significant development was the Venture Capital initiative. This was a concept that was relatively unused in Northern Ireland when the International Fund was established in 1986, but it also proved to be very successful. When Enterprise Equity (Northern Ireland) Ltd was set up, the Fund allocated or invested some £7 millions, and this investment will be returned when the Fund is wound up.

A similar enterprise in the South was established – with the title Enterprise Equity (Ireland) Ltd, and funding equivalent to Euros 9.4 millions. This whole initiative was established purely as a business proposition, and the project proved successful. The Northern company, based in Belfast, and the Southern company based in Dundalk, were set up basically to stimulate economic and business development in Northern Ireland and the Southern border counties. They achieved this primarily by providing venture capital on normal commercial criteria to existing enterprises and start-up projects.

One good example of the success in the North was the Ben Sherman shirt-making factory in Lurgan which was in financial difficulties in the late Eighties. The IFI, through Enterprise Equity (NI) Ltd, secured equity in the company which kept it afloat and helped it eventually to prosper. Later it was sold to an American manufacturer, at a profit of some £15 millions.

In fact the Venture Capital initiative has been so successful in the North that the company now has a portfolio of some £27 millions of equity in local companies, with some £18 millions in cash or shares with local companies. When the International Fund finally winds up, it will leave a legacy of expertise in venture capital to Northern Ireland and the border counties.

There have also been successes in the South, including Euros 925,000 invested in Clontibret in Co. Monaghan to develop a truck mounted forklift with Moffett Engineering, and other investments.

Another important initiative by the Fund was the Research and Development Programme, which was designed to help small

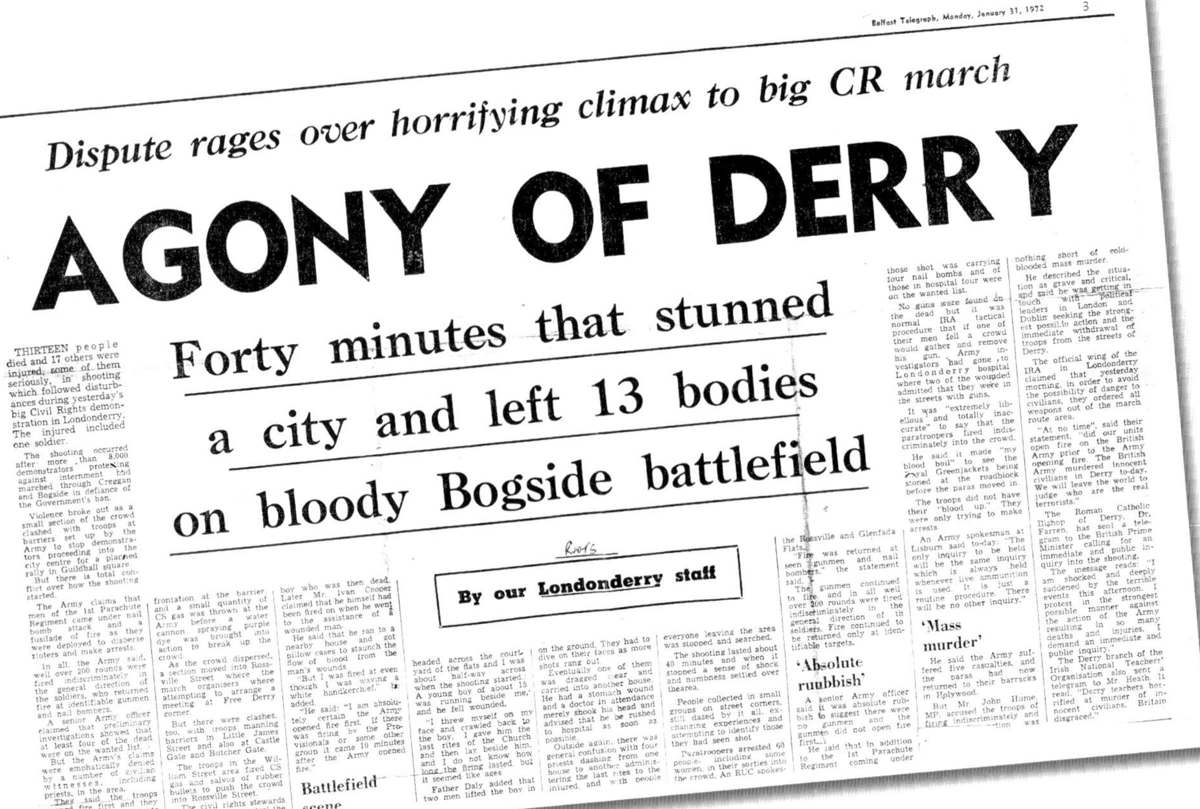

Belfast Telegraph, Monday, January 31, 1972 3

Dispute rages over horrifying climax to big CR march

AGONY OF DERRY

Forty minutes that stunned a city and left 13 bodies on bloody Bogside battlefield

By our Londonderry staff

THIRTEEN people died and 17 others were injured, some of them seriously, in shooting which followed disturbances during yesterday's big Civil Rights demonstration in Londonderry. The injured included one soldier.

The shooting occurred after more than 8,000 demonstrators protesting against internment had marched through Creggan and Bogside in defiance of the Government's ban.

Violence broke out as a small section of the crowd clashed with troops at barriers set up by the Army to stop demonstrators proceeding into the city centre for a planned rally in Guildhall square.

But there is total conflict over how the shooting started.

The Army claims that men of the 1st Parachute Regiment came under nail bomb attack and a fusilade of fire as they were deployed to disperse rioters and make arrests.

In all, the Army said, well over 200 rounds were fired indiscriminately in the general direction of the soldiers, who returned fire at identifiable gunmen and nail bombers.

A senior Army officer claimed that preliminary investigations showed that at least four of the dead were on the wanted list.

But the Army's claims were emphatically denied by a number of civilian witnesses, including priests, in the area.

They said the troops opened fire first and they alleged indiscriminate shooting at civilians by

frontation at the barrier, and a small quantity of CS gas was thrown at the Army before a water cannon spraying purple dye was brought into action to break up the crowd.

As the crowd dispersed, a section moved into Rossville Street where the march organisers where attempting to arrange a meeting at Free Derry corner.

But there were clashes, too, with troops manning barriers in Little James Street and also at Castle Gate and Butcher Gate.

The troops in the William Street area fired CS gas and salvos of rubber bullets to push the crowd into Rossville Street.

The civil rights stewards did their best to control the

boy who was then dead. Later Mr. Ivan Cooper claimed that he himself had been fired on when he went to the assistance of a wounded man.

He said that he ran to a nearby house and got pillow cases to staunch the flow of blood from the man's wounds.

"But I was fired at even though I was waving a white handkerchief," he added.

"He said: "I am absolutely certain the Army opened fire first. If there was firing by the Provisionals or some other group it came 10 minutes after the Army opened fire."

Battlefield scene

headed across the courtyard of the flats and I was about half-way across when the shooting started. A young boy of about 15 was running beside me, and he fell wounded.

"I threw myself on my face and crawled back to the boy. I gave him the last rites of the Church and then lay beside him, and I do not know how long the firing lasted, but it seemed like ages

Father Daly added that two men lifted the boy in

on the ground. They had to dive on their faces as more shots rang out.

Eventually one of them was dragged clear and carried into another house. He had a stomach wound and a doctor in attendance merely shook his head and advised that he be rushed to hospital as soon as possible.

Outside again, there was general confusion with four priests dashing from one house to another administering the last rites to the injured, and with people

everyone leaving the area was stopped and searched.

The shooting lasted about 40 minutes and when it stopped a sense of shock and numbness settled over the area.

People collected in small groups on street corners, still dazed by it all, exchanging experiences and attempting to identify those they had seen shot.

Paratroopers arrested 60 people, including some women, in their sorties into the crowd. An RUC spokes-

the Rossville and Glenfada Flats.

"Fire was returned at seen gunmen and nail bombers," the statement said.

The gunmen continued to fire, and in all well over 200 rounds were fired indiscriminately in the general direction of the soldiers. Fire continued to be returned only at identifiable targets.

'Absolute ruubbish'

A senior Army officer said it was absolute rubbish to suggest there were no gunmen and the gunmen did not open fire first.

He said that in addition to the 1st Parachute Regiment coming under

those shot was carrying four nail bombs and of those in hospital four were on the wanted list.

No guns were found on the dead but it was normal IRA tactical procedure that if one of their men fell a crowd would gather and remove his gun. Army investigators had gone to Londonderry hospital where two of the wounded admitted that they were in the streets with guns.

It was "extremely libellous and totally inaccurate" to say that the paratroopers fired indiscriminately into the crowd.

He said it made "my blood boil" to see the Royal Greenjackets being stoned at the roadblock before the paras moved in.

The troops did not have their "blood up." They were only trying to make arrests.

An Army spokesman at Lisburn said to-day: "The only inquiry to be held will be the same inquiry which is always held whenever live ammunition is used. It is just a routine procedure. There will be no other inquiry."

'Mass murder'

He said the Army suffered five casualties, and the paras had now returned to their barracks in Holywood.

But Mr. John Hume, MP, accused the troops of firing indiscriminately and [illegible] was

nothing short of cold-blooded mass murder.

He described the situation as grave and critical, and said he was getting in touch with political leaders in London and Dublin seeking the strongest possible action and the immediate withdrawal of troops from the streets of Derry.

The official wing of the IRA in Londonderry claimed that yesterday morning, in order to avoid the possibility of danger to civilians, they ordered all weapons out of the march route area.

"At no time", said their statement, "did our units open fire on the British Army prior to the Army opening fire. The British Army murdered innocent civilians in Derry to-day. We will leave the world to judge who are the real terrorists."

The Roman Catholic Bishop of Derry, Dr. Farren, has sent a telegram to the British Prime Minister calling for an immediate and public inquiry into the shooting.

The message reads: "I am shocked and deeply saddened by the terrible events this afternoon. I protest in the strongest possible manner against the action of the Army resulting in so many deaths and injuries. I demand an immediate and public inquiry."

The Derry branch of the Irish National Teachers' Organisation also sent a telegram to Mr. Heath. It read, "Derry teachers horrified at murder of innocent civilians. Britain disgraced."

businesses in Northern Ireland which could not afford to undertake these necessary steps on their own. The aim was to link them with suitable partners in the United States and Europe to help them bring an embryo idea to the stage of commercial production.

These were purely commercial measures by the Fund, but they helped local communities by securing jobs, by assisting small businesses to grow and by helping them to launch their products on the national and international stage. In this process there were some spin-offs to universities, but the IFI did not fund universities directly.

Another economic initiative, though on a much smaller scale, was the AMBIT Programme (American Business Internship). The idea was to team up local business leaders with large US companies to give them first-hand experience of established commercial enterprises. Many Northern Ireland people came back with ideas that helped to turn their business around, and one good example of this was Patsy O'Kane of the Beech Hill Country House Hotel in Drumahoe, near Londonderry.[2]

In recent years the AMBIT Programme changed in character, particularly as the Northern Ireland economy began to improve. AMBIT took on a more community-based flavour. Some of those who travelled to the US more recently included people from the Police Service of Northern Ireland and also from political parties. The AMBIT participants met some of the people in America who had experience in similar areas of operation.

This new development in AMBIT was fully supported by the Board of the IFI, and it underlined the significant change in this area of its support to keep pace with changing circumstances. This also linked in well with the Fund's strategy of moving from purely economic development to other important integration issues.

Patsy O'Kane with memorabilia from the US Marines display at the Beech Hill Country House Hotel

Ambition Achieved

One of the most striking successes of the AMBIT Programme was that of Patsy O'Kane, the proprietor of the Beech Hill Country House Hotel at Ardmore, near Londonderry.

The history of this distinctive Irish country house goes back to the early 17th century, when two former buildings were located on the site at different times. The third house, which has direct links with the hotel of today, was constructed in 1729 by a Captain Thomas Skipton, and named Beech Hill because of the large number of beech trees in the area.

The house remained in the Skipton family for several generations, and its members included some of the leading scholars, merchants and adventurers of the day who also modified the building, but in a way which helped it to retain its unique character.

During the Second World War, the house was used as the headquarters for several companies of the US Marines who established the US Navy's first base in Europe, on 5 February 1942. The American forces played a vital role in the Allied war effort, and the history of their time in the Derry area is carefully preserved in a unique exhibition which remains permanently on show at Beech Hill.

The House later became the property of a legal family in Belfast, but in 1989 it was bought by the O'Kanes who had had previously owned a licensed restaurant in Magherafelt. Patsy O'Kane, who was a trained paramedic and occupational therapist, also had a deep interest in the hotel and catering business. She helped to persuade her family to make a considerable investment in the Beech Hill property and run it as a hotel.

They had the difficult task of keeping their Country House financially viable at a time when visitors were not coming to Northern Ireland because of the continuing violence and the resultant bad publicity. Beech Hill did benefit, however, from a small but steady trickle of American visitors who came to the North in search of their family roots.

The hotel also received a considerable boost when, in 1998, the British Government set up the Saville Inquiry into the shooting dead of 13 civilians in Londonderry by the Army on 30 January 1972 - which became widely known as "Bloody Sunday." A 14th person died later. The establishment of the Inquiry led to the engagement of a large team of lawyers and other legal and support staff - many of whom regularly stayed in Beech Hill.

To provide a high-quality service, Patsy O'Kane employed expert staff, and the high cost of doing this was met by the corresponding accommodation and catering revenue. However, when the Saville Inquiry began to hear evidence from British Service personnel in 2002, it decided to move its deliberations to London, for security reasons. Pasty O'Kane's regular business disappeared almost overnight, and she was forced to try to fill the gap.

She recalls "I began to develop a programme featuring short breaks and specialist holidays. I was aware that technology and web-sites were providing the way forward with on-line booking, but I did not have a clue as to how it all worked. Meantime I was losing money month after month, and the financial situation was becoming extremely difficult.

"However, I was not prepared to lock the door and walk away. I was looking for help and I answered a newspaper advertisement on the AMBIT Programme. I was successful in obtaining a place, and that was the beginning of a process that turned things around for me completely."[3]

Patsy joined 11 other people on an AMBIT course in Washington DC in November-December 2003, and she began to learn about the latest developments in marketing and technology which might provide her business with a lifeline. Initially she was slightly overawed by the technological expertise of some of the other participants, who were already experienced in the use of online sales, but she found the course tutor – Jan Hepola from Minnesota – to be an enormous help.

Patsy says "She really had her finger on the pulse. She was able to relate to those who were so far advanced in this area, but she could also relate to me on the bottom rung of the ladder. To try to get me back on track again, she worked with me well beyond her remit, even spending periods long past the normal business hours in trying to help me sort things out."

One of the lessons she taught Patsy was about the importance of proper marketing. She recalls "I was ready to spend thousands of pounds on computers because I thought that these were the answer, and that technology was going to help me in a big way. Jan made the point, however, that what I really needed was people who understood what I was trying to do, and who could point me towards the right questions – what were my targets, how was I going to achieve them, and who was going to help me?"

As well as this, Patsy O'Kane learned more about the latest technology. She says "The AMBIT course made me even more determined to succeed. It also inspired me, and helped to give me a sense of direction. Jan was wonderful, because she felt a loyalty to the IFI and to me, and she kept me going to the next stage, and then the next stage, and the stage after that. She also kept in touch long after the course ended, and she even came across to Beech Hill and helped me to establish our present website."

Armed with the new technological knowledge and advice, Patsy O'Kane's business not only survived but expanded, and today in the more relaxed atmosphere of the peace process, the bookings are coming in on-line from all over the world.

She says "I had been running around with blinkers on, and feeling sorry for myself. Maybe I would have ended up like the proprietor of one of those little hotels which never move with the times. However, the AMBIT Programme changed all that for me. It gave me much more knowledge and technological expertise and comradeship, as well as a focus. It also gave me the stability and confidence to stand alone, and to source out people who could help me at each stage.

Patsy O'Kane: "Every day something new happens".

"I am passionate about the Beech Hill property, and every day something new happens, and I get another link. I have discovered that people will pay for quality if they know about it, but that there's no point in spending time planning something if you don't know how to tell the world about it. I learned that from the AMBIT Programme and from the IFI. It was a marvellous experience, which has paid great dividends for me and for the business, and I am very grateful for the help which I received at exactly the right time when I needed it most."

Young At Heart

Two of the most important projects supported by the International Fund concentrated on young people between the ages of 12 and 16, and gave them an understanding of simulated business development and enterprise.

The LET Programme (Learning and Educating Together) and KEY (Knowledge through Enterprise for Youth) brought secondary school children out of their local communities on both sides of the Border, and gave them the opportunities to meet and to learn from one another in a neutral space, which they might not otherwise have experienced.

The LET Programme, which was run by Young Enterprise Northern Ireland and Junior Achievement Ireland, catered for those aged 12-13 who were also given the opportunity to find out something about entrepreneurship, and they were also encouraged to take part in a wide range of outdoor pursuits including canoeing, and rock-climbing.

The students who came from areas or situations of disadvantage were selected because they had shown initiative and leadership potential. They attended three residential courses between October and May at an activity outdoor centre in the North. Each school was partnered with two others from different community backgrounds.

The concept for the KEY Programme was similar, and it catered for the older age group of 14-16. The emphasis was also on personal development, and the Programme tried to impress on pupils the importance of staying on at school.

The KEY students attended four residential sessions from May to September, and as with the LET Programme, pupils from each school were grouped with those from two other schools from a different cross-community and cross-border background. Over the years, the KEY/LET Programmes catered for thousands of young people, most of whom gained personal confidence and stature as a result.

Fiona McCabe, who played a key management role in helping to run both Programmes, explained to me more about the background. She said "We are not miracle workers, but what I have learned most is not just from the young people but from our training staff who really believe in what they are doing. They have faith in the young people, many of whom have their own problems and challenges, and our staff engage with them from day one as if everybody is coming with a clean slate to the project."[4]

Fiona McCabe. "Young people need to understand that there are rules in life".

It was important to give the young people support and encouragement and to help them not only to look beyond the confines of their own communities, but also to look to the future. Fiona said "There are opportunities to grab, and we are trying to get them to dream a little. Our training staff are young themselves and they would be seen very much as a role model for the youngsters."

There were many individual success stories, including that of a young man who had serious behavioural problems at school and had a high level of truancy. Fiona said "He was always in the Headmaster's office for the wrong reasons, but he went on one of our Programmes, and there was a dramatic change in his attitude to the school and to himself.

Canoeing on Carlingford Lough

"That young lad went on to be one of our nominees for a visit to Canada as recognition of his achievement over the year, and as far as I know he is now in full-time employment and doing well. Whereas many of his teachers, and perhaps even his parents and his family, had written him off, they were completely shocked and surprised by his turnaround, and by the dramatic change he had undergone within a 1-year period."

Not everyone, however, was successful. "The last thing we want to do is to expel a young person but if they consistently break the rules, people have been expelled. It's a huge blow and we are reluctant to go down that road, but if we allow a certain type of behaviour to persist, it sends out the wrong message to others. Young people need to understand that there are rules in life, and that that is part of their journey."

This young man's experience was not an isolated one. The following evidence was gathered from qualitative research conducted with teachers in a pilot study examining the impact of the KEY Programme on truancy levels.

One teacher reported "With the kids who are willing to give it a go, their confidence and self-esteem has definitely improved. Their attitude to each other, and even some of the teachers, has improved. It helps, you know. It means that things are less of a struggle when they do come into class. Their whole attitude has improved."

Another teacher said "I thought it was a super Programme, well-delivered, and the kids got a lot out of it, to the extent that they are meeting other kids from the Programme at weekends, from Catholic and Protestant schools. Those relationships have lasted, and it's not been about going down to residentials and getting a few days here and there. It continued, and you can see the benefits."

To find out something about one of the Programmes at first hand, I visited a KEY group at the Killowen Residential Centre in Rostrevor. This is a beautiful coastal area on the Northern side of Carlingford Lough, on the opposite side from Co. Louth and the rugged backdrop of the Cooley peninsula.

The pupils from schools in the North and South were enjoying themselves and had just taken part in a classroom session where they were preparing to go to Newry the

L-R: Della Clancy, Executive Director Junior Achievement Ireland; Denis Rooney, Chairman of the International Fund for Ireland; Valerie Ingram, CEO, Young Enterprise Northern Ireland; and Jackie McManus, Carrick-on -Shannon Community School, Co Leitrim; pictured at the official launch of a new residential camp based at The Share Centre, Lisnaskea

next day on a joint business enterprise and marketing project. In the meantime they were sharing in a canoeing exercise in the Lough, under the watchful eye of the outdoor pursuits experts.

Back at the residential centre Bernard Thompson, a Senior Training Officer with KEY, told me some of the experiences of his five years with the Programme. He said "It's a difficult job because you spend so much time away from your family, with a lot of travelling, but the work inspires me so much. When you meet the students, the experience drives you on to give them an opportunity that not everyone can get."

On one course there was a young girl who had a fear of water. Bernard said "We told her that we were not going to push her into the waves! However, we encouraged her to put on her wet gear and maybe dip in and out of the shallow parts. By the end of the fourth residential course the same young girl was driving a speed-boat on Carlingford Lough at high speed, and she took part in pier-jumping as well. She was one of the many students who overcame their fears, who believed in themselves and who became young adults."

Rebecca Stranney, a then newly-qualified teacher, told me that she had recently joined the KEY Programme as a Trainer and was enjoying it thoroughly. She said "You try to achieve the balance between discipline and letting them know you're in charge when you are up there in front of them, but not acting like a school-teacher. They need to feel like young adults who are being trained and it's important not to give them the impression that I'm standing up preaching to them and that they therefore have to listen."

The inter-community theme is also handled sensitively. Rebecca said "We don't ram it down their throats. It's a subtle undertone, the very fact that they are down here working with each other and engaging with young people from other communities, without us pointing that out. We just let it happen."

The dynamics of each residential session, like each group, is different. Meike White was brought up in East Germany, and later married a Northern Ireland man and came to live in the Province in 1989. Meike, who trained in Berlin as a teacher, became a Trainer with the KEY Programme. She talked to me about her five years of experience in dealing with hundreds of students.

KEY Staff – Meike White (left), Bernard Thompson and Rebecca Stranney

She said "The Programme is amazing. From day one when the students arrive to the time they go home, they are changed people. We do switch on something in them and help them to realise what they could be doing with their lives. It just opens everybody's horizons."

There is no danger of being stereo-typed as a trainer. Meike says "The dynamic of each group is totally different. For example, the group this week is relatively quiet whereas last week the students were 'mad'. Each group has its own qualities, and each training day is never, ever the same."

It is not only the trainers and the students who appreciate the courses, but also the parents. One parent said "Students from different areas and different religions normally would not get the chance to come together and to experience the good points of working together. It gives them an opportunity to break down the barriers and to see the benefits of teamwork."

Each year, the students from the LET/KEY Programmes attend a "Graduation "Ceremony in Belfast, where the enthusiasm of such shared experiences and achievements is obvious. The ethos of both Programmes was well-summarised by the IFI Chairman Denis Rooney at one of the KEY Graduation ceremonies, on 21 May 2007.

He told a large audience at the Europa Hotel in Belfast " Each one of you is sitting here today because during the past year you have shown spirit and drive, that you can work together with other young people from other communities and from across the border in the spirit of enterprise and entrepreneurship.

"That's what the International Fund for Ireland is most interested in and why we, with the generous support of our donors – the US, the European Union, Canada, Australia and New Zealand - provide the money to run the Programme every year."

The Chairman underlined that this was "a great investment." He said "When you put money into something, as you all now know, you want to make some profit at the end of it - you want to get something more out of it.

"At the International Fund, we're not really thinking so much about how many pounds sterling or euros we can make from all of you, but we are thinking about investing in the future of Northern Ireland and the border counties. Our profit is to see all of you working together, across the community and across the border, as role models for your generation."

Notes

1 This was discussed in more detail in Chapter 11.

2 See Separate Story.

3 In an Interview with the Author at Beech Hill on 22 June, 2007.

4 In an Interview with the Author in Belfast, in April 2007.

CHAPTER FIFTEEN

Sharing This Space

ONE OF THE MOST IMPORTANT DEVELOPMENTS IN THE recent history of the International Fund was the decision to adopt a significant new strategy with the theme of "Sharing This Space." The emphasis on the new approach had four key elements - building the foundations for reconciliation in the most marginalised communities, building bridges between divided communities, moving towards a more integrated society, and looking ahead to ensure sustainability in the longer term.

At first glance these objectives were not all that dissimilar from what had gone on before, but the incoming Chairman Denis Rooney, who had succeeded William McCarter in 2005, outlined to me the thinking behind the new initiative. He said "When I was appointed to the Chair I understood that the Fund had spent almost 20 years changing many parts of Northern Ireland and the border counties for the better, and that although the economic circumstances had improved in most of the areas, the Fund still had a vital role to play in underpinning the Peace Process which was then at a very sensitive stage."

Rooney said that on his first trip to Washington he was surprised firstly at the access which the Fund enjoyed at the very highest political level. "We were received warmly by many of the top US Senators and Congressmen and Congresswomen in a series of meetings. Although the meetings were most cordial and supportive of the Fund's great achievement, they gave a clear message that many thought that the Fund's role was less relevant in the new circumstances and I felt that there was a real danger that our funding would be under threat."

"We then did what any organisation has to do from time to time and held an in-depth strategy review, the product of which was the 'Sharing This Space' document. This realignment of the Fund's strategy, together with the unambiguous declaration of a time-frame which we believed it would take to achieve, rekindled the US interest and reinforced the EU commitment and has secured confirmed financial support from Europe and likely matching contributions from US until 2010. More importantly, it has enabled the Fund to continue to challenge our society to change for the better in areas where it would have been unlikely to have happened through any other means, whilst at all times continuing to underpin the Peace Process." Denis Rooney outlined the new strategy in a keynote speech delivered on 18 January 2006 in the Harbour Commissioners' historic building in Belfast.

Mr Rooney began his speech by paying tribute to those he succeeded and by taking stock of what had already been achieved. He noted, rightly, that when the Fund had been established in 1986, few people would have expected its life-span to have existed beyond four or five years. It was a major achievement, he said, to have remained in existence for over two decades and, by the start of 2008, to have contributed some £600 millions/Euros 870 millions to more than 5,700 projects.

Rooney paid tribute to the Fund's sponsors in North America, Europe, Canada, Australia and New Zealand, and noted that the IFI had been "an incredibly effective funding agency." He added "From its controversial beginnings, when many viewed it with suspicion, the Fund has concentrated on the needs of the community and has implemented a series of innovative and well-managed programmes."

When Denis Rooney had taken over as Chairman the previous March, the Fund had carried out a review of its role. It concluded that "while the Fund had some very important work still to do, it could not go on for ever in its present form." Rooney acknowledged that it was up to the British and Irish Governments to indicate when they believed the work of the Fund should end, but he suggested that a further five years of international support " would enable the Fund to go a long way towards achieving its' long-term objectives."

The Chairman sent out a clear signal that he and his colleagues wanted to ensure "that the Fund will not jog gently on to a passive sunset, but that we will continue to take risks on behalf of the communities and deliver the full quarter century of effective intervention."

There was no illusion, he said, that the IFI's level of funding or its expertise were sufficient in themselves to address adequately the scale of the problems. He added "We are simply recognising that circumstances have changed and that our resources, for however long they remain, might now be usefully deployed to promote attempts to enable people to live together more amicably, and for young people to share their formative years more effectively."

In a particularly important passage the Chairman noted that "Together, we need to explore ways of sharing

Denis Rooney, Chairman International Fund for Ireland with some of the young people who were selected to go to the Canadian Junior Achievement Conference in Montreal, (L-R) Rory Maguire, O Fiach College, Dundalk; David Maye, Dungannon Integrated College; Deirdre Dolan, Community School Carrick on Shannon; and Philip Trueman, Aughnacloy College.

this space. Over the remaining four years of the Fund's life, the Board wishes to signal an intention of assisting communities who wish to explore these themes with us." The task, of course, was to choose the priorities for the new direction.

In this context, it is important to remember the political background in early 2006 when the Board's new direction was being announced. Some two decades years earlier when the Fund had been established it faced intense political opposition and suspicion from many quarters, as has been noted before, but the paramilitary cease-fires, (however fragmentary some of them proved to be), and the political progress through the Downing Street Agreement of 1993 and the Good Friday Agreement of 1998 had changed the landscape enormously for the better.

By the beginning of 2006 there was still bickering between some of the major parties and an apparent deadlock on key political issues of power-sharing including recognition of the police and the whole question of security. No-one at that time, including the Chairman and the Board of the IFI, could have predicted the eventual rapprochement between the Democratic Unionists and Sinn Fein which in May 2007 paved the way for a new and stable arrangement acceptable to both communities.

However in the 2005 Annual Report, the IFI Chairman underlined succinctly the Fund's impending change in its policy. He stated "As for the future, the political and social environment within Ireland has changed significantly, and what was required in the 1990's is not necessarily what is needed now. Our 5-year strategy gives us the tools necessary to focus on reconciliation and create a better tomorrow for future generations."[1]

The point was well-summarised in the outline in the Annual Report which described the new 5-year strategy as the launching of "a final phase of activity to promoting reconciliation in Ireland. The Fund's existing Community programmes have been extended, with a view to building a sustainable infrastructure for reconciliation, operating beyond the Fund's lifetime. As a consequence of this, much of the Fund's traditional economic-based activities have ceased, with resources diverted to grass-roots community development."[2]

This was perhaps easier said than done. The Fund acknowledged that the problems of economic deprivation had not been solved, and it recognised that there were appropriate agencies North and South which had this as their sole statutory remit. The Chairman, in his speech on 18 January 2006, recognised, for example, the sterling work of the Northern Ireland Housing Executive, but added that if it was felt the Fund could make a contribution "in promoting the sharing of the spaces where people live.... we would signal our willingness to become involved, if that would be helpful." In essence the Chairman was suggesting that the Fund was moving from a major involvement in bricks and mortar to the promotion of ideas, though the further provision of capital costs was not being ruled out - depending on the circumstances.

The Fund was also placing an emphasis on supporting community groups which saw potential opportunities and advantages in integrating their work. This was intended to go beyond the benefits of community engagement at its simplest level. The Chairman noted that "there are groups who have an interest in pursuing this kind of integration, and we would encourage them to engage with us on how we might be of assistance."

In one new, and intriguing, development the Fund was recognising the need to tell its own story more widely. Denis Rooney noted that the International Fund had developed particular kinds of programmes and their

Pictured from left. Denis Rooney Chairman of the International Fund for Ireland, Professor Tony Gallagher, School of Education, Queen's University Belfast, and Padraic Quirk, from Atlantic Philanthropies, with a pupil from Limavady High School, one of the participating schools

management, in a climate which had developed out of conflict. He also admitted that in the past the Fund had been reticent about publicising part of its success story, for obvious reasons arising out of the earlier hostility from those who objected to the very establishment of the Fund itself.

The Chairman, like others, recognised the degree of conflict that existed in places outside Northern Ireland. He said, however, that it was a measure of the progress in the North that the Board now considered the "time to be ripe for sharing with other regions the approaches that have benefited the communities in Northern Ireland and the border counties." He added "It is the intention of the Board to attempt to share the experiences.... with other groups who might find the Fund useful as a model that could be adapted for use in their own particular circumstances."

The wording here was important, in that the Fund recognised that its experience in Ireland - North and South - was not necessarily a blue-print for all situations, but that the model might be adapted for use in other regions and circumstances where historical conflict needed to be resolved.

Significantly, in June 2008 the IFI produced an information booklet titled "Effective Peace Building", which was intended to have a wide circulation. It outlined in some detail the establishment and role of the IFI, and indicated that its Programmes were characterised by, inter alia, "a clear focus on reconciliation as the over-riding objective; an independent and credible approach with strong international backing; a willingness to take risks on behalf of those communities we work with; a willingness to innovate and to break new ground in support of reconciliation, and a responsive approach to donor priorities."

In the Chairman's foreword, Denis Rooney underlined that Northern Ireland and the border counties were not alone in dealing with conflict and unrest. He added "Other regions of the world are also dealing with conflict. Given its history over the last 20 years, the Fund is committed to sharing its experiences as a model for intervention with other organisations and regions seeking to move beyond conflict to creating more stable civic societies."

One of the first practical examples was the Sharing Education Programme which was launched formally at Queen's University, Belfast in 2008, and involved more than 60 schools. It was developed by the IFI Board in association with The Atlantic Philanthropies, an American organisation. The idea was to offer students from all backgrounds an opportunity to share enhanced education and development while building up positive relationships with those from a different culture and tradition.

The Programme was administered by Queen's University and it featured 12 projects which were shared by the 60-plus schools involved. Significantly, these included Northern Ireland's first Specialist Schools, which had been designated (ie specially recognised) by the Department of Education because of their commitment to collaboration and excellence in key areas. These Specialist Schools worked with partners from all over Northern Ireland.

Professor Tony Gallagher from Queen's explained the importance of the SEP project. He said "Despite intensive efforts over many years, work in education which was aimed at promoting reconciliation had limited impact. The Sharing Education Programme is based on the premise that reconciliation is more likely to occur if cross-denominational collaboration is focused on high status activities, involving large numbers of pupils who are working together on a sustained basis."[3]

The ultimate goal of the SEP project was to encourage all schools to make inter-community collaboration an integral part of their everyday life. As part of this work, the participating schools shared their experiences of partnership with the rest of the education community through conferences, seminars, publications and the Sharing Education Programme website - http://www.schoolsworkingtogether.co.uk".

One key aspect of the concept of "building integration" was the drive to promote integrated housing. One of the major problems of Northern Ireland had long been the segregation in public sector housing which was intensified and maintained by the Troubles. This

The Butterfly Garden Project, Broughshane, Co Antrim

Murals in Northern Ireland had their own direct message including those from Loyalists (top) and Republicans (bottom). Many are now a tourist attraction

affected many important areas of daily life, including employment, schooling and recreation, at a time when people were unwilling, or even afraid, to enter those areas which were perceived to have a different culture from their own.

For example, the whole area of West Belfast was perceived to be "Catholic" and "Nationalist" despite the presence of some "Protestant" and "Unionist" individuals and enclaves, and the same applied to East Belfast, though in reverse order, where the Protestants were in the majority. The Board of the IFI was aware that it would be a massive task to change the pattern of housing, but it worked closely with the Northern Ireland Housing Executive to try to achieve this objective.

The first major initiative was the Shared Future Neighbourhood Programme, in association with the Shared Future Advisory Panel. It involved a wide range of civic and voluntary groups, and concentrated on providing support in those housing areas which wished to be associated with the Programme.

This involved training for local community workers who would become "champions" of shared housing in their own areas. It also facilitated the development of a Neighbourhood charter, and also

the delivery of a "Good Relations Plan" for the areas involved. The expectation was the creation of up to 30 Shared Future Neighbourhoods within the first three years of operation.

All of this was very different from the more straightforward projects of earlier years which had a major focus on the development of buildings and which had demonstrated the importance of bricks and mortar in helping to contribute to shared community identities and achievements.

The new emphasis was in many ways more difficult to implement, and none more so than the Re-Imaging Communities Programme. This imaginative project was intended to help communities in urban and rural areas to think about positive ways to express a new self-generated image of themselves, and the idea was to encourage the creation of shared public space through the use of the creative arts.

This was seen most clearly in the attempts to replace some of the distinctive political and paramilitary murals, graffiti and historical slogans which resonated with the majority of people in one community, but which were highly offensive to others. This was evident, for example, in the Nationalist and Unionist murals in West and East Belfast respectively, and other areas. Artistically a number of these were not without merit, while others had flawed historical concepts, and yet others were nakedly sectarian in nature.

The idea of providing funds to change these images proved controversial, with critics suggesting that the money could be better used for other purposes. It was also a sensitive issue, in that many people in the areas felt that the murals, however repugnant to others, were part of their heritage, and it was a major step to move towards the creation of neutral or culturally-relevant images.

However, the IFI and its associates persisted with their re-imaging objective, and with some success. In East Belfast, for example, some of the images of hooded gunmen were replaced by those of the legendary and ill-fated Titanic, which was built in the nearby shipyard of Harland and Wolff. This re-imaging was only the first part of a very long process, but many people felt that these were steps in the right direction.

The Re-Imaging Communities Programme was funded through the Shared Communities Consortium, which itself had a wide representation ranging from the Arts Council to Government Departments and the Police Service of Northern Ireland, and the Programme was open to all communities which sought the renewal and reclamation of their shared public spaces.

One particularly good example of this was the Butterfly Garden Project in the attractive floral-decked village of Broughshane in Co. Antrim, not far from Slemish Mountain where – according to tradition – St. Patrick herded animals as a slave, before escaping from Ireland and returning later to convert its peoples to Christianity.

The main purpose of the proposal was to reclaim a hitherto drab gable wall in the village, and to prevent it from being used for a political, and some would claim, "sectarian" mural. People were so apprehensive of this happening that, in the meantime, they had placed old signs on the wall to prevent it being taken over.

A local group applied to the Shared Communities Consortium and stated clearly their objective to "give the community an area which all can take ownership of, depicting a theme that no-one need feel

Hope for the future. Julia and Zoista at Mums and Tots, The Link, Newtownards, which is supported by the Fund

excluded from. In addition, it presents the opportunity to remove the flagpole holders and replace them with plants."

The application was successful, and a most beautiful wall display of butterflies became one of the outstanding features of Broughshane, which in its own right had won more than one major award – despite the seasonal political and other displays which had contrasted with the overall image of the village. In 2007 it won the Gold Award as Champion of Champions in the Britain in Bloom Competition, and no doubt the splendid Butterfly Wall helped to create a good impression.

Another important element in the overall strategy of "Building Integration" was the work in bringing community groups closer together. The Integrating Community Groups Programme, in association with the Rural Development Council for Northern Ireland, offered to build confidence and to promote opportunities for integration, participation and communication between Unionist and Nationalist groups in Northern Ireland and also on a cross-border basis.

The participants were asked to take part in "good relations and diversity" training, and the Programme also offered support for greater personal contact, including study visits, resources for project development and assistance to develop agreements with other groups. A key part of this was to match participants, with a view to working more closely together on shared projects.

In addition, a number of distinctive collaborative projects were funded. In Eglinton, Co. Londonderry, the two housing estates – one predominantly Nationalist, and the other predominantly Unionist – had separate children's play facilities. With the help of the IFI, community groups from each estate began to work together to change attitudes and hopefully to build shared facilities for the children from both estates.

One significant illustration of the International Fund's new direction was the support given to a pilot study to support training for members of Northern Ireland's District Policing Partnerships. The Partnerships were a politically sensitive issue, given that the Republican movement had been unwilling to give any formal recognition to the Police Service of Northern Ireland, or its predecessor the Royal Ulster Constabulary.

This aspect of the Fund's work was of particular interest to Congressman Chris Smith from New Jersey, who assisted greatly with the legal challenges in making this a success. He also sustained his interest in this work, and encouraged the International Fund in its continued intervention in this area.

L-R: Denis Rooney, Chairman of the International Fund for Ireland with Josep Borrell Fontelles, then Chairman of the European Parliament; and Dermot Ahern TD, the then Minister for Foreign Affairs during a visit to Dundalk.

This attitude of Republicans changed in the aftermath of the St. Andrew's and Stormont Agreements, but policing remained a politically-sensitive issue. However, the International Fund's initiative with the Policing Partnerships was intended to help members – who were drawn from local communities – to deal with issues such as sectarianism and racism. The ultimate objective was to enable the Partnerships and the people to work together with the PSNI to create stronger and safer local communities, and also to build trust and confidence in policing.

Another important measure of the IFI's Building Integration Programme was the assistance given to help the Orange Order to move beyond its historical activities and to assist it in maintaining its focus on wider community issues and involvement. Not surprisingly, this proved to be controversial, and some members of the general public objected to funds being made available to what they regarded as a "sectarian organisation."

However the IFI's policy was in accord with one of the Orange Order's own aims which was to change its image and to help "celebrate a Unique Cultural Heritage and Tradition." This was no easy task, given the history of previous years, and the IFI may well have laid itself open to misinterpretation and misunderstanding.

However Sandy Smith, the Joint Director General of the IFI based in Belfast, explained some of the background. He said "We were trying to provide training to help members to engage in work and activities beyond those immediately associated with the Orange Order. That was misunderstood by some people who believed that the Fund was giving money directly to the Order for its traditional activities. This was not so. The funding was given to help the Order to make its activities much more acceptable to everyone in the community and its premises accessible to all."

This policy of the IFI required a steady nerve to withstand the predictable criticism, but the initiative was important at a time when a number of Orange Halls and GAA buildings were being destroyed or damaged by sectarian arsonists.

Only time will tell how far this policy of the IFI with regard to the Orange Order proves successful, but the fact that it was being tried at all gave some hope about the future of community relations in Northern Ireland. The overall strategy of "Sharing This Space" was never going to be easy, but that was no reason for not attempting it.

Denis Rooney, the Chairman of the IFI, summarised well the new strategy in his remarks in the 2007 Annual Report. He stated "The International Fund continues to lead the way in identifying and piloting new interventions in education, housing and community structure which can make a meaningful and lasting contribution to creating a society that is genuinely integrated and living in peace, rather than one which is merely enjoying a cessation of violence."

He added "While we can look back on many significant achievements, we must now focus on ensuring that we can deliver initiatives and interventions which will have long-term impact, and be sustainable as the Fund's time draws to a close."[4]

A Helping Hand

Denis Rooney, a well-known Belfast chartered surveyor and businessman, was invited to become Chairman of the International Fund for Ireland in 2005.

Reflecting on the progress of the past few years, he said "I had worked occasionally with people from the IFI, but not in any great depth. When I became Chairman it took me a long time to appreciate fully the complexity of its range of projects, and the impact they have made on so many people."[5]

Pictured at a St. Patrick's Day reception in the White House from left to right: Denis Rooney, Chairman of the International Fund, Father Patrick Whyte, the former Taoiseach Bertie Ahern and US President George W Bush

He continued "After several years as Chairman I continue to be impressed by that range of activities and their collective and individual impacts. However, I believe that the work of the IFI is not as well known as it should be, except to those who are the direct recipients, and this is something which we have been taking steps to counter.

"Looking back over its work since 1986, there has been a slow but definite realisation of the part the International Fund has played in helping society to be able to make the changes of direction, in a long process which is still being worked out. It is my firm belief, however, that without the Fund's work, those changes in society would have been harder to achieve."

The Chairman said it was important to stress that the International Fund still had an important amount of work to do. He added "The Fund has created a series of networks and connections which are both at the macro political level and at community level, both of which are needed to have a successful impact."

Denis Rooney said that there was also enormous personal fulfilment for people working with the Fund. He said "When you are engaged with any organisation, you can judge how good it is by the commitment of the people who are involved with it. The reaction to the International Fund has been positive in all senses, and that is rare for any organisation I have encountered very little negative comment, or negative emotion about the IFI.

"People who connect with it become involved very quickly, as I have done, and there's a saying that even when you've gone, 'you never really leave the Fund.' That is very true. People who have been involved even for a short while always retain a warm place in their hearts for the Fund. Not many organisations have that kind of legacy."

Notes

1 Op. Cit. Page 5.
2 Ibid Page 7.
3 IFI Annual Report 2007, Page 30.
4 Op. Cit. Pages 6-9.
5 In an interview with the Author in Belfast in 2008.

CHAPTER SIXTEEN

Leaving A Legacy

ONE OF THE MAJOR OBJECTIVES OF the International Fund for Ireland has been to improve community relations in Northern Ireland and also across the border. In 1988 a Community Relations Programme was set up to help organisations working for reconciliation and peace-building.

The range of grants was varied, and funding was given to Co-Operation North for its programme of cross-community and North/South exchange visits. The Northern Ireland Voluntary Trust, an umbrella organisation funding a wide range of community organisations, was helped with a new programme of support for the improvement of areas experiencing great community stress in Northern Ireland.

In the South, financial assistance was given to the Presbyterian Youth Centre in Lucan to improve its facilities for a programme of North/South visits. Help was also given to the Irish School of Ecumenics, the Belfast-based Ultach Trust which aimed to increase the knowledge of the Irish language in Northern Ireland, and also the Ulster People's College, a cross-community adult education establishment based in South Belfast. There was a steady stream of grants for improving community relations, over the next few years.

In 1995 the Board developed a new focus for this type of work, and introduced a Community Bridges Programme, which - as was noted earlier - was further developed in 2007. The Fund provided a full-time co-ordinator to ensure that the enhanced Programme remained both effective and pro-active. It also operated a Community Leadership Programme to support volunteers in some of the most disadvantaged areas to acquire skills, experience and techniques for tackling economic and social problems in their localities. In 1995 alone, some 140 people from 90 community groups in Northern Ireland and the border counties took part in this Programme.

In 1995 also the Fund launched its Communities in Action Programme as a 3-year pilot scheme. This Programme provided support for people in some of the most disadvantaged areas to try to break the cycles of deprivation - particularly those affecting children under five, young people and also women who wanted to return to work. Thus in a very broad way the Fund supported community-building

The founder of the Corrymeela Community Dr Ray Davey and his wife Kathleen at a meeting with the Dalai Lama at the Corrymeela Centre in Ballycastle

initiatives across a wide geographical and social spectrum and a large number of organisations were helped in simple yet practical ways to begin or to continue their work.

It was well-known and widely-accepted that the work of peace-building and reconciliation was a long-term process, given the depths of the animosities and cultural differences in Northern Ireland. The physical toll of the Troubles could be assessed all too well in the number of human beings killed and injured, and also in the damage done to buildings and physical structures of all kinds.

However, the corresponding damage to community relations was literally incalculable, and much work was done by many organisations over a long period not only to minimise that damage but also to try to sow the seeds of peace in a hostile climate. In this respect the International Fund provided constant and much–needed support for four of the important institutions working in this field - namely the Corrymeela Community in Northern Ireland, the Glencree Community near Dublin, An Teach Ban at Downings in Donegal, and the Crossfire Trust in South Armagh.

The Corrymeela Community is a Christian-based organisation which was established at Ballycastle in 1965. Its visionary Founder is the Reverend Dr Ray Davey, a Presbyterian Minister from Belfast who chose to serve as a chaplain with the YMCA during the Second World War. His recently-published war dairies give a vivid account of his experiences in the North African desert, where he was captured by the Germans in Tobruk. He spent several years in prison camps in Italy and Germany, during which time he learned a great deal about the whole concept of community living, and how this helped people to survive and to make a contribution in situations of great stress.[1]

Davey returned to Northern Ireland, and in 1946 he became the first Presbyterian Dean of Residence at Queen's University, Belfast. He did not forget his war experience of community life, albeit in prison camps, and he was acutely aware of the need for better relationships in a deeply-divided Northern Ireland. His central philosophy was simple and profound - "If we Christians cannot speak the language of reconciliation, then we have nothing to say." Davey had a remarkable ability to make friends and to get the best from people, but behind the gentle exterior was a man of great determination.

The current Corrymeela Community Leader Dr David Stevens

The Corrymeela Centre in Ballycastle and its distinguished visitors, Archbishop Desmond Tutu and Mother Teresa

He was also ahead of his time. One of his successors as Leader, Dr David Stevens, said recently “Ray spoke the language of reconciliation and about the importance of relationships, at a time when this was unfashionable. Today, that language is mainstream; it is on the lips of church leaders, politicians and Government Ministers. This is a mark of Ray's success. He is a prophet of a shared future.”[2]

Ray Davey gathered around him a group of like-minded people, including other Presbyterian Ministers and Queen's students, and they established the Corrymeela Community in a former Holiday Fellowship Centre. It was situated on a hill-top outside Ballycastle, with stunning views of Rathlin Island and the North Channel. It is important to note that Corrymeela, which later opened a centre in Belfast, was established well before the outbreak of the Troubles in the late 1960's.

It was meant to be a meeting place, not just for Protestants and Catholics, but also for management and trade unionists, for professional people, for craft-workers and volunteers who could make their own contribution, and also for churches and faith-based groups. The idea was to provide a safe meeting-space in beautiful surroundings, where people had an opportunity for reflection,

Prince Charles at the Corrymeela Centre with Chairman Willie McCarter and the then Leader of Corrymeela Trevor Willams who subsequently became the Church of Ireland Bishop of Limerick

and also to take time to listen to what one another had to say.

However, within only a few years of its establishment, Corrymeela – like much else in Northern Ireland – was engulfed in the Troubles. To its great credit, Corrymeela did not just preach about what should be done – instead it opened its doors to the victims of violence and their families right across the divide. In doing so it offered comfort over many years, and it provided a safe haven where people, from different political, cultural and social backgrounds could meet together for discussion and dialogue, and to try to find some common ground.

This work was not easy, and the Community grappled not only with the major divisions within Northern Ireland society, but also with its own internal problems of dealing with conflict, and yet remaining true to its principles in a vastly-changing world. It received help from various quarters, and the International Fund made a major contribution to the rebuilding of the main house at Ballycastle. This was officially opened on 2 June 1998 by Prince Charles, during a visit to Northern Ireland.

Colin Craig, the then Corrymeela Director at Ballycastle said "We think of ourselves as peace-builders who strive to break down historical barriers. These new buildings stand as a testimony to that effort, and to the IFI's commitment to establishing peace. We are also grateful to the IFI for its help through the Community Bridges Programme of work in the interface areas, particularly in North Belfast and in isolated rural areas where the divisions run very deep."

The Corrymeela Community continued its work throughout the Troubles, and won many accolades at home and abroad. Its many distinguished visitors included Mother Teresa, who visited the Ballycastle site at a time when community tensions were high, during the Republican hunger-strikes. The Reverend Doug Baker, the Summerfest organiser, recalls "Her message was 'Love till it hurts', but her sub-text both in public and in private meetings, about Corrymeela was encouraging. She told us, in effect, 'This is good. What you are doing here is important'".[3]

Ronnie Miller, Director of Corrymeela at Ballycastle. "Volunteering lies at the heart of our community".

Another distinguished world figure was the Dalai Lama, who visited Corrymeela and told the Community "My spirit is with you, and please carry on your work tirelessly. You can consider me as a member." President Mary McAleese, a strong supporter of the Community, summarised well one of its main characteristics. She said "Corrymeela set an agenda and was uncompromising in what that agenda was. It was an utter belief in the capacity of the human person to change for the better."

The Stormont Agreement of May 2007 was a vindication of the work of Corrymeela and many other organisations and individuals committed for so long to the difficult objective of creating a permanent peace. Ironically, however, the advent of peace made the funding of Corrymeela more difficult.

Its Leader Dr David Stevens outlined the problem thus "We are in a place of change, and change is happening to us. Lots of resources – both Government and voluntary – were put into Northern Ireland from the early 1970's, and we have had our fair share. Some of that is ending, and there is nothing we can do to stop it. We are reverting to normality; there are going to be less resources around. This is not about failure and blame, but about facts and living in reality."[4]

The Founder of Corrymeela also gave the Community wise advice. Speaking in his 92nd year, and reflecting on his long life, he said "Don't be afraid of change. Life is dynamic, not static. It is important to have flexibility, and life and circumstances are changing all the time. Don't tie your tiller down. If you are not able to change, you may become shipwrecked."[5]

This was advice which could well have been the motto of the International Fund, which was aware of changing circumstances and of the need for flexibility. The Board was also conscious that the Fund, after more than 21 years of achievement, would be wound down.

Accordingly one of the significant and later programmes was Leaving a Legacy, which was aimed at providing long-term help for institutions which would remain relevant and effective when the Fund itself was no longer in existence. This objective was neatly summarised thus "In pursuit of our aim to leave a lasting legacy, we have provided significant support to a range of projects which will ensure that the expertise we have acquired over 20 years of peace-building will not be lost."[6]

In 2006, before the recent Agreement had been achieved, the Fund was already laying a foundation for Corrymeela's future work in providing £1 million for a new long-term volunteers centre on the Ballycastle site. The Board also indicated that if this project had developed satisfactorily, a further £1m would be available for the redevelopment of an outdated chalet village and other accommodation at Ballycastle.

The Director Ronnie Millar said "Volunteering lies at the heart and soul of our community. We value fairness, diversity and inter-dependence within the volunteering programme. In the past we had a large number of younger long-term residential volunteers from all over the world, and now we want this to develop further by accommodating older volunteers, who bring specific skills. This new building enables us to do this. It is not a question of economics – our investment in volunteering brings us back to the basics of the Community as we move forward."[7]

The International Fund also provided help for the Volunteering Development Project to improve the recruitment and quality of its training. Millar said "Our aim is to equip people better to be peace-makers and reconcilers in their own community, when they return home from Corrymeela."

Dr David Stevens, the Leader said "The funding for the new volunteers centre and for the Volunteering Programme is linked, and this constitutes a step-change in the approach to this important aspect of our work. All of this is helping to provide new ways to benefit from the skill of volunteers."

The refurbished accommodation is also important for outside groups visiting the Ballycastle site. Stevens said "The expectations of people about accommodation have increased over the years, and without suitable advances in this respect there would be a slow decline in what we have to offer. People will no longer come if the accommodation is not suitable. Without this help from the IFI our anchor projects would not be happening, and we are now being helped to equip ourselves on site for the work of the next 30 years. I am impressed that the IFI is prepared to put such serious money into legacy issues. The Fund's representatives asked us tough questions, and it was not just a cosy relationship. However it was also a great challenge, and that is rare in today's grant-aided world. It's been a good experience to work with the International Fund."[8]

The Corrymeela experience has been a salutary example of an important Community evolving with the times, but without losing its core Christian principles and outreach. With the help of the IFI and its own fund-raising initiatives it is enabled to remain fresh and challenging in its unique Christian witness.

The Glencree Centre for Reconciliation near Dublin is another important institution which is benefiting from the Leaving A Legacy Programme. Like Corrymeela it enjoys a remarkable physical setting, but whereas the former is

Glencree. A former British military barracks established in the 19th Century, with a Garrison Church

situated on a hill with stunning views over the north-east coast, Glencree is virtually hidden away in the Wicklow Hills.

The first-time visitor, like this writer, can drive for miles along a relatively straight road which seems to have been constructed amid rugged scenery in the middle of nowhere. Then, with not a little difficulty amid poor signposting, the Glencree Reconciliation Centre can be located in a deep hollow amid the hills.

Suddenly the penny drops – this was not merely a random construction in a wilderness. In fact it was an early 19th century British military barracks, which was completed and operational by 1806. It was designed to accommodate an officer and 400 men, and was one of five similar barracks built in the area and linked by a military road.

The purpose was to provide a collective base from which British soldiers could combat armed Irish rebels in the Wicklow Hills, in the aftermath of the 1798 Rising. However with the termination of the Napoleonic Wars in 1815, the string of barracks became obsolete, although the military road survived to provide splendid access to the Wicklow Hills - not only for the locals, but for generations of tourists to come.

The Glencree buildings, however, were left largely unattended until 1856 when they were turned into an Oblate Fathers' Reformatory to help young offenders in the harrowing period after the Irish Famine. A Protestant church was built on the site to complement the military garrison, and this was taken over by the Oblate Fathers.

The church remains operational today, and no doubt it provided Christian succour for many generations in their times of trial. However, the remoteness of the location and the establishment of the Reformatory in the mid-19th century conjure up visions of strict discipline in a setting from which there seems to have been little chance of escape.

The Oblate Fathers, like the British military presence earlier, were overtaken by time. In 1945 the buildings were used by the International Red Cross to accommodate displaced people from Europe in the aftermath of the Second World War, and in 1957 Glencree was again opened up to

Chairman Denis Rooney and Congressman Richie Neal with young people at Glencree

help refugees fleeing from the Hungarian uprising.

In 1974 the buildings were yet again put to good use when the Glencree Centre For Reconciliation was set up, principally in response to the violence in Northern Ireland. Its main aim was to promote good relations between people in both parts of Ireland and their neighbours. In the first phase of its operation the Centre carried out important work, but in the mid-1980's it experienced difficulties, and closed for several years while its friends and supporters worked out a better way to carry out its function.

It re-opened in the early 1990's and the important decision was taken to adopt a non-church approach to its work. Mairín Colleary, the Chief Executive from 2004 until her retirement in 2007, was a Council Member from 1992-2000, and then Chair of Council until 2004. She says "We decided that there would be nothing that would exclude anyone and that we would work with many groups including the churches, but because we were not Christian-based we could ask the right questions without having a particular agenda. Our values are totally inclusive and non-judgmental."[9]

The International Fund provided help in the mid-Nineties to help refurbish the old Reform School dormitories which were in a spartan condition, and this helped Glencree to offer courses on a residential basis, and to provide for the needs of volunteers. The Centre also developed its Education Programme, partly with IFI funding, and built a high reputation for the quality of its work.

Another important programme was Sharing the Learning. Mairin Colleary says "This helped people to deal with what we called the 'curved ball' which others might throw at them when they least expected it. People are good at building things, but they are much more nervous about entering in to discussions that might cause divisions and upsets. Even though there is still an elephant in the room, nobody wants to talk about it."

Over the years, Glencree offered a wide range of courses and programmes, including those for young people, schools, victims and survivors and former combatants, as well as political, religious and community groups from within Ireland, and between Ireland and Great Britain and beyond.

Glencree received funds from the Community Bridges Programme to facilitate cross-community and North-South development mainly for schools, and another project in helping with a long-term volunteer programme.

In September 2006, Glencree also received a significant grant of Euros 1.8 millions to upgrade its existing residential facilities, and to provide extra space and accommodation for its work. The remainder of the Euros 3.2 millions total was being provided by the Office of Public Works and also by the Centre, through its own fund-raising.

Eamon Hickey, Joint Director General of the Fund at its Dublin office, says that the work at Glencree is entirely consistent with the Fund's objectives

Mairín Colleary, the former Chief Executive of Glencree. "The work of the IFI has been an incredible gift to the people of Ireland North and South".

"Equally important, however, is that through Glencree we are helping to give effect to the Fund's aim of leaving a legacy of sustainable projects in support of peace and reconciliation in Ireland."

At this time of writing the Centre resembles in part a huge building-site as this work is being completed, but it also underlines the vibrancy and relevance of an organisation which learned from its past and is currently providing an important reconciliation and peace-making service within its unique geographical context, and elsewhere.

Mairín Colleary says "The work of the IFI has been an incredible gift to the people of Ireland, North and South. It minimises red tape, gets things done and is prepared to take risks. The current wisdom, however, is that economic progress alone will not bring reconciliation, and that we need to dig deeper. Because of the speed at which the Stormont Agreement progressed, many people felt isolated, marginalised and betrayed, especially on the Loyalist side. There is still enormous ignorance between North and South."

She added "People are who they are, and they are not willing to part with their identity. If we are to get out of the cycle of violence every 30 years, the work of reconciliation has to continue. It is slow, hard and painful and will not be accomplished only in a few years."

The Glencree Centre, situated on a location associated formerly with repression and harsh discipline, is now hugely symbolic of the renewing power of peace and reconciliation in a setting where people can look on themselves as "oppressed" or "oppressors", and continue their personal journey in an atmosphere where they feel safe to confront and to explore further.

A third organisation to benefit from IFI funding is the An Teach Bán Centre for Peace Building at Downings in Co. Donegal. Like Corrymeela and Glencree this Centre has its own distinct ambience, and is set in an area of great natural beauty.

It has been active as a cross-border community since 1988, and became a dedicated Peace Centre in July 2002. The Centre and its various programmes have grown, and continue to grow, out of a long-term relationship with the community at large in the North/West, and also further afield. Its role is to provide a residential centre, which is regarded by its participants as a "safe place", where they are welcomed and allowed to meet one another as human beings.

People come from all backgrounds, including paramilitaries and their families, former policemen and soldiers, victims and survivors groups, as well as women's' groups and young people. Its ethos is firmly based in the community. The Director Dr Kate O'Dubhchair, says "The Centre evolved from the late 1980's, mainly working with community groups. Part of the uniqueness of this place is the site, overlooking Sheep Haven Bay, and right in the village of Downings. It is safe and homely, and we try to keep that homeliness and intimacy, which provides a particular setting for the work we do."[10]

The Centre's connections are to an existing group or institution, rather than to individuals, and participants are chosen carefully. Usually about 12 people are invited and they spend time in small groups telling their own stories. Kate O'Dubhchair says "People are amazed at their ability to travel such a distance in terms of experience, in such a short time. We prepare them carefully beforehand, and they know that

Dr Kate O'Dubhchair Director of An Teach Bán Centre for Peace Building in Donegal. "It is safe and homely, and we try to keep that homeliness and intimacy, which provides a particular setting for the work we do".

they will be meeting people they might not otherwise want to meet. In many cases they have said 'I'll come and talk, but I don't want to have anything to do with him or her'."

"Most often they not only find themselves talking to the other person, but embracing each other at the end. They come to understand that they have walked along the same path of their journey at the same time. They have been connected by the same event, though they may come to it from different sides, and yet they realise that their lives have been totally changed by it."

Kate tells the story of two women, one from a Provisional IRA background and the other from a police family, who came to the Centre full of a general anger, and also angry with each other. "We ask people to use a 'prop' while telling their story, and we encouraged these two women to make a necklace, each with beads that represented different parts of their lives."

"At the end of that workshop each woman was wearing her own necklace. Some time later I met both of them at a reception in Derry, and they approached me and said 'We have a present for you!' I noticed that each of them was wearing a necklace, but I noticed that it was each other's necklace which they were wearing, because they had come to realise that in their lives they were, in effect, carrying each other's story. That, to me, was a great 'present' from the two women. It was really marvellous."

Kate O'Dubhchair has her own inspiring story to tell. In mid-life she developed breast cancer, but with characteristic strength and courage she overcame the illness, and wrote a book titled 'I've Got Cancer But it Hasn't Got Me'. She says "I wrote it to help anyone else with the illness. It's a devastating experience, but also a chance to re-evaluate and to work out any lack of balance in your life."

Kate, then a leading academic with the University of Ulster, had a growing family of four boys and also a high-pressure job. She took a career break, and decided that she no longer wanted a full-time job. However, she had been involved with An Teach Bán and eventually applied successfully for the post of Director. She says "The experience of a life-threatening illness and a major family crisis gives you an empathy with people who have had different experiences, but also things that changed their life in a moment."

The importance of inner peace, she believes, is vital. "If people can find inner peace, then they can begin to spread this to others. However, if they don't have peace with what has happened to themselves, they are not going to find their way forward. So we try to work with people towards that. It is important to tell your story and to have others hear it."

The Centre received help from the International Fund under the Community Bridges Programme to improve its facilities, but in the long-term its future depends on new and much more comprehensive accommodation in which it can develop its work. It needs more bedroom and conference space, and the need for an entirely new building on the original site became obvious.

Accordingly, in November 2007 the International Fund approved a grant of E2m under its "Leaving A Legacy" Programme to underpin and assist the Centre's long-term mission. This is all part of the Fund's intention to leave a legacy, quite literally. Dr O'Dubhchair says "It's a legacy to future generations, both to ensure that the conflict does not start all over again, and also to demonstrate that the Centre will continue to stand for the values which are important to the International Fund - a shared society living in peace, investing in youth, valuing people and their contribution, and of generosity in giving to others."

Kate sums up "One of our core values is that we treat everybody as equals. We create a community which is An Teach Bán, and we hope that people feel a part of that. I first came here as a participant, when I had cancer, and to me the house kind of wraps its arms around you. You have that sense of being welcomed by the place, with its atmosphere and serenity, and we try to uphold that. The house has so many stories - it's heard so much laughter, and also tears. It's the same for everybody who comes here - for a little while our life journeys overlap and we are all the richer for it."

L-R: Ian Bothwell; Sheila Masters; Alison Flannagan; and Dave Masters from Crossfire Trust, at the site of the Coach House Regeneration Project

Darkley

The village of Darkley, in the border area of South Armagh, is situated in a hilly area of rural beauty, but it has known more than its share of hardship and tragedy. In the late 1950's it suffered the closure of the local textile mill, and this was an economic blow from which it never fully recovered.

Then it became engulfed in the Troubles, as did the rest of South Armagh which was referred to disparagingly as "Bandit Country." There were numerous killings, ambushes, and attacks all across the area and one of the worst of these took place on 20 November 1983.

During Sunday evening service at the small Mountain Lodge Pentecostal Church, gunmen from

the outlawed Irish National Liberation Army opened fired on the 60-strong congregation and shot dead three worshippers. The sound of hymn-singing was punctuated by the crack of rifle-fire, as gunmen continued to shoot into the church, and wounded several other people.

This vicious attack on such a soft target was one of the worst incidents of the Troubles. The perpetrators of the violence claimed that they were retaliating against attacks on Catholics by another shadowy outlawed group, the Protestant Action Force. Such feeble attempts at justification, and the attack itself, were widely condemned by community figures and politicians on all sides. The leaders of the four main Churches said that the Darkley incident was "an act of sectarian slaughter on a worshipping community which goes beyond any previous deed of violence."

One of the more disturbing aspects of the incident was that it involved a church, with people at worship on a Sunday evening. The situation in Northern Ireland generally was bad throughout the 1980's, with widespread violence including sectarian murders affecting both communities, but no-one had envisaged that terrorists would attack innocent victims within the confines of a church building.

A new Church was opened on the same site several years later, but the task of building bridges in the wider community – and in South Armagh as a whole – was an even greater challenge. At that time, and given what had happened before – including the murder of ten Protestant workmen in the Kingsmills massacre more than seven years earlier, and other atrocities, the darkness of South Armagh appeared to have few shafts of light.

One man who had set out to improve the situation in part of South Armagh, even before the Darkley murders took place, was Ian Bothwell, the founder of the Crossfire Trust. He was a young evangelical Christian who by his own admission "wanted to change the world." He thought that this mission might take him to places overseas, but instead, he ended up by trying to change the world in his own backyard, in South Armagh.

He told me, during an interview in Darkley House, "I had watched a BBC television programme about nearby Crossmaglen, and it was all about bullet-holes, fear and division. So that made me resolve to do something positive in the area. I knocked on doors, and did some 'informal' community work. But it was lonely work too, and you were always in danger of being misunderstood. I believe that love does not fail - it heals, and it deals with fear and division. I have the conviction that the story of the Good Samaritan means that we build up relationships with people 'on the other side' and that we try to help them."[11]

In 1981 he established the Crossfire Trust, and two years later the charity bought the sprawling yet attractive Darkley House, which has roots going back to the 17th century. In 1986 Ian married Pauline, a local girl, and they worked hard with others in the Crossfire Trust to provide for the physical and emotional needs of vulnerable people in the area who were suffering because of the Troubles.

Ian Bothwell- he"Wanted to change the world".

Ian recalled "It was a full-time job just to survive from day to day. We were not supported by grant-aid or by Government agencies. In those days anyone with a religious background, tended to be regarded as part of the problem, and maybe we had motives which funders could not easily support. Life was tough, and we did well even to survive daily in South Armagh."

The Trust did get support from some individuals and from churches in England and America, but the breakthrough came in 2003 when Bothwell was awarded the "President's Peace Prize" by two Northern Ireland newspapers, the Irish News and the News Letter. Part of that prize was a visit to Washington by Ian Bothwell, who

Belfast Telegraph, Monday, November 26, 1984 5

Tears and tributes for Darkley dead

Mrs. Elizabeth Browne, whose husband Harold was one of the three murdered elders, unveils the plaque in their memory. Pastor Robert Bain (left), and Pastor Jack Gibson look on. Pictures by Harold Ford.

A GRANITE memorial wall tablet has been unveiled at the Mountain Lodge Pentecostal Church in memory of the three elders shot dead in the Darkley massacre a year ago this month.

The rugged South Armagh countryside echoed to voices raised in song yesterday, as 300 people gathered to remember the victims described by one speaker as "martyrs".

Security was discreet around the isolated church which stands by the roadside, just half-a-mile from the border. The church was packed to overflowing for the service at which the tablet, lettered in gold and erected by the congregation, was unveiled.

The church has been re-decorated, but it still bears the marks from bullets which ripped into the wooden structure. Paint and fillers could not wipe out the scars.

Children

The three elders who died were Harold Browne (59), David Wilson (44) and Victor Cunningham (39). They were cut down by a hail of bullets as they stood in the porch waiting to welcome latecomers to the evening service. Although fatally wounded, Mr. Wilson staggered down the aisle, shouting to the congregation to take cover, before dropping dead.

The three masked gunmen struck just as the 60 worshippers, including two dozen children, were singing the last verse of the opening hymn "Are You Washed In the Blood of the Lamb".

Yesterday, armed police patrolled the grounds and surrounding area as the congregation's spiritual leader, Pastor Bob Bain (59), a local farmer, led the singing of the opening hymn, "Stand Up, Stand Up, For Jesus".

Piper

A year ago Pastor Bain, his son Bobbie (36) and seven-month-old grandson Darrell miraculously escaped death when the gunmen sprayed the church. His daughter Minnie, who playes the organ, was also unhurt, but her sister Sally was injured.

The memorial, unveiled by Mrs. Elizabeth Browne, whose late husband was a founder member of the church, reads: "In loving memory of our three elders who were killed by terrorists in this church on Sunday, November 20, 1983, during our evening church service. Sadly missed by all". The text, "Who would separate us from the love of Christ," is added.

After the dark blue velvet curtains had been drawn aside a lone piper played a gospel hymn in tribute. Earlier, the piper had played on the porch steps to greet worshippers as they arrived.

Memories

There were few dry eyes among the assembly as Pastor Bain recalled the atrocity. Several had been at the fateful service and there were those who still bore the signs of their injuries. There are others who find the memories too painful and have never returned to the church.

Seven people had to be treated in hospital for injuries received when the wooden building was raked

emphasised that nothing would dampen the word of God or the courage of God's people.

expressions of sympathy, along with the prayers from the Roman Catholic community were

Pictured at yesterday's service is Mr. David Browne, whose father died in the attack last year.

Mr. William White, who was seriously injured in the raid.

met other community groups and also President George W. Bush.

Ian, who is very much his own man, recalled "I told the President that 'a blessing is greater than a bombing' and he just nodded. I think he was a bit taken aback that someone who had gone to receive a prize would take the opportunity to have a word in his ear!"

CHURCH LEADERS UNITED IN SORROW

22 NOV 1983

File Darkley

By Tim Cooke
and Graham Bardgett

PROTESTANT and Roman Catholic church leaders and lay people today joined in a public demonstration of their united horror at the massacre of three church elders at the Mountain Lodge Pentecostal Assembly.

The Roman Catholic Primate, Cardinal Tomas O'Fiaich; the Church of Ireland Primate, the most Rev. John Armstrong; the Presbyterian Moderator, Dr. Tom Simpson, and the president of the Methodist Assembly, the Rev. Cecil Newell, visited the homes of all three murder victims.

And thousands of mourners of all denominations walked side-by-side at the funeral of the first murdered elder in Armagh this afternoon.

Father-of-two Mr. Victor Cunningham (39) was buried at the Presbyterian New Cemetery after a service in his home at Drumconwell Road, Ballinagallia. Mr. Cunningham died in a hail of bullets as he handed out hymnbooks in the church porch.

Freedom

The Roman Catholic Primate, Cardinal Tomas O'Fiaich, speaks to a brother-in-law of Mr. Victor Cunningham, one of the victims of the gospel hall shooting. The cardinal called at the homes of the three victims along with Dr. Tom Simpson, Moderator of the Presbyterian Church; the Most Rev. John Armstrong, of the Church of Ireland, and the Methodist Church leader, the Rev. Cecil Newell.

During that visit, Bothwell became known to other funders in Washington, including representatives from the IFI, as "the guy who had no funding". However, that did not last for long. Back home he soon became linked up to the International Fund who developed with him a project to support the establishment of the Coach House Project, just behind Darkley House.

This involved the establishment of 12 units for a 3-storey business park on the site of a former coach house, at a cost of £1,020,720. The IFI agreed to provide £347,875 of this from its Community Based Economic and Social Regeneration Programme. Plans were also made for the development of Darkley House and the improvement of its facilities, at a further cost of around £240,889 which was met by the IFI.

Ian said "We regarded this funding as a line in the sand. After the failure of the local textile industry, there was little or no employment, but now we will be bringing business opportunities to the village.

"Our vision is that Darkley House will continue as a Care Home for vulnerable people, and when some of them have recovered sufficiently, they can walk across the court-yard to find a job with a sympathetic employer in the new business park who wants someone to work on a part-time or a casual basis."

Ian Bothwell and his colleagues are greatly appreciative of the help from the International Fund. He said "It's amazing that the village has attracted such major funding to an isolated rural area, but it also says a lot about the hearts of the funders that they are prepared to go to where the pain is. In the past, the Government and other agencies did not seem to want to know us, partly because of our ethos, or perhaps because we did not use the language they understood.

"The IFI were more approachable, their application forms were shorter and they were prepared to take risks. They understood that we were not geared to paper exercises, but that we were very committed to people, and flexible to their needs."

Ian Bothwell is optimistic about the future, but with certain reservations. He said "We were accustomed to the challenges of conflict, but for peace-builders the issues are more heart-penetrating. After the cease-fires, when you open yourself up, it can be frustrating when people retreat back. It's a very big challenge to go deeper than words and to develop relationships that go beyond verbal contacts. We need to revisit history and to discover the causes of the conflict."

"We could settle for what we have now, which is an uncertain relationship, but this is not the kind of 'good news' story which some funders want to hear. The Promised Land is in sight but we still have to press through some difficult territory to get there.

"I don't think that we are quite at the place where the media portrays we are. We want to be positive, to endorse peace, and to leave the past behind. Yet the challenge of dealing with the conflict and guilt in South Armagh is enormous. The political structures are not yet secure enough for people to discuss their own involvement in the Troubles or their motive, and yet this insight needs to be shared in order for the other side to understand why some of the kindest people imaginable carried out some of the most hateful acts." This observation applies to Northern Ireland in general.

Meanwhile Ian Bothwell and his colleagues are looking forward to the completion of the IFI project at Darkley. He said "In this project, reconciliation is combined with regeneration, and this wonderful mix of healing and skill will allow the wounds and hurts of yesterday to be the well of hope for tomorrow. We know our past, the pain is engraved in our minds, but business plans, ideas, and strategic initiatives are beginning to focus us on the future."[12]

He added "It really is a new day, and the teenagers of Darkley and their parents ask weekly when will the business park be opened. We are very grateful for this lifeline. Thanks are also due to the staff for their administration skills, and to the generosity of the IFI, whose funding made this happen."

Notes

1 The War Dairies by Ray Davey Published in 2005 by the Brehon Press.
2 "In War and Peace – The Story of Corrymeela" by Alf McCreary, Published in October 2007 by the Brehon Press, Page 19.
3 Op. Cit. Page 146.
4 Ibid Page 244.
5 Op. Cit. Page 85.
6 Chairman's Foreword in the 2006 Annual Report Page 5.
7 In an Interview with the Author at Ballycastle in October, 2007.
8 In an Interview with the Author in Belfast in November 2007.
9 In an Interview with the Author at Glencree in August, 2007.
10 In an Interview with the Author in September, 2007.
11 The interview took place on 7 April 2008.
12 IFI Annual Report 2007, Page 14.

Community Bridges

In 1996 the International Fund established the Community Bridges Programme to help people on each side of the border to develop new projects to deal with issues of difference and of division.

Dave O'Brien, the former Carlingford Project Manager. "I have met terrific people from all backgrounds and we have managed to get beyond the traditional labels and mind-sets".

This innovative Programme was managed by the Community Relations Council for Northern Ireland, and it carried out valuable work over a wide spectrum of projects. The outcome was so successful that the Fund re-launched its programme in May 2007, with the announcement of £9 millions (Euros 13 millions) for a further three years to promote and to encourage better community relations, as well as reconciliation and cross-border activities.

Those institutions which benefited from the new funding included the 18/25 project in Craigavon, the 174 Trust in Belfast, the Irish Peace Institute in Limerick, the Sesame Workshop, and a partnership between Donegal Youth Service and Tyrone Donegal Partnership.

The 174 Trust was an inter-denominational faith community development organisation in North Belfast, where there were few cross-community groups or neutral venues. The role of the Trust was to help local people to identify and meet needs in the area, and to provide a non-threatening venue where people could take part in a wide variety of programmes, ranging from a pre-school group to activities for senior citizens.

At the other end of the island, almost literally, the Fund supported the Irish Peace Institute's year-long programme, with the University of Limerick, to develop a capacity to create and sustain peace-building network across Ireland. This project attempted to tackle conflict and division, and to build good cross-border relationships.

Another fascinating project, supported by the Fund, was the development of Sesame Tree. This was a co-production between Sesame Workshop, the non-profit organisation behind Sesame Street (the well-known television programme for children) and a Northern Ireland production company.

The new programme was written and produced for children aged from 3-6 years of age in Northern Ireland, and its aim was to address issues of conflict, discrimination, prejudice and sectarianism. The series of twenty 15-minute episodes was broadcast on BBC Northern Ireland in the Spring of 2008, and one of the target audiences was the parents, as well as the children.

The International Fund also supported the important work of the New Border Generation group, based in Carlingford and the wider Cooley Peninsula area of Co. Louth. This organisation's imaginative programme helped to establish relationships between groups in its own area and also groups from Belfast, particularly from the interface areas.

This significant work helped to develop cultural understanding across the community and also across the border, and also to provide leadership as well as business and community-conflict training, and lasting cross-border relationships.

Dave O'Brien, the then Project Manager at Carlingford, is a Dubliner with an encyclopaedic knowledge of the contribution of Irish soldiers from North and South in the First and Second World Wars, and he used the knowledge to help to educate and to widen the horizons of those who were not aware of the range and commitment of this Irish involvement in the conflicts.

He brought together groups from traditionally Loyalist and Republican areas of East Belfast who developed greater understanding while in Carlingford, and who brought this back home with them to develop further their contacts.

He brought people from Loyalist backgrounds to Dublin where they discovered a different perspective to Irish history, and this helped with important conflict transformation initiatives. Dave also facilitated contacts between people from the North and those in the Carlingford area.

He said "I tried to help people from both sides to work 'outside the box', and I discovered that if I treated them as human beings without preconceptions, in the vast majority of cases they responded in a positive way. I met terrific people from all backgrounds and we managed to get beyond the traditional labels and mind-sets. Without the full support of the International Fund, I could not have carried out this work."

The wide range of activities within the Community Bridges Programme has been central to the International Fund's philosophy of working towards reconciliation for a shared future, and the development of projects which could help the emergence of a peaceful and shared future for the island as a whole.

The success of such projects was harder to measure than a programme of building with bricks and mortar, but these in themselves could become part of the building bricks for a new society - and it was significant that the Community Bridges Programme was being sustained even after the Stormont accord of May 2006. This was further evidence, if evidence was needed, that the journey to ultimate peace at all levels, including the grass-roots, was going to be a long haul, but certainly worth the continuing effort.

CHAPTER SEVENTEEN

Past, Present and Future

WHEN THE INTERNATIONAL FUND FOR IRELAND WAS established in 1986 there was no certainty that it would last for more than a few years. Nothing like it had been tried before, and there were no guidelines from previous experience.

Capitol Hill in Washington DC

There were, of course, certain broad outlines for the first Board and its Chairman Sir Charles Brett, but there was also concern about funding. As Brett noted later on "Uncertainty as to the future life-span of the Fund.... always restricted the Board's ability to plan ahead. Indeed, this was to be a source of some friction between the Board and Advisory Committee: the latter argued that over-programming was essential to ensure a full take-up of funds: the Board took a more cautious view, and feared over-committing its resources."[1]

However, the money came in with relatively few restrictions, and the Chairman and Board guarded their independence jealously. Despite the understandable apprehension of Sir Charles, the International Fund not

Pictured at the launch of the Fund's community Bridges Programme from left: the then Minister for Foreign Affairs, Dermot Ahern TD with Deirdre Ryan, Fund Board Member and Duncan Morrow, Chief Executive, Community Relations Council

only survived, but prospered to carry out work which helped to pave one of the foundations for the eventual "Peace Process."

There were many reasons for this success. The Board's independence gave it the freedom to act outside the restrictions of both Governments, and the 'diktats' of senior ministers and political parties. The donor countries could, if they wished, make suggestions as to the use of their money – notably in the case of the Canadian donation which contributed to broadening the experience of young people through the Wider Horizons Programme. However, the donors could not impose their policy on the Fund, and neither could the Administrations in Dublin or London. Only in very special circumstances could the British or Irish Governments intervene. The independence of the Fund was so great, in fact, that its business was even outside the jurisdiction of the all-embracing Freedom of Information Act.

Though the architects of the Fund had put in place a structure which guaranteed its independence, the real success of the project was its impact on the people whom it was trying to help. In the early days it was seen by the Unionists and Loyalists, not surprisingly, as a "green" tool of Irish-American policy for intervention in Northern Ireland, but in practice they accepted it eventually. As John McGuckian pointed out, the complaints by the majority community that they were not included in the Fund's largesse meant that they were beginning to take it seriously.

It would be inspiring to assume that this acceptance was a direct response to the altruism of the Fund and its donors. This may have been partly so, but there was also the down to earth realism that there was something in it for them as well. One leading Loyalist told an important American visitor "We don't care where the money comes

A cartoon from the Belfast Telegraph illustrates a remarkable political and personal relationship, and a reflection on the Battle of the Boyne

from. It can come from the Pope himself, and we'll use it for our community."

People may wish to build bridges, with the best of motives, but there is more likelihood of them doing so if all sides can benefit from the process. The hidden agenda, however, was not just the relevance and practicality of a particular project, but the fact that it encouraged personal contacts which helped to develop respect across the divides.

It is also important to remember that the Fund was by no means welcomed at the start by Nationalists either – including many in Fianna Fail, whose leader Charles Haughey opposed the Anglo-Irish Agreement of 1985. Haughey, however, was nothing if not a pragmatist and he accepted the outworking of the Agreement, and its offshoots, including the IFI.

The Fund was also successful because it provided relatively few hostages to fortune. The work of the Development Consultants was vital, as the longest-serving Chairman Willie McCarter pointed out. He stated, in a paper delivered to an international Conference after his tenure as Chairman, "This feature was extremely important because it enabled the Fund to take a 'bottom-up' approach in its development activities. The use of Development Consultants was a key instrument in the success of a number of the Fund's economics-based programmes."

The pro-active approach of the Fund was also important in developing initiatives with communities which needed help, as in Greysteel, Poyntzpass and elsewhere. The policy of making available the "first money on the table" was also crucial, as it was important in encouraging others to put up money. This was evident in many of the projects in all the border counties, and not least in Donegal – some of which have been mentioned earlier.

The Fund also had the ability to take risks, and to open new channels of communication which had not existed, or which had been blocked or fallen into disrepair. As has been noted elsewhere, this was illustrated – literally - in the first major Flagship Project, to restore the Ballyconnell Canal linking the Shannon and Erne waterways. There was uncertainty – even scepticism – about the viability of the project until funding was provided for a feasibility study which concluded that this ambitious venture could be successful.

The Fund also showed foresight in helping to set up other Flagship

Chairman Denis Rooney with former Minister for Foreign Affairs, Dermot Ahern TD

projects such as Navan Fort and the St. Patrick's Centre in Downpatrick. Due to reasons beyond the Fund's control these projects did not flourish as well as had been hoped, but they continued to provide a resource for the preservation of the island's heritage and culture. Without the IFI's initiative it is doubtful of other funders could have or would have been able to do so.

Another major factor in the success of the Fund was its international dimension. Dean Pittman, a former US Consul-General in Northern Ireland with a direct experience of the work of the Fund, spoke to me shortly before he left Belfast in 2007. He said "It's a rare opportunity for a diplomat to have a resource like the IFI, and a lot of Ambassadors around the world would be green with envy to have something like that, with a substantial amount of money to focus on projects and to move the overall agenda towards stability, a shared future, and reaching a political settlement."

"Now you have both sides working in a constructive way, because they want to make it work. From what I've been hearing across Northern Ireland, no-one wants to go back to the way it was. I think that everybody feels a sense of relief to see that both sides can work together in a positive way towards a better future for Northern Ireland, and I can see no reason why that this should not continue."[2]

Tony Culley-Foster, a Washington business consultant who comes from the North of Ireland told me "The Irish-American community was very concerned, and they knew how difficult it was to stabilise the economy of Northern Ireland against the backdrop of a virtual civil war. At that time the brightest and the best were getting on planes and boats and moving out."

"The Americans wanted to do something that was tangible to make an impact on individuals and smaller communities, and they believed that if the economy improved, then the likelihood of young people being marginalised or unemployed or being drawn into paramilitarism would be diminished. They weren't looking at funding large companies or thriving enterprises. The real focus for the IFI has always been community-based organisations, and trying to make a difference. That's how you change the world – one heart, one mind and one soul at a time."[3]

Duncan Morrow, Chief Executive of the Community Relations Council, also spoke to me in the summer of 2007 and he underlined the sense of hope and of a new beginning. He said "We cannot draw on the history of the past to predict the future, and so we are still at this stage of a kind of open page. Nobody quite knows how that is going to be filled, including – I suspect – the leadership of Sinn Fein and the DUP. What we do know is that it's a new world, and we are in a new context."

"I believe that the IFI was the song-bird singing before the dawn broke. It was a very big statement of international intent to put in a

Tony Culley-Foster a Washington Business Consultant with deep roots in Donegal

Micheál Martin, TD, the current Minister for Foreign Affairs, who succeeded Dermot Ahern in May 2008

degree of support behind a shared future, and not just to support one side or the other. It was the symbol of a clear international direction, and they did it not by force, but by trying to invest in the quality of life and to demonstrate what might be possible on that basis."

Morrow believes that, within the American context, "the IFI was something which Irish America in particular was happy to identify with, and the role of those people in the different political parties in Congress needs to be acknowledged. It was their way to show an interest which did not simply repeat 'Irish Republicanism' but which, on the other hand, represented a traditional Irish Nationalist interest in the long-term good of Ireland."

"So America was in a position to guarantee to both Britain and Ireland that this was not a project that was aimed at either of them, but was actually a collective project. In that sense they were able to play a significant role."[4]

In the end, of course, all politics are "local", as one of the main instigators of the Fund – Tip O'Neill – never tired of pointing out. In that "local" perspective, therefore, one of the most interesting examples of the Fund working well at grass-roots level was in the improvements in and around Dundalk in Co. Louth, where the local TD was Dermot Ahern.

He became the Minister for Foreign Affairs in September 2004, after holding a number of other important Cabinet posts. He was first elected to the Dail (Irish Parliament) in February 1987. On 7 May 2008 he was appointed Minister for Justice, Equality and Law Reform by the new Taoiseach Brian Cowen, who took over from the former Taoiseach Bertie Ahern, after his resignation the previous day.

Incidentally, in one of the most symbolic and stage - managed farewells in Irish history, Bertie Ahern and the Reverend Dr Ian Paisley, who was also soon to resign as First Minister at Stormont, met on 6 May 2008 at the site of the Battle of the Boyne to open a new Boyne heritage centre. In a ceremony of warm and mutual appreciation, they demonstrated that, at last, the old enmities between Orange and Green were beginning to wane. It was an extraordinary day at the end of an extraordinary year in Irish politics, North and South.

This was tangible evidence of the success of the painstaking, and sometimes disheartening peace process, in which the International Fund had played its part. In an interview with me some weeks earlier Dermot Ahern recalled "My election more or less coincided with the start of the International Fund, at a time when Dundalk was regarded as a 'For Sale" town, because there were so many 'For Sale' signs on the main streets. It was economically deprived, and it had fallen so far down that it could only go up.
It also had difficulty in attracting industry because it had a bad name due to the reflected difficulties from the North."[5]

The support from the International Fund was indubitably welcome. Ahern said "We were not getting any special recognition from the Government in the Republic, but if the International Fund looked favourably on a project, there would be an onus on the Government to provide some assistance as well.

The County Council also used the help from the Fund to upgrade the urban landscape and to make the place look a bit better."

This meant that "to a certain extent, the International Fund gave us the recognition that we did not really get from the Government, which looked at all the regions of the South as being equal. However, the International Fund was indicating clearly that the border counties North and South were a special case."

People were not always happy with all the Fund's decisions "but, by and large, they were good decisions. The Fund was a vehicle which was not caught up in bureaucracy. It provided economic opportunities, it was flexible and it tried to heal wounds. It wasn't just about physical things, but about bringing people across the border in both directions, including young people."

"I have always been a strong supporter of the Fund, which has been of enormous assistance to us as we sought to overcome the effects of the Troubles in the border region. It helped to regenerate areas, and it helped people to make connections who might not otherwise have communicated with one another. I would have regarded it as one of the most important examples of assistance that could be given to coax people forward. From my own point of view, it helped this area immeasurably, and Dundalk changed beyond all recognition."

The wider potential of the Fund's story did not go unmentioned. The Minister spoke to me just after his return from an official visit to East Timor which is one of the poorest countries in Asia. He said, "They now have an agreement with Australia for sharing the proceeds of oil extraction in the seas between the two countries. This is likely to be of substantial financial benefit to East Timor but, at the same time, they need help to develop their capacity to make best use of these resources. One of the things we suggested to them is to look at the experience of the International Fund, many aspects of which could be useful to them as a model for assisting their development."

This is in accord with one of the broad strategies of the Fund, which is to share its knowledge with those other areas of the world which might benefit from such experience, though no two situations are ever quite the same. This is an important strategy, but of itself it is not sufficient to justify the continued existence of the Fund.

So what of the future? At this time of writing, the Fund is in its "Sunset" years. This term in itself is a clever way of indicating that it may not end abruptly, but that it might evolve into something rather different – but still retaining some of the essential elements which made the Fund so successful. Minister Ahern echoed the views of many people when he said to me "Come the day that the International Fund ends, the work will still have to be taken forward by some means, because the work of reconciliation in Northern Ireland is far from over."

The future of the International Fund, and what may replace it, or evolve from it, is outside the scope of this volume. However, to my mind, it would be a great pity if the experience and expertise of the Fund during the past 21 years and more were not put to good use. How that will happen is a matter for others.

For now, it is timely to recognise the work of people at all levels who contributed to the International Fund's success. There were, of course, failures but on balance the number of successes were by far in the majority. That success can be measured by all kinds of statistics compiled by independent analysts, and some of these figures have been included elsewhere in this publication.

However, some of the most impressive successes have been

The former US Consul General in Belfast Dean Pittman, Paula Dobriansky, the US Special Envoy to Northern Ireland, and Fund Chairman Denis Rooney

almost immeasurable in the way that the Fund has helped to change the lives of individuals. When I was researching and writing this book, I was moved and deeply impressed by the courage and vision of so many men and women, and groups, who tried to achieve the best of things in the worst of times, and who kept alive the light of hope when there seemed only darkness on the horizon.

It has been to the credit of the International Fund, and its donors, staff and advisers, that it has encouraged and underpinned that hope in a practical way, while ensuring that its beneficiaries also played their part in the healing process, and in a businesslike manner.

This year marks the tenth anniversary of the Good Friday Agreement, which – after a long period of uncertainty and mutual recrimination – has proved to be a watershed in the relationships and peaceful aspirations of the peoples of these islands. It would be naive to suggest that there will be no setbacks, but it is more than wishful thinking to suggest that peace while "dropping slow" will eventually settle on our troubled past.

Already memories are short concerning the sheer misery and awfulness of the years of the Troubles, and this is as it should be, as society moves on to better things – while trying to find a formula where the victims of violence and their families can achieve closure on the past.

Perhaps the most abiding success of the International Fund for Ireland, apart from its tangible achievements, is its legacy of goodwill and hope. The Fund expressed the goodwill of those from outside who wanted to help in an even-handed way, and it also gave hope to those on the island who were looking for a way out of the morass.

These observations were well – expressed to me by the American Congressman Richie Neal who said "People saw the Fund as an act of goodwill, and it also brought together those who might not have otherwise come in contact with one another."

The element of hope was highlighted by an Irish civil servant who told me "In those dark days of polarisation, terrible things were happening. What was needed was hope, and the International Fund helped to provide the hope. It wasn't just the money."

Over the past 21 years and more, many people have contributed to the success of the Fund, and a representative number of their individual and collective achievements has been recognised in this anniversary record, and elsewhere. However, the final words should come from the first Chairman of the Fund Sir Charles

Brett who, with his hardy pioneer colleagues, entered uncharted territory in the difficult and dangerous years of more than two decades ago.

In one of his last public statements, Sir Charles was both reflective and visionary. Then out of office as Chairman in 1990, he wrote "Some fundamental changes on both sides are going to be needed before any solution to the dreary old Northern Ireland problem comes into sight. Though never a Unionist, I have always been very conscious of the social, as well as the economic, benefits to the people of Northern Ireland of the British connection."

He added "At the same time, I should dearly wish to see a far happier relationship between North and South, Protestant and Catholic. If the two parts of Ireland are ever to draw closer together, many old habits of thought are going to have to be abandoned on both sides of the border. I think that the International Fund has made a significant contribution to prosperity, and so (it is to be hoped) to the reconciliation of the two communities within the twelve Northern counties of Ireland."

"Its most important achievement may prove to be to have broken down some of the barriers between people of different traditions and loyalties, at many levels – in the Board itself; amongst the supporting civil servants and public bodies; amongst those concerned with the North-South or cross-community projects on the ground. It has provided, for the first time ever, a practical mechanism for cross-border co-operation without political or constitutional implications. Much more than this, I think, money alone – the mainspring of the Fund – cannot achieve.[6]

Sir Charles and his colleagues could not know then that the International Fund would go on to do so much more, and that it would establish a broad foundation which, with the assistance of many others, would help – in the compelling words of the poet Seamus Heaney – to make "hope and history rhyme."

That, by any standards, was a considerable achievement.

Notes

1 The Political Quarterly Vol 61, No 4 October-December 1990, Page 433.

2 In an Interview with the Author on June 21, 2007.

3 During an Interview in Washington in July 2007.

4 In an Interview with the Author in Belfast in July 2007.

5 At a meeting with the Author in Dundalk on 25 February 2008.

6 Op. Cit. Pages 439-440.

Appendix A

CHAIRMEN

Name	Start Date	Finish Date
Sir Charles E B Brett	December 1986	October 1989
Mr J B McGuckian	October 1989	November 1992
Mr W T McCarter	February 1993	February 2005
Mr D Rooney	March 2005	

John McGuckian Pictured with the Board of the Fund at Ballycastle.
"There's nothing I have done that I enjoyed quite as much."

Appendix B

BOARD MEMBERS

Name	Start Date	Finish Date
Sir Ewart Bell	December 1986	October 1989
Sir Gordon Booth	December 1986	April 1989
Mr Michael Canavan	December 1986	February 1987
Mr Gerald Dempsey	December 1986	October 1989
Mr Neil McCann	December 1986	March 1991
Mr Alastair McGuckian	December 1986	October 1989
Mr J Doherty	April 1987	October 1989
Mr J Craig	April 1989	February 1996
Mr J V D Calvert	October 1989	November 1992
Mr P A Duffy	October 1989	September 1995
Mr P Kenny	October 1989	February 1996
Mr W T McCarter	October 1989	November 1992
Mr P McKillen	September 1991	November 1992
Ms J McCrum	February 1993	December 1999
Ms C Murphy	February 1993	December 1999
Mr B Slowey	February 1993	December 1999
Mrs L Steele	April 1996	February 2003
Mr E Hanna	April 1996	February 2003
Mr Haslett	April 1996	February 2003
Ms H Kirkpatrick	February 2000	December 2005
Mrs C Lynch	February 2000	December 2005
Mr E Murtagh	February 2000	December 2005
Mr J Hewitt	April 2003	-
Mr J McDaid	April 2003	-
Ms D Ryan	April 2003	-
Mrs A Henderson	March 2006	-
Ms A Bonner	March 2006	-
Mrs M Southwell	March 2006	-

Appendix C

OBSERVERS

Name		Start Date	Finish Date
Mr Bob Bell	Deputy Assistant Administrator USAID	December 1986	January 1987
Mr Michael Phillips	Canadian High Commission London	December 1986	September 1988
Mr W Fine	US Observer	January 1987	March 1990
Mr D Leask	Alternate Observer (New Zealand)	June 1987	February 1989
Mr D Smith	Canadian Observer	October 1988	December 1989
Mr C Trojan	European Communities Observer	February 1989	April 2000
Mr C Pearson	Alternate Observer (New Zealand)	February 1989	March 1990
Mr T J McConnell	Canadian Observer	December 1989	September 2003
Mr E McCaffrey	US Observer	May 1990	March 1993
Ms C McDonald	New Zealand Observer	May 1990	September 1991
Ms B Brown	New Zealand Observer	November 1991	September 1994
Mr J Lyons	US Observer	November 1993	February 2001
Mr T Quinn	Alternate US Observer	November 1993	April 2001
Mr M Chilton	New Zealand Observer	November 1994	December 1997
Ambassador E Stevens	Australia Observer	April 1995	September 1998
Ms G Rush	New Zealand Observer	February 1998	June 1999
Ambassador R Halverson	Australian Observer	February 1999	December 2002
Ambassador P East	New Zealand Observer	September 1999	November 2001
Mr G Crauser	EU Observer	September 2000	March 2004
Mr E Gillespie	US Observer	June 2001	September 2003
Mr J Palma Andres	EU Alternate Observer	March 2002	
Hon R Marshall	New Zealand Observer	June 2002	March 2005
HE Dr John J Herron	Australian Observer	February 203	December 2005
Ms P Noonan	US Observer	December 2003	June 2008
Mr C Millikin	Canadian Observer	December 2003	March 2006
Mr R T Waters	Alternate US Observer	March 2004	
HE The Rt Hon J Hunt	New Zealand Observer	June 2005	February 2008
HE Anne Plunkett	Australian Ambassador to Dublin	June 2006	
Mr B Doherty	Canadian Observer	June 2007	
Ambassador D Leask	New Zealand Observer	June 2008	
Mr G McKelvey	US Observer	June 2008	

Appendix D

ADVISORY COMMITTEE

North	South	Start Date	Finish Date
	Mr E O Tuathail	December 1986	October 1987
Dr G Quigley		December 1986	April 1988
	Mr D A Gallagher	October 1987	May 1991
Mr J Semple		April 1988	June 2000
	Mr S O'Huiginn	September 1991	June 1997
	Mr D A Gallagher	September 1998	April 2000
	Mr D O'Ceallaigh	June 2000	June 2001
Mr G Loughran		September 2000	March 2002
	Mr B Scannell	September 2001	June 2006
Mr W Haire		May 2002	December 2003
Mr J Hunter		March 2004	June 2007
	Mr P Hennessy	December 2005	
Mr B Robinson		November 2007	June 2008

The current Board of the International Fund for Ireland.
Back (L-R) Jackie Hewitt, Chairman Denis Rooney, John McDaid. Front (L-R) Dierdre Ryan, Mary Southwell, Anne Henderson and Anne Bonner.

Appendix E

JOINT DIRECTORS GENERAL

North	South	Start Date	Finish Date
	Mr B T Lyons	December 1986	September 1989
Mr J Hunter		December 1986	June 1988
Mr A I Devitt		June 1988	May 1991
	Mr D Hamill	September 1989	May 1993
Mr H Moore		June 1991	June 1992
Mr C Todd		September 1992	November 2001
	Mr B Scannell	September 1993	June 1995
	Mr T Russell	September 1995	June 1999
	Mr D Brangan	September 1999	May 2002
Mr A Smith		March 2002	
	Ms O O'Hanrahan	September 1992	June 2004
	Mr N Burgess	September 2004	June 2005
	Ms M Collins	September 2005	November 2007
	Mr E Hickey	November 2007	

Other titles by Alf McCreary

THE TROUBLES
Corrymeela - In War And Peace
Survivors
Profiles of Hope
Marie - A Story from Enniskillen
An Ordinary Hero - the Biography of Senator Gordon Wilson
All Shall Be Well (with Joan Wilson)

THIRD WORLD
Up With People
Peace In Our Time

CORPORATE AND INSTITUTIONAL HISTORY
Spirit of the Age -The Story of Old Bushmills
By All Accounts - The History of the TSB
Degrees of Excellence - The Queen's University of Belfast 1845-1995 (with Professor Brian Walker)
A Vintage Port-Larne and Its People
A Passion for Success - the History of the Coca-Cola Corporation
St. Patrick's City - The Story of Armagh
Faith, Friendship, Service - Fleming Fulton School

BIOGRAPHICAL
St. Patrick's Footsteps
Nobody's Fool - The Life of Archbishop Robin Eames

AUTOBIOGRAPHICAL
Remember When

ESSAYS AND COLLECTED JOURNALISM
Princes, Presidents and Punters
The Good, The Bad and the Barmy

TRAVEL
An Ulster Journey
This Northern Land

SPORT
Going for Goal
Blue is the Colour

PICTURE	CREDITED TOO	PAGE No
Lord Brooke, former Secretary of State	Alf McCreary	P16
Seddie McGovern	Alf McCreary	P43
Joe Gillespie, Waterways Ireland	Alf McCreary	P46
Donegal Skyline	Alf McCreary	P56
Coastal photograph	Alf McCreary	P57
Donal MacLoughainn & Winston Patterson	Alf McCreary	P61
A welcome from Bart Simpson at the St Patrick's Centre	Alf McCreary	P63
Monreagh Church	Alf McCreary	P65
Gemma Havlin	Alf McCreary	P79
Jim McClenaghan	Alf McCreary	P79
The Jeanie Johnston	Alf McCreary	P83
Patrick & Breda McGinnis	Alf McCreary	P103
Congressman Neal	Alf McCreary	P117
Dr Garret Fitzgerald	Alf McCreary	P124
Carlo Trojan, Eamon Hickey & Sandy Smith	Alf McCreary	P125
Dr Hübner	Alf McCreary	P127
Canoeing on Carlingford Lough	Alf McCreary	P137
KEY staff	Alf McCreary	P139
Mairín Colleary former Chief Executive of Glencree	Alf McCreary	P160
Ian Bothwell at Crossfire	Alf McCreary	P163
Dave O'Brien, the former Carlingford Project Manager	Alf McCreary	P166
Capitol Hill in Washington	Alf McCreary	P168
Tony Culley - Foster, a Washington Business Consultant	Alf McCreary	P171
Padraig O'Dochartaigh	Alf McCreary	P71
Rathlin Island	Alf McCreary	P49
The Canal Basin	Alf McCreary	P60
Signing of the Anglo - Irish Agreement	Belfast Telegraph	P10
Reaction on the Streets of Belfast	Belfast Telegraph	P10
Dr Ian Paisley and Martin McGuinness in US	Belfast Telegraph	P121
Dr Paisley & Jose Manuel Barroso	Belfast Telegraph	P127
Newspaper Cuttings about Darkley	Belfast Telegraph	P164
Cartoon of the Battle of the Boyne	Belfast Telegraph	P170
Sir George Quigley	Bombardier	P9
The current Board of the Fund.	Catherine McAviney	P179
Cardinal Sean Brady	Catholic Press Office	P123
Dr Ray Davey founder of Corrymeela	Corrymeela	P153
Dr David Stevens, Current leader at Corrymeela	Corrymeela	P153
Corrymeela and some of its distinguished guests	Corrymeela	P154
Young band member	Declan Doherty - Donegal News	P62
Marching Bands	Declan Doherty - Donegal News	P63
The Old Courthouse in Lifford	Declan Doherty - Donegal News	P58
Inside the Lifford Courthouse	Declan Doherty - Donegal News	P59
Cathal MacSuibhne	Declan Doherty - Donegal News	P61
Denis Rooney, Father O'Ferraigh & Pat 'The Cope' Gallagher	Declan Doherty - Donegal News	P62
Rannafest in West Donegal	Declan Doherty - Donegal News	P64
The Jeanie Johnston	Declan Doherty - Donegal News	P66
Maurice Harron Sculpture	Declan Doherty - Donegal News	P68
Dr Kate O'Dubhchair Director An Teach Bán	Declan Doherty - Donegal News	P161
Dermot Gallagher, Secretary General at DFA	Department of Foreign Affairs Dublin	P39
Brendan Behan	DFA	P81
The Irish Minister for Foreign Affairs Micheál Martin	DFA	P172

The former Irish Minister for Foreign Affairs Peter Barry	DFA	P16
John Hunter	DFP Press Office	P22
Julia and Zoista at the LINK	Diane Holt (The Link, Newtownards)	P149
Jacques Delors	European Commission	P125
Former Taoiseach Albert Rynolds	Fianna Fail Papers, University College Dublin Archives	P40
Former Irish Ambassador in Washington Sean Donlon	Fine Gael	P12
Former Taoiseach Dr Garret Fitzgerald	Fine Gael	P13
Former Taoiseach Bertie Ahern	Forum on Europe	P123
Lord Mayhew, former Secretary of State for Northern Ireland	Harrison Photography	P39
Lord Eames, the former Church of Ireland Primate	Harrison Photography	P52
Butterfly Garden	Harrison Photography	P146
Willie McCarter Chairman 1993 to 2005	IFI	P8
Sir Charles Brett, the First Chairman of the International Fund	IFI	P18
The first Annual Report	IFI	P19
One of the early meetings of the Board	IFI	P19
The first Board Meeting	IFI	P23
John McGuckian, the second Chairman of the International Fund	IFI	P26
Peter Brooke MP, John McGuckian and Gerard Collins TD	IFI	P27
John McGuckian launching the CRISP Programme	IFI	P29
Canadian PM Brian Mulroney, Toiseach Charles Haughey & The Chairman	IFI	P30
John McGuckian and Senator Ted Kennedy	IFI	P30
John McGuckian & Hon Tom Foley, Speaker US House of Representatives	IFI	P31
Carlingford	IFI	P32
The new Board of the International Fund from 1989	IFI	P33
The Carlingford Waterbus	IFI	P35
Cross Border Tourism	IFI	P35
Labour Sheet	IFI	P37
Aerial view of the Shannon Erne Waterway	IFI	P38
Former Chairman Willie McCarter and former PM Sir John Major	IFI	P49
Inner City Trust	IFI	P49
Derry / Londonderry	IFI	P50
Former President Bill Clinton with the Chairman and Jim Lyons	IFI	P53
Bill Clinton and Tony Blair	IFI	P54
Willie McCarter with former US Vice, President Al Gore	IFI	P76
The Chairman and former Irish President Mary Robinson	IFI	P77
Chairman with John Reid, Des Brown and Brian Cowen	IFI	P75
Joan Wilson with former Canadian Prime Minister Jean Chrétien	IFI	P88
Stewartstown Road	IFI	P95
Guy Crauser, Jean Brown, Willie McCarter & Renee Crawford	IFI	P96
Jean Brown, Denis Rooney & Commissioner Hübner	IFI	P97
Business and the Community	IFI	P105
The different stages at Greysteel	IFI	P106
Townsend Enterprise Park	IFI	P109
Neil Kinnock 'hands on' at Townsend	IFI	P110
Causeway Steam Train	IFI	P114
The Chairman with Jim Walsh, John Hume, Newt Gingrich and Joe Millan	IFI	P118
Willie McCarter and Senator Tom Foley	IFI	P118
The Chairman, and Senator Ben Gilman	IFI	P119
John Hume and Jim Dougal	IFI	P126
The Ben Sherman Company	IFI	P131
Murals	IFI	P147
Prince Charles at Corrymeela	IFI	P155

Ronnie Millar, Director at Corrymeela	IFI	P156
Glencree	IFI	P158
Denis Rooney & Dermot Ahern	IFI	P171
An early Board of the International Fund at Ballycastle	IFI	P176
The Chairman with Congressman Richie Neal at Glencree	IFI	P159
Drawing of Willie McCarter	Irish Times	P80
The Queen and President McAleese	Irish Times	P124
Denis Rooney, current Chairman of the International Fund	John McVitty	P4
John Waddell	John Waddell	P104
Dermot Ahern, Deirdre ryan and Duncan Morrow at CBP Launch	Justin MacInnes	P169
Tony Blair and Bertie Ahern	Maxwell Photographers	P129
Dr Ian Paisley and Martin McGuinness in Europe	Office of NI Executive in Brussels	P128
Former Prime Minister Margaret Thatcher	Pacemaker	P25
Ian Bothwell at Crossfire	Parkway Photography	P162
Fishing Villages	Parkway Photography	P48
Help for Rathlin Island	Parkway Photography	P54
The Chairman at four different International Fund events and openings	Parkway Photography	P73
Bernard McGuinness, Jose Palma Andres and Willie McCarter	Parkway Photography	P74
The uptake of the new ferry	Parkway Photography	P78
President McAleese at Poyntzpass	Parkway Photography	P107
St Patrick's Centre	Parkway Photography	P115
People selected for Canadian Junior Achievement Conference	Parkway Photography	P142
John Hume with President Ronald Reagan, Tip O'Neill and Edward Kennedy	Pat Hume	P11
Denis Rooney, Josep Borrell Fontelles and Dermot Ahern	Presseye	P150
Stuart Moffett & Tony Clarke	Presseye	P86
Bronagh Lawson & George Briggs	Presseye	P89
Jean Brown & Renee Crawford	Presseye	P93
Jean Brown	Presseye	P94
Renee Crawford	Presseye	P94
Jean Brown & Renee Crawford	Presseye	P98
Hugh Nicholl	Presseye	P101
Dedication to those who lost their lives at Greysteel	Presseye	P102
Barney McCaughey	Presseye	P111
Jackie Hewitt	Presseye	P112
Jackie Hewitt & Barney McCaughey	Presseye	P113
Patsy O'Kane	Presseye	P133
Patsy O'Kane	Presseye	P135
Fiona McCabe	Presseye	P136
Dean Pittman, Denis Rooney and Paula Dobriansky	Presseye	P174
Denis Rooney, Professor Gallagher and Padraic Quirk	Presseye	P144
Della Clancy & Denis Rooney at KEY/LET	Presseye	P138
The late David Ervine	PUP	P87
Joan Bullock	Steve Rogers Photography	P41
Graham Thomas	Steve Rogers Photography	P42
President Jimmy Carter	The Carter Library	P12
Former President Ronald Reagan and former Prime Minister Margaret Thatcher	The Reagan Library	P14
Coalisland CRISP	The then DOE Regional Development Office	P29
The re-opened waterway	Waterways Ireland	P45